PCs
FOR
DUMMIES®
8TH EDITION

PCs

FOR

DUMMIES®

8TH EDITION

by Dan Gookin

Hungry Minds™

Best-Selling Books • Digital Downloads • e-Books • Answer Networks • e-Newsletters • Branded Web Sites • e-Learning

New York, NY ◆ Cleveland, OH ◆ Indianapolis, IN

PCs For Dummies, 8th Edition

Published by
Hungry Minds, Inc.
909 Third Avenue
New York, NY 10022
www.hungryminds.com
www.dummies.com

Library of Congress Control Number: 2001118278

ISBN: 0-7645-0838-5

Printed in the United States of America

10 9 8 7 6 5 4 3 2

8B/QU/QR/QS/IN

Distributed in the United States by Hungry Minds, Inc.

Distributed by CDG Books Canada Inc. for Canada; by Transworld Publishers Limited in the United Kingdom; by IDG Norge Books for Norway; by IDG Sweden Books for Sweden; by IDG Books Australia Publishing Corporation Pty. Ltd. for Australia and New Zealand; by TransQuest Publishers Pte Ltd. for Singapore, Malaysia, Thailand, Indonesia, and Hong Kong; by Gotop Information Inc. for Taiwan; by ICG Muse, Inc. for Japan; by Intersoft for South Africa; by Eyrolles for France; by International Thomson Publishing for Germany, Austria and Switzerland; by Distribuidora Cuspide for Argentina; by LR International for Brazil; by Galileo Libros for Chile; by Ediciones ZETA S.C.R. Ltda. for Peru; by WS Computer Publishing Corporation, Inc., for the Philippines; by Contemporanea de Ediciones for Venezuela; by Express Computer Distributors for the Caribbean and West Indies; by Micronesia Media Distributor, Inc. for Micronesia; by Chips Computadoras S.A. de C.V. for Mexico; by Editorial Norma de Panama S.A. for Panama; by American Bookshops for Finland.

For general information on Hungry Minds' products and services please contact our Customer Care Department within the U.S. at 800-762-2974, outside the U.S. at 317-572-3993 or fax 317-572-4002.

For sales inquiries and reseller information, including discounts, premium and bulk quantity sales, and foreign-language translations, please contact our Customer Care Department at 800-434-3422, fax 317-572-4002, or write to Hungry Minds, Inc., Attn: Customer Care Department, 10475 Crosspoint Boulevard, Indianapolis, IN 46256.

For information on licensing foreign or domestic rights, please contact our Sub-Rights Customer Care Department at 212-884-5000.

For information on using Hungry Minds' products and services in the classroom or for ordering examination copies, please contact our Educational Sales Department at 800-434-2086 or fax 317-572-4005.

For press review copies, author interviews, or other publicity information, please contact our Public Relations Department at 317-572-3168 or fax 317-572-4168.

For authorization to photocopy items for corporate, personal, or educational use, please contact Copyright Clearance Center, 222 Rosewood Drive, Danvers, MA 01923, or fax 978-750-4470.

Hungry Minds is a trademark of Hungry Minds, Inc.

About the Author

Dan Gookin got started with computers back in the post vacuum tube3 age of computing: 1982. His first intention was to buy a computer to replace his aged and constantly breaking typewriter. Working as slave labor in a restaurant, however, Gookin was unable to afford the full "word processor" setup and settled on a computer that had a monitor, keyboard, and little else. Soon his writing career was under way with several submissions to fiction magazines and lots of rejections.

The big break came in 1984, when he began writing about computers. Applying his flair for fiction with a self-taught knowledge of computers, Gookin was able to demystify the subject and explain technology in a relaxed and understandable voice. He even dared to add humor, which eventually won him a column in a local computer magazine.

Eventually Gookin's talents came to roost as a ghostwriter at a computer book publishing house. That was followed by an editing position at a San Diego computer magazine. During this time, he also regularly participated on a talk show about computers. In addition, Gookin kept writing books about computers, some of which became minor bestsellers.

In 1990, Gookin came to IDG Books Worldwide (now Hungry Minds, Inc.) with a proposal. From that initial meeting unfolded an idea for an outrageous book: a long overdue and original idea for the computer book for the rest of us. What became *DOS For Dummies* blossomed into an international bestseller with hundreds of thousands of copies in print and many translations.

Today, Gookin still considers himself a writer and computer "guru" whose job it is to remind everyone that computers are not to be taken too seriously. His approach to computers is light and humorous yet very informative. He knows the complex beasts are important and can help people become productive and successful. Gookin mixes his knowledge of computers with a unique, dry sense of humor that keeps everyone informed — and awake. His favorite quote is "Computers are a notoriously dull subject, but that doesn't mean that I have to write about them that way."

Gookin's titles for Hungry Minds include *Word 2002 For Windows For Dummies, C For Dummies, Buying a Computer For Dummies,* and the *Illustrated Computer Dictionary For Dummies.* All told, he's written more than 50 books about computers, some of which he's written more than once. Gookin holds a degree in communications from the University of California, San Diego, and lives with his wife and four boys in the hinterlands of Idaho.

Dan can be contacted by e-mail at dang@idgbooks.com.

Publisher's Acknowledgments

We're proud of this book; please send us your comments through our Online Registration Form located at www.dummies.com.

Some of the people who helped bring this book to market include the following:

Acquisitions, Editorial, and Media Development

Project Editor: Paul Levesque

Acquisitions Editor: Jill Byus Schorr

Copy Editors: Kim Darosett, Rebecca Huehls, Amy Pettinella

Technical Editor: Allen Wyatt

Editorial Manager: Constance Carlisle

Editorial Assistant: Amanda Foxworth

Production

Project Coordinator: Maridee Ennis

Layout and Graphics: Joyce Haughey, Jill Piscitelli, Jacque Schneider, Julie Trippetti, Jeremey Unger, Erin Zeltner

Proofreaders: John Greenough, Marianne Santy, TECHBOOKS Production Services

Indexer: TECHBOOKS Production Services

Hungry Minds Technology Publishing Group: Richard Swadley, Senior Vice President and Publisher; Mary Bednarek, Vice President and Publisher, Networking; Joseph Wikert, Vice President and Publisher, Web Development Group; Mary C. Corder, Editorial Director, Dummies Technology; Andy Cummings, Publishing Director, Dummies Technology; Barry Pruett, Publishing Director, Visual/Graphic Design

Hungry Minds Manufacturing: Ivor Parker, Vice President, Manufacturing

Hungry Minds Marketing: John Helmus, Assistant Vice President, Director of Marketing

Hungry Minds Production for Branded Press: Debbie Stailey, Production Director

Hungry Minds Sales: Michael Violano, Vice President, International Sales and Sub Rights

Contents at a Glance

Cartoons at a Glance

By Rich Tennant

page 7

page 339

page 105

page 249

page 371

page 273

page 41

Cartoon Information:
Fax: 978-546-7747
E-Mail: richtennant@the5thwave.com
World Wide Web: www.the5thwave.com

Table of Contents

Introduction

*W*elcome to *PCs For Dummies,* the fresh new 8th Edition. This is the book that answers the question, "How does a computer turn a smart person like you into a dummy?"

Computers are useful, yes. And a fair number of people — heaven help them — fall in love with computers. But the rest of us are left sitting dumb and numb in front of the box. It's not that using a computer is beyond the range of our intellect; it's that no one has ever bothered to sit down and explain things in human terms. Until now.

This book talks about using a computer in friendly, human — and often irreverent — terms. Nothing is sacred here. Electronics can be praised by others. This book focuses on you and your needs. In this book, you'll discover everything you need to know about your computer without painful jargon or the prerequisite master's degree in engineering. And you'll have fun.

What's New in This Edition?

This book contains plenty of new and up-to-the-minute information about the technology that has changed since the previous edition. I've tossed out about 80 pages of what I felt was no longer needed, and tossed in about 80 pages of information on today's computers, options, software, the Internet, and lots of troubleshooting that readers have requested over the years. Just about all the important stuff for today's PC user can be found right here betwixt these covers.

This edition contains the following information not found in any previous edition of *PCs For Dummies*:

- ✔ Coverage of Windows 98, Windows Me, Windows 2000, and the new Windows XP
- ✔ The latest information on USB and FireWire
- ✔ New hardware information, including LCD monitors, optical mice, and the latest modems
- ✔ Brand-new CD-R and CD-RW "burning" information
- ✔ Scanning and digital photography
- ✔ Plenty of new Internet information

✔ Tips and advice for using Internet Explorer and Outlook Express

✔ Tons of new troubleshooting and prevention information

✔ Appreciation for what you already know about computers

Regarding that last point, I've updated lots of the basic information in this book under the assumption that many people understand a few simple computer concepts, such as sending e-mail or starting a program in Windows. Although this information remains in the book, I've cut it back a tad to allow for more information on immediate and advanced topics that are certainly not beyond the range of any PC user.

As always, all the information is presented in the same soothing, gentle tones that calms even the most panicked computerphobe.

Where to Start

This book is designed so that you can pick it up at any point and start reading — like a reference. There are 31 chapters. Each chapter covers a specific aspect of the computer — turning it on, using a printer, using software, kicking it, and so on. Each chapter is divided into self-contained nuggets of information — sections — all relating to the major theme of the chapter. Sample sections you may find include:

✔ Your Basic Hardware (A Nerd's-Eye View)

✔ Learning which buttons you can ignore

✔ "My taskbar is gone!"

✔ Creating a signature

✔ Where you cannot get a virus

✔ Running a troubleshooter

You don't have to memorize anything in this book. Nothing about a computer is memorable. Each section is designed so you can read the information quickly, digest what you've read, and then put down the book and get on with using the computer. If anything technical crops up, you'll be alerted to its presence so you can cleanly avoid it.

Conventions Used in This Book

This book works like a reference. Start with the topic you want more information about; look for it in the table of contents or in the index. Turn to the area of interest and read the information you need. Then, with the information in your head, you can quickly close the book and freely perform whatever task you need — without learning anything else.

Whenever I describe a message or information on the screen, it looks like this:

```
This is a message on-screen.
```

If you have to type something, it looks like this:

> **Type me in**

You would type the text **Type me in** as shown. You'll be told when and if to press the Enter key.

Windows menu commands are shown like this:

> Choose File⇨Exit.

This means to choose the File menu and then choose the Exit command.

Key combinations you may have to type in are shown like this:

> Ctrl+S

This means to press and hold the Ctrl (control) key, type an *S*, and then release the Ctrl key. It works just like the way pressing Shift+S on the keyboard produces an uppercase *S*. Same deal, different shift key.

What You Don't Need to Read

A lot of technical information is involved with using a computer. To better insulate you from it, I've enclosed such material in sidebars that are clearly marked as technical information. You don't have to read that stuff. Often, it's just a complex explanation of information already discussed in the chapter. Reading that information will only teach you something substantial about your computer, which is not the goal here.

Foolish Assumptions

I am going to make some admittedly foolish assumptions about you: You have a computer, and you use it somehow to do something. You use a PC (or are planning on it) and will be using Windows as your PC's operating system or main program.

This book does not cover DOS, Windows 95, or any previous Windows versions. It does cover Windows 98, Windows Me, Windows 2000, and Windows XP. If information relates to a specific version of Windows, I'll name the version. Otherwise, when I use the term "Windows," it applies to all versions.

(For coverage of DOS or earlier editions of Windows, refer to *DOS For Dummies*, 3rd Edition, published by Hungry Minds, Inc. Windows 95 coverage is included in *PCs For Dummies*, 6th and 7th Editions.)

Icons Used in This Book

 This icon alerts you to needless technical information — drivel added because I just feel like explaining something totally unnecessary (a hard habit to break). Feel free to skip over anything tagged with this little picture.

 This icon usually indicates helpful advice or an insight that makes using the computer interesting. For example, when pouring acid over your computer, be sure to wear a protective apron, gloves, and goggles.

 Ummm, I forgot what this one means.

 This icon indicates that you need to be careful with the information presented; usually, it's a reminder for you not to do something.

 This icon marks the special, and often strangely different, methods by which Windows XP accomplishes many of the tasks in this book. If you have Windows XP, look for these icons. If you don't have Windows XP, then you're truly blessed!

This icon flags Q&A topics that I've culled from my reader mail. Because many questions deal with topics that affect a lot of people, I've placed the original questions and my replies in the various "Ask Dan" sidebars throughout this book. Speaking of which. . . .

Getting in Touch with the Author

My e-mail address is listed here if you'd like to write me on the Internet:

```
dgookin@wambooli.com
```

Yes, that is my address and I personally respond to every e-mail message I get. However, remember that you paid others for your technical support and you should try there first: Phone your dealer for hardware support, software developer for software assistance, and your ISP for various Internet trouble.

You can also visit my Web site, which is chock full of helpful support pages and bonus information. You can also subscribe to my various e-mail newsletters at the site:

```
http://www.wambooli.com/
```

Where to Go from Here

With this book in hand, you're now ready to go out and conquer your PC. Start by looking through the table of contents or the index. Find a topic, turn to the page indicated, and you're ready to go. Also, feel free to write in this book, fill in the blanks, dog-ear the pages, and do anything that would make a librarian blanch. Enjoy.

Part I
Introducing the PC

The 5th Wave • By Rich Tennant

"The new technology has really helped me get organized. I keep my project reports under the PC, budgets under my laptop, and memos under my pager."

In this part . . .

A special operator's license is not required to use a personal computer. No, you need a license to do other dangerous things, such as drive a car or get married. But no one needs a license to own or operate a computer. That might imply that computers aren't that dangerous (and they aren't), but more than that it means that just about anyone can, after a fashion, use a computer. You don't even need thick, horn-rim glasses or a white lab coat.

This part of the book covers the very basic computer concepts. It's designed to get you up to speed on computer stuff, whether you're just starting out, or haven't even bought a computer yet, or perhaps you're buying a new computer after "retiring" your old clunker, or maybe you just bought a shotgun and need to know what to shoot at. Whatever the case, this part of the book is for you.

Chapter 1

Hello, Computer!

• •

• •

*P*ersonal computers, or *PCs*, are nothing to fear. They're not like personal robots, or *PRs*. No, personal robots start out nice and friendly and then, after a while, you and the entire human race become way too relaxed and dependent on them. Then guess what? They turn on you! In mere moments, we're history, and intelligent cockroaches are running the planet. (Think of the smell!) That will never happen with a PC.

Computers are nothing to fear, but they won't go out of their way to help you either. Don't for once think that the computer will pop out of the box, shake your hand, and then instantly become your best friend. That just ain't gonna happen. On the other hand, you do have this friendly book, which starts out with this "Hello, Computer!" chapter introducing you to everything you need to know about the PC.

✔ If you don't already own a PC, I can recommend a great book: *Buying a Computer For Dummies,* written by yours truly and available from Hungry Minds, Inc. It covers the basics of the PC, how to select one just right for you, and how to set it up for the first time.

✔ This book tries its best to be jargon free or at least explain terms before using them. Other books and magazines cannot make the same promise, so I can recommend a good computer dictionary: *The Illustrated Computer Dictionary For Dummies,* also written by yours truly and available from Hungry Minds, Inc.

✔ I promise not to plug any of my other books for the remainder of this chapter.

What Exactly Is a PC?

A PC is a personal computer, named after its earliest ancestor, the IBM PC. IBM (International Business Machines) created the PC (Personal Computer) after years of making larger, more impersonal computers (IPs).

Today, most computers are known as PCs, whether you're buying them for the home or office. They don't have to be made by IBM. Heck, even the Macintosh is a PC. If it's yours and it's a computer, then it's a PC.

- ✔ Technically, a PC is a large calculator with a better display and more buttons.

- ✔ PCs are as adept with words as they are with numbers. It's the software that controls things, which is covered later in this chapter.

- ✔ Though the Macintosh, Sony PlayStation, PalmPilot, and even the Nintendo Game Boy are all technically personal computers, they aren't covered in this book. This book concentrates on PCs that run the Windows operating system. [Windows is defined later in this chapter, in the section "The operating system (Or Who's in charge here?)."]

- ✔ Laptops and notebook computers are lighter and more portable versions of the traditional desktop PC. They allow people to do important computing tasks on the go, such as playing computer games on airplanes. Although a laptop may not be your first PC, I mention various laptoppy things throughout this book just to amuse my managing editor.

- ✔ I just made up the term IP (for impersonal computer). Larger computers are called *mainframes*. Feel free to ignore them.

- ✔ Computers are not evil. They harbor no sinister intelligence. In fact, when you get to know them, they're rather dumb.

What does a PC do?

Computers defy description. Unlike other tools that have definite purposes, a computer can do a number of different things, solving an infinite number of problems for an infinite number of people. Just about anything that can be done with words, numbers, information, or communication can be done with a computer.

In a way, a computer is just another electronic gadget. Unlike the toaster and your car's fuel injection system, which are programmed to do only one thing each, a personal computer can be *programmed* to do a number of interesting tasks. It's up to you to tell the computer what you want it to do.

- ✔ The computer is the chameleon of electronic devices. Your phone can be used only as a phone, your VCR only records and plays videos, and your microwave oven only zaps things (food, mostly). A computer's potential is limitless.

- ✔ Computers get the job done by using *software*. The software tells the computer what to do.

- ✔ Software is only half of the computer equation. The other side is *hardware*, which I cover later in this chapter.

- ✔ No, you never have to learn about programming to use a computer. Someone else does the programming, and then you buy the program (the software) to get your work done.

- ✔ Your job, as the computer operator, is to tell the software what to do, which then tells the computer what to do.

- ✔ Only on cheesy sci-fi shows does the computer ever tell *you* what to do.

- ✔ You can always *verbally* tell the computer what to do with itself. This happens millions of times a day, by programmers and nonprogrammers alike.

What does a PC not do?

The PC does not give off a pleasing odor, nor does it hum.
And while it can do many things at once, it just cannot chew gum.

A PC is happy to do Windows, but it won't clean the house.
It makes an okay companion, but it's not really a spouse.

With your PC you can play games, interactive and chess.
But if you need a hug, the computer could really care less.

The PC does work, calculating, storing, and retrieval.
But while it may seem really smart, it's certainly not evil.

And above all, remember this handy PC rule:
It's not you but the computer that's really dumb, dumb, dumb, dumb.

Hardware and Software

Two separate things make up a computer: hardware and software. They go hand in hand. You cannot have one without the other. It would be like romance without the moon, lightning without thunder, macaroni without cheese, Yin without Yang, Frankincense without Myrrh.

Everyone say "Hardware." Say it hard: *Hardware*.

Hardware is the physical part of a computer, anything you can touch and anything you can see. Yet, hardware is nothing unless it has software to control it. In a way, hardware is like a car without a driver or a saw without a carpenter; you need both to make something happen.

Everyone say "Software." Whisper it: *Software*.

Software is the brains of the computer. It tells the hardware what to do. Without software, hardware just sits around bored and unappreciated. You must have software to make a computer go. In fact, software determines your computer's personality.

- ✔ If you can throw it out a window, it's hardware.

- ✔ Computer software is nothing more than instructions that tell the hardware what to do, how to act, or when to lose your data.

- ✔ Computer software is more important than computer hardware. The software tells the hardware what to do.

- ✔ Although computer software comes on disks (CDs or floppy disks), the *disks* aren't the software. Software is stored on disks just as music is stored on cassettes and CDs.

- ✔ Without the proper software, your computer is merely an expensive doorstop.

Your Basic Hardware (A Nerd's-Eye View)

Figure 1-1 shows what a typical computer system looks like. I've flagged the most major computer things you should identify and know about. These are the basics. The rest of this book goes into the details.

Console: The main computer box is the console, though it might also be called the *system unit* (geeky) or the *CPU* (incorrect). It's a box that contains your computer's guts plus various buttons, lights, and holes into which you plug the rest of the computer system.

Monitor: The monitor is the TV-set-like thing on which the computer displays information. It sits to the right or left of the console, or if you put the console beneath the table, the monitor sits on top of the table. (Putting the monitor beneath the table is a silly idea.) I cover monitors in detail in Chapter 11.

Keyboard: It's the thing you type on. Clackity-clack-clack. Chapter 13 cusses and discusses the computer keyboard.

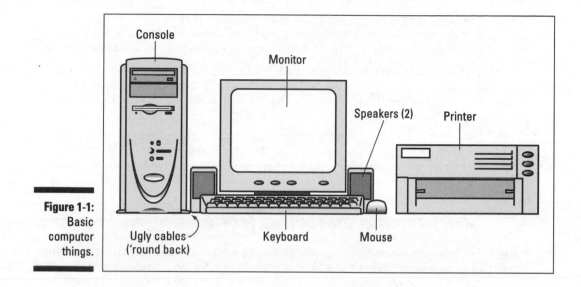

Figure 1-1:
Basic
computer
things.

Mouse: Ah, the computer mouse. No rodent or pest, it's a helpful device that lets you work with graphical objects that the computer displays on the monitor's screen. See Chapter 12 for more mouse information.

Speakers: Most PCs can bleep and squawk through a set of stereo speakers, either external jobbies you set up, as shown in Figure 1-1, or speakers that are built into the console or the monitor. Pay more money, and you can even get a subwoofer to sit under the desk. Now *that* will frighten the neighbors.

Printer: It's where you get the computer's output: the printed stuff, also called *hard copy.* Sashay off to Chapter 14 to increase your PC printer knowledge.

Scanner. This item, not shown in Figure 1-1 (because, like your desktop, there just isn't room!), is used to scan in graphic images and printed material, transforming them into graphics you can manipulate, e-mail, or do a number of interesting things with inside the computer. Mince up to Chapter 17 for the lowdown.

Lots of ugly cables: One thing they never show you — not in any computer manual and especially not in advertisements — is the ganglia of cables that lives behind each and every computer. What a mess! These cables are required to plug things into the wall and into each other. No shampoo or conditioner on earth can clean up those tangles.

✔ These parts of the computer are all important. Make sure that you know where the console, keyboard, mouse, speakers, monitor, and printer are in your own system. If the printer isn't present, it's probably a network printer sitting in some other room.

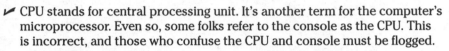

✔ A computer really exists in two places. Most of the computer lives inside the console. Everything else, all the stuff connected to the console, is called *peripherals*. See Chapter 18 for more information about peripherals.

✔ If your computer has a modem, it's usually located inside the console. You can see it from the back, as shown in Figure 1-3. Some modems do live outside the console, but that's less common today than it was ten years ago.

✔ CPU stands for central processing unit. It's another term for the computer's microprocessor. Even so, some folks refer to the console as the CPU. This is incorrect, and those who confuse the CPU and console must be flogged.

Stuff on the console (front)

The console is the most important part of your computer. It's the main thing, the Big Box. Every part of your computer system either lives inside the console or plugs into it. Figure 1-2 shows what a typical PC console may look like. I've flagged the more interesting places to visit, although on your computer they may appear in a different location than shown in the figure.

CD-ROM or DVD drive: These high-capacity drives read discs that look exactly like musical CDs, although they contain computer information. Chapters 4 and 9 cover how you use and abuse CD-ROM and DVD drives and discs.

DVD drives have the "DVD" logo on them. If you don't see the DVD logo, then your PC has a mere CD-ROM drive. That's okay for now, because little software is available exclusively on DVD discs.

Future expansion: Ah, potential! You can add a whole grab bag of goodies to a computer, and most consoles have plenty of room for it. Any blank spots or covers on the front of your computer mean that you can add even more junk later. Such a space may already be taken, filled with such goodies as a tape backup unit, Zip drive, another CD-ROM or CD-R/RW drive, another hard drive, or an assortment of other computer things many folks eagerly spend their hard-earned money on.

Floppy drive: This slot eats floppy disks. Some software comes on floppy disks, and you can use these disks to move files from one PC to another.

Zip drive: A common option found on many PCs is the Zip drive, which is like a super-dooper floppy drive. On a Zip disk, you can store the equivalent of 100 floppy disks worth of information, or more! Not every PC has a Zip drive, however.

Air vents: Okay, this one isn't truly important, but most consoles sport some type of air vent on the front. Don't block the air vents with books or sticky notes! The thing has gotta breathe.

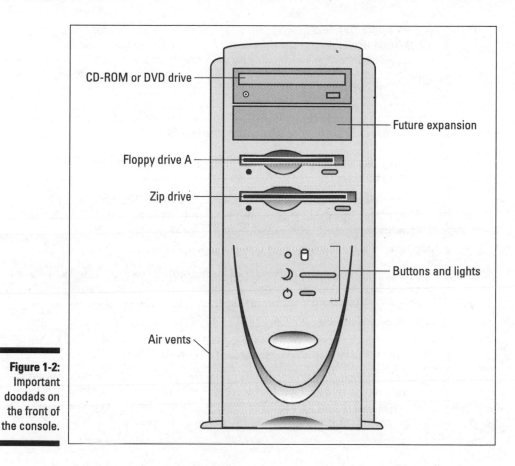

CD-ROM or DVD drive

Future expansion

Floppy drive A

Zip drive

Buttons and lights

Air vents

Figure 1-2:
Important
doodads on
the front of
the console.

Buttons and lights: Most of the computer's buttons are on the keyboard. A few of the more important ones are on the console, and these buttons on fancier PCs are accompanied by many impressive tiny lights. These buttons and lights include the following:

✔ **On-off button:** The PC's main power button, the one you use to turn the darn thing on. A light usually accompanies the on-off button, although computers make enough racket that you can usually hear when they're turned on.

✔ **Reset button:** This button allows you to restart the computer without going through the bother of turning it off and then on again. Chapter 2 explains why anyone in his right mind would want to do that. Note that not every PC has a reset button.

✔ **Sleep button:** Pressing this button causes your PC to go into a coma, suspending all activity without turning the computer off. On some computers, this button and the on-off button are the same. Read all about this craziness in Chapter 2.

✔ **Disk drive lights:** These lights flash when the hard drive, floppy drive, CD-ROM drive, or Zip drive is working. For a hard drive, the light is your reassurance that it's alive, happy, and doing its job. For all other types of drives (with removable disks), the light indicates that the computer is using the drive.

Other fun and unusual things may live on the front of your console, most of which are particular to a certain computer brand.

✔ Older computers sported such things as locks and keys and "turbo" buttons.

✔ Some newer computers have stickers that show Windows' secret installation number, or proclaim such nonsense as "I was built to run Windows 3,000,000" or "A Pentium XIX lurks inside this box."

✔ Rarely, if ever, will you find a Panic button.

✔ The console isn't the only part of your computer system that sports an on-off switch. Your PC's monitor, printer, modem, and almost everything else also have their own on-off switches. See Chapter 2 for more information about turning everything on.

✔ Do not block the air vents on the front of the console. If you do, the computer may literally suffocate. (Actually, it gets too hot.)

✔ A hard drive light can be red or green or yellow, and it flickers when the hard drive is in use. Don't let it freak you out! It's not an alarm; the hard drive is just doing its job. (Personally, I find the green type of hard drive light most comforting — reminds me of Christmas.)

Stuff on the console (back)

The console's backside is the busy side. That's where you find various connectors for the many other devices in your computer system: a place to plug in the monitor, keyboard, mouse, speakers, and just about anything else that came in the box with the PC.

Figure 1-3 illustrates the typical PC's rump, showing you where and how the various goodies can connect. Your computer will have most of the items shown in the figure, although they'll probably be in different locations on the PC's backside.

 Power connector: This thing is where the PC plugs into a cord that plugs into the wall.

 Keyboard connector: The keyboard plugs into this little hole. The wee li'l picture is supposed to be a keyboard. Note that some keyboard holes may be labeled *KBD* or even say *Keyboard* with all the vowels and the *R*.

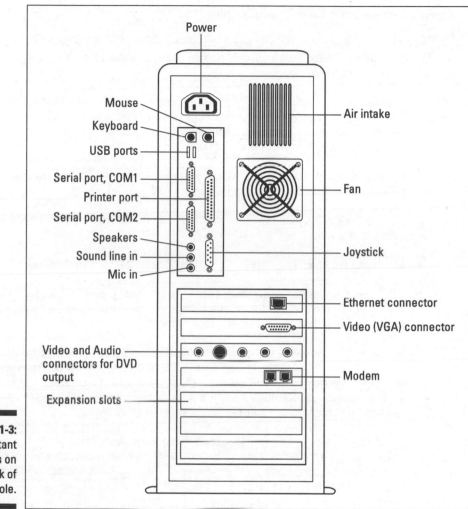

Figure 1-3:
Important
doodads on
the back of
the console.

 Mouse connector: It's generally the same size and shape as the keyboard connector, although this hole has a mouse icon nearby to let you know that the mouse plugs in there.

USB port: Plug snazzy USB devices into these Certs-size slots. If you have a USB mouse, keyboard, speakers, or printer, it plugs in here, not in the other ports. See Chapter 8 for more USB information.

Serial, or COM, ports: Most PCs have two of these ports, labeled COM1 and COM2, though often they're labeled with a series of Is and Os. This is where an external modem or sometimes a mouse is plugged in.

Printer port: The PC's printer plugs into this connector.

Joystick port: This port is used mainly for scientific applications. The port may be identified by an image (shown in the margin), or it may say *Joystick* or *Game controller.*

 Monitor connector: Your PC's monitor plugs into this hole. Sometimes the hole is on an expansion slot and is unlabeled. If so, you can tell what the monitor connector is because it has 15 little holes in it — more than the serial port, which is the same size but has only 9 holes.

 Speaker/sound-out jack: It's where you plug in your PC's external speakers or where you would hook up the PC to a sound system.

Line-in jack: This jack is where you plug in your stereo or VCR to the PC for capturing sound.

Microphone jack: The computer's microphone plugs into this hole.

Ethernet (network) connector: This is where you plug in a local area network (LAN) connector, which looks like a huge phone connector. Not every computer will have one of these connectors.

Modem: The modem can have up to two connectors, though some modems have only one. One of the two connectors, or the only connector, is where you plug the modem to the phone jack in your wall. The other connector, if available, is used to connect a telephone to the computer so that you can answer the phone. See Chapter 15 for more on modems.

S-Video out: If your PC sports a DVD drive, it probably has several additional connectors for video and audio output. The S-Video connector allows you to connect an S-Video-happy TV to your PC. Other video connectors let you pump a DVD movie out to a TV set or VCR.

 If your computer has a DVD drive, then you need to use the sound jacks on the DVD expansion card, not the sound jacks as shown in Figure 1-3. So, for example, if you plug your speakers into the plug as shown in the figure and you get no sound, look for an identical hole on one of the expansion cards.

In addition to the ports, jacks, and holes on the back of the console are expansion slots. They're the backsides of various expansion cards you plug into your PC. Some expansion slots have connectors for other PC goodies as well.

The good news? You connect all this stuff only once. Then your PC's butt faces the wall for the rest of its life, and you never have to look at it again.

Oooh! It's color-coded!

The new trend in computer hardware is to color-code the connectors on a PC's rump. So in addition to the intergalactic icon for speaker or sound-out, you now have the color green. That's the good news.

The bad news is that each computer manufacturer tends to use its own color-coding for everything. So what's red on one computer may be violet on another. Such illogic is the earmark of the computer industry. Fortunately, the connectors still look different and are still tagged with the international symbol or text. Even so, I thought I'd list the common colors used by most manufacturers in Table 1-1.

Table 1-1	PC Connector Color Codes
Port/Connector	*Color*
Keyboard	Purple
Mouse	Green
Serial port(s)	Cyan
Printer	Violet
Monitor	Blue
Line out/speakers	Lime
Microphone	Pink
Audio line in	Grey
Joystick	Yellow

Variations on the typical computer theme

Not all computers look like the image shown in Figure 1-1. The type of PC shown there is currently the most popular, called the *mini-tower*. It can sit upright on your desk or be tucked away out of sight beneath the desk. And it's sleek and sexy.

PCs need not all be configured as mini-towers. For the first ten years or so of the PC's life, the desktop model was the most popular. Other models exist as well, each with an orientation, size, and enough blinking lights to please any particular person.

The following list describes the various types and models of PCs:

Mini-tower: The most popular PC configuration, where the computer sits upright on a desktop or beneath the desk (refer to Figure 1-1).

Desktop: Formerly the most popular PC configuration, with a slab-like console lying flat on the table top with the monitor squatting on top.

Desktop (small footprint): A smaller version of the desktop, typically used in low-priced home systems. (A PC's *footprint* is the amount of desk space it uses. A small footprint desktop model is just tinier than the full-size desktop model. Of course, in the end, it makes no difference: The amount of clutter you have always expands to fill the available desk space.)

Notebook/laptop: A specialty type of computer that folds into a handy, lightweight package, ideal for lugging around airports. Laptop PCs work just like their desktop brethren; any exceptions are noted throughout this book.

Towers: Essentially a full-sized desktop standing on its side, making it tall, like a tower. These PCs have lotsa room inside for expansion, making them the darlings of power-mad users. They typically sit on the floor, usually propping up one end of the table.

Your Basic Software

Computer software doesn't get the credit it deserves for running your computer, which is probably why it's overpriced. In any event, you need the software to make your hardware go.

The operating system (Or "Who's in charge here?")

The most important piece of software is the *operating system*. It's the computer's number-one program — the head honcho, the big cheese, Mr. In Charge, Fearless Leader, *le roi*.

The operating system rules the computer's roost, controlling all the individual computer components and making sure that everything gets along well. It's the actual brains of the operation, telling the nitwitted hardware what to do next.

The operating system also controls applications software (see the next section). Each of those programs must bend a knee and take a loyalty oath to the operating system.

Finally, it's the operating system's job to communicate with you, dear human. On this level, it does a truly mediocre job, which is why you see so many books on using computer operating systems in the bookstore.

- ✔ The computer's most important piece of software is the operating system.

- ✔ The operating system typically comes with the computer when you buy it. You never need to add a second operating system, although operating systems do get updated and improved from time to time. See Chapter 19 for information about upgrading the operating system.

- ✔ When you buy software, you buy it for an operating system, not your brand of PC. In the olden days (the 1980s), you would walk to the Apple or IBM or Commodore section of the software store. Today, you browse either in the Macintosh or Windows or even Linux aisles.

- ✔ For the PC, the operating system is Windows. It comes in various flavors: Windows 98, Windows Me, Windows 2000, and Windows XP.

- ✔ Chapter 3 chitty-chats about Windows, all flavors.

Software that actually does something

The operating system is merely in charge of the computer. By itself, an operating system doesn't really do anything for you. Instead, to get work done, you need an application program.

Application programs are the programs that do the work.

Application programs include word processors, spreadsheets, and databases. Whatever it is you do on your computer, you do it using an application program.

Other types of programs include utilities and games and educational and programming software. And then there are all the Internet applications: Web browsers, e-mail programs, and software of that ilk.

Some Consoling Words of Advice

The biggest problem I encounter with people new to the world of computers is that they quickly blame themselves when something goes wrong.

Honestly, people! It's not your fault!

Computers goof up. Programs have bugs. Things go wrong, and sometimes they would do so even if you weren't sitting there at the controls.

Please, don't assume you've goofed up or somehow wrecked something. True, that does happen. But a good deal of the time, the computer is just acting dumb.

- ✔ Blame the computer or the software first! The stuff sometimes doesn't work.

- ✔ See Chapter 27 for more information on troubleshooting your PC should it do something wrong or happen to explode.

Chapter 2

The Big Red Switch

Compared to a car, turning on a computer is a cinch. Computers have only one switch. Cars have one ignition switch, which has two positions, plus you have to take the car out of gear and often press on the brake pedal. And if you screw up, the car could lurch forward or back, making various ugly grinding noises. By contrast, computers are far easier to get going. Never mind that the switch is neither big nor red.

This chapter covers the basics of turning on a computer. No, you don't woo the computer with flowers and love sonnets; you turn on a computer simply by flipping its power switch. Of course, that would make for a rather short chapter, so I've tossed in information about what to do *after* flipping the switch, plus important info on when (if ever) to turn the computer off.

To Turn the Computer On, Throw the Switch

Click.

Perhaps the toughest part of turning the computer on is *finding* the switch. Most PCs put the switch on the front of the console. On others, you may find the switch on the side or even the back.

Some switches are the on-off flip or rocker type. Other switches are push buttons that turn the system on and turn it off.

- ✔ The power switch on your PC is most likely labeled in the international manner. The | (bar) means "on," and the O (zero) means off. I think.

- ✔ Laptop computers have strange on-off switches. Some of them are on-off push buttons beneath a stiff rubber top. Other switches may be a "slide-and-release" job. And there's no telling which side of the slab the button is on; just get used to wherever it is.

- ✔ If the computer doesn't turn on, check to see whether it's plugged in. If it still doesn't turn on, refer to Chapter 27.

- ✔ Some nerdy terms for turning on a computer: *power-on*, *power-up*, and *boot*. To *boot* a computer merely means to turn it on. You don't have to kick the thing.

- ✔ Some newer computers have on-sleep switches instead of on-off switches. The on-sleep switch turns the computer on and puts it to sleep. It does not turn the computer off. See the sections "Turning the Computer Off (Shutdown)" for more information.

- ✔ Make sure there isn't a floppy disk in drive A when you start your computer. If there is, then the computer may not start from the hard drive like it's supposed to. (See Chapter 4 for more information about drive A.)

Oops! Other things to turn on

Just about everything connected to your PC has an on-off switch, which sometimes means that turning on the console by itself doesn't complete the job. Instead, you should turn on other devices you may need.

Here is the list of things you should turn on in the general order they should be turned on:

1. **The monitor.** Get this warmed up and ready to display text.

2. **Peripherals.** Turn on any external devices you plan on using: external disk drives, CD-Rs, and so on. Turning these on now means that the computer will *see* them once it gets up and running.

3. **The console.** Turn this on last.

Or you can turn everything on at once, which is okay. Otherwise, the console should come on last.

- ✔ Most computer devices have their own on-off switches.

- ✔ The largest button on the front of the monitor turns it on. Some older models may have the on-off switch in back.

✔ You don't need to turn on an external modem right away. Don't bother turning it on until you're ready to use it. Or, you can be like me and just leave the external modem on all the time.

✔ You don't need to turn on your printer until you're ready to print something. Or (again), you can be like me and leave your printer on all the time. (I have one of those *power-saving* printers, so it's environmentally safe and all that.)

✔ Another no-need-to-turn-on-at-first item is the scanner. You need to switch on most scanners only just before you plan on scanning a photo or document (though some of the newer scanners are on all the time).

The best solution for turning on a PC

Because the computer has so many devices that must be plugged in and turned on, most people buy a power strip. The power strip comes with six (more or less) sockets into which you can plug every part of your computer. Then you just plug the power strip into the wall. Flipping the switch on the power strip then turns on the console, monitor, and everything.

Here are some power strip hints and suggestions:

✔ Set everything up by plugging each of your PC's parts into the power strip: console, monitor, modem, scanner, printer, and so on.

✔ Don't plug a laser printer into a power strip. The laser printer draws too much juice for that to be effective — or safe. Instead, you must plug the laser printer directly into the wall socket. (It says that in your laser printer's manual, if you ever get around to reading it.)

✔ Try to get a power strip with *surge protection*. They're a little more spendy than plain-old power strips, but they offer a level of power protection that could save your PC should a power surge occur.

✔ A power surge is a gradual increase in the amount of voltage coming from the power company. A power spike is a sudden increase in the amount of voltage, such as when lightning strikes. Both things are nasty. (The opposite of a surge is a dip; the opposite of a spike is, well, the power goes out.)

✔ For even more protection, get a *UPS*, which I cover in the next section.

✔ I recommend the Kensington SmartSockets power strip. Unlike cheaper power strips, the SmartSockets lines up its sockets in a perpendicular arrangement, making it easier to plug in bulky transformers.

✔ Plugging everything into a power strip sure solves the problem of "which part of the computer do I turn on first?"

✔ With a power strip, you can turn on your computer system with your foot (providing that the power strip is on the floor). Or if you take off your shoes, use your big toe. And if you're really classy, use your big toe sticking out of a hole in your sock.

✔ The medical name for your big toe is *hallux*.

An even better power solution (the UPS)

Perhaps the best thing to plug your computer into is a UPS or uninterruptible power supply. It's like a large battery that keeps your computer running even if the power goes out.

Depending on the number of outlets on the UPS, you can plug in your monitor and console, plus other items in your computer system. For example, I also plug my external modem and external CD-R drive in my UPS (it has four sockets). That setup keeps me up and running during minor power outages.

Figure 2-1 illustrates one approach to how a UPS could work along with a power strip to power your computer system. Note that only the console and monitor are plugged into the UPS. Everything else goes into a power strip. The following dramatization illustrates my reasons for this:

A large boom is heard. The lights flicker, then go out. STAN *is left sitting in the dark, but his computer is still on.* GINGER *rushes in.*

> **GINGER:** The power is out! Those croissants I put in the toaster oven are ruined! Did you lose that life-saving doodle you were creating in Paint?
>
> **STAN:** No, darling, I'm still working on it. See? Our UPS has kept the computer console and monitor on during this brief outage.

The urge to surge

Q: I am a bit unsure of how you feel about surge protectors. I was under the impression that most computer gurus think everyone should have a surge protector, even if the power in the area is usually stable and lightning doesn't strike more than normal. Maybe the big chain stores just push surge protectors to make more money; I'm not sure. So, do you think everyone who buys a PC should also purchase a surge protector?

A: Yes. Buying a power strip with surge protection is the best of both worlds: It gives you more sockets to plug things into, and it adds surge protection. Also, you should know that surge protection does nothing against lightning strikes. For that you need spike protection, which is offered in a UPS.

GINGER: Well, hurry up and print it.

STAN: Nay! I shan't print. Printing can wait, which is why I did not connect the printer to the UPS. It is as powerless as the toaster oven.

GINGER: What can you do? Hurry! The UPS battery won't last forever!

STAN: Relax, gentle spouse. I shall save to disk, thus. [Ctrl+S] Now I can shut down the computer, assured with the knowledge that my doodle file is safely stored on the internal hard drive. There. *(He turns off the computer and monitor.)* Now we can weather out the storm with peace of mind.

Two hours later, after the power is back on. GINGER *and* STAN *are sipping wine.*

GINGER: Honey, you sure are smart the way you used that UPS.

STAN: Well, I am just thankful I read Dan Gookin's book *PCs For Dummies,* published by Hungry Minds, Inc. I think I shall buy more of his books.

They kiss.

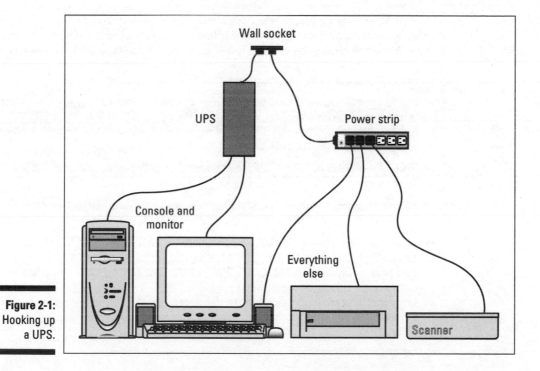

Figure 2-1:
Hooking up
a UPS.

Despite the advertising, a UPS gives you maybe five minutes of computer power. So be like Stan and save your stuff to disk and then shut down Windows and turn off the computer. You can print, scan, modem, or whatever when the power comes back on.

- ✔ A UPS works best for brief power outages. For example, those little power burps that may just flicker the lights can reset your PC. A UPS prevents that reset.

- ✔ Never plug a laser printer into a UPS.

- ✔ In addition to emergency power, a UPS also provides higher levels of electrical protection for your equipment. Many models offer surge, spike, and dip protection, which keep your PC running smoothly despite any nasties the Power Company may throw your way.

Here Comes Windows!

After starting your computer (the hardware), the operating system (the software) takes over. Remember that the software controls the hardware, and the main piece of software is the operating system. So the operating system is the first program that your computer runs. That operating system is called Windows.

As Windows comes to life, you see various messages displayed on the screen. Whatever. Just sit and watch; most of it has low entertainment value, kind of like a long list of credits before a good film . . . or a mediocre film, in this case.

- ✔ Lots of chaos occurs as Windows loads. Don't fret over any of it.

- ✔ For everyone reading this book, the operating system is Windows, either Windows 98, Windows Me, Windows 2000, or possibly Windows XP. Subtle differences and specifics between the various Windows versions are noted throughout this book.

- ✔ Earlier versions of Windows are covered in earlier editions of *PCs For Dummies*.

- ✔ Before Windows, the PC's operating system was called DOS. See *DOS For Dummies* (Hungry Minds, Inc.) for more information.

- ✔ Some monitors may display text before Windows starts up. The text is basically telling you that the monitor is not receiving a signal from the computer. Rather than just say, "I'm not getting any signs of life from the computer," the monitor instead says `Invalid Sync` or `Error on input` or something even cruder. Ignore the message; it vanishes when the console comes to life.

"My computer was shut down improperly!"

There's a right and wrong way to do everything. To shut down a computer, you don't just throw the big red switch the other way. That just won't do. A few years back, it was okay. Today, however, you have to shut down *properly*. If you don't, Windows may warn you the next time you start the computer.

Don't fret over the warning. There is no shame in having Windows tell you it was shut down improperly. It's actually a good thing! The warning tells you that the ScanDisk program is about to run, which fixes any problems caused by the improper shutdown.

TIP

✔ If you never see this error message . . . good!

✔ If ScanDisk finds any errors, fix them by pressing the Enter key.

✔ You don't need an *undo disk,* so select the Skip Undo option if you ever see it offered.

✔ See the section "Turning the Computer Off (Shutdown)," later in this chapter, for information about how to properly turn off your computer.

"My computer says 'Non-system disk.' What gives?"

It happens frequently, even to Bill Gates!

```
Non-system disk or disk error
Replace and strike any key when ready
```

Lightning strikes

Q: I unplugged my computer during a recent lightning storm. Even so, a nearby strike zapped my hard drive. Fortunately, my dealer replaced the computer. But how did it get zapped if the computer was unplugged?

A: Most likely the spike came in through the phone line, into the modem, and then right to the computer's motherboard. *Zap!* Whether you unplug the computer or use a spike-protection UPS, the computer can still be damaged through the phone line. So as an extra precaution, I recommend unplugging the phone line during an electrical storm. Or, if you have a UPS, check to see if it has a socket for the phone line, which means it offers phone line spike protection. That's a very nice thing to have.

If you see this message, remove the floppy disk from drive A and press the Enter key. Your computer then starts up normally.

The reason you see the message is a floppy disk was left in your PC's drive A. The computer has tried to start itself up by using software on that disk and — whaddya know? — no software is on that disk! The software (your PC's operating system) is really on your PC's hard drive, which can't be loaded until you remove that dern floppy disk from drive A and whack the Enter key.

Log in, mystery guest

The final step into the Windows prison is for the inmates to identify themselves to the warden. In technical parlance, this is to *login* or *logon*. This happens for several reasons:

- ✔ To connect you and your computer onto a network (mostly at the office or, if you're *really* into computers, at your home)
- ✔ To identify you as one of several people who use the same computer
- ✔ To annoy the bejeezus out of you

Logging in works differently, depending on your version of Windows and whether or not it's networked.

Figure 2-2 shows the silly logon dialog box for Windows 98 and Windows Me. It's silly because it offers no security and can easily be bypassed by pressing the Esc key or clicking the Cancel button. Otherwise, you type in your user name and password, or only the password if your user name is already shown, as illustrated in Figure 2-2.

Don't mess with system passwords

Some PCs have the capability to have a system password. This sounds nifty: A prompt appears right after you turn on your computer, preventing unauthorized access. If you don't know the password — or you forget it — you can't use the computer. A password is great for security, but it's a serious risk should your brain suddenly forget it.

My advice: Don't bother with system passwords.

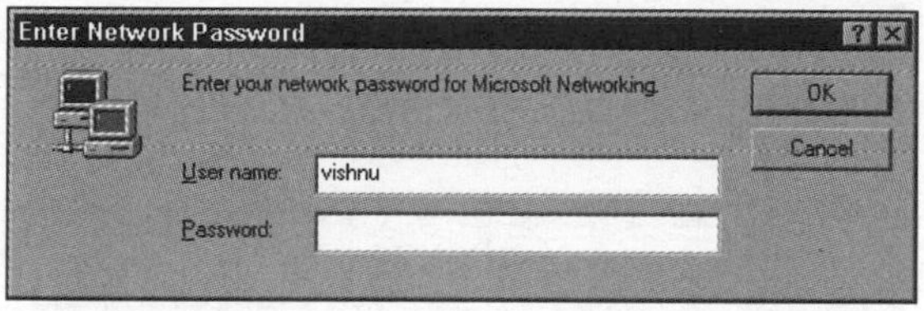

Figure 2-2:
The silly
Windows
98/Me logon
dialog box.

Enter Network Password

Enter your network password for Microsoft Networking.

OK

Cancel

User name: vishnu

Password:

Windows 2000 has a different logon scheme: First you must press
Ctrl+Alt+Delete to summon the logon dialog box. Then you must type in a
recognized user name and enter a proper password, or Windows 2000 just
won't let you in. Nasty, huh? But that's because Windows 2000 offers sincere
security.

For Windows XP, you click your user name from the list shown on the
Welcome screen. Unless you've created more user accounts, you'll see only
two: yours and one called *Guest.* If a password is needed, a box appears after
you click the user name; type your password in the box and press Enter.

No matter which version of Windows you're using, type your user name or
just accept the name that automatically appears in the dialog box (Vishnu in
Figure 2-2). Then enter a password. Or, for Windows 98/Me, just click the
Cancel button.

Ta-da. You're in.

- ✔ Press the Tab key to move between the User Name and Password text
  boxes.

- ✔ If you're lucky enough to be on a Very Large Impersonal Network, a text
  box may be available for you to type in the network's name or domain.

- ✔ If you're on a network, then you *need* to type in the password to access
  network devices. Network passwords offer *real* security.

- ✔ It's possible to disable the password dialog box in Windows 98/Me. Refer
  to the following Web page: www.wambooli.com/help/Windows/logon/.

- ✔ In Windows 2000, you can also remove the password dialog box, providing that you're the only person who uses the computer and you're not
  on a network. From the Start button, open the Control Panel and then
  open the Users and Passwords icon. Remove the checkmark by the item
  Users Must Enter a User Name and Password to Use This Computer.
  Click OK.

- ✔ You cannot get around logging in under Windows XP. No, after years of
  lax benevolence, the folks at Microsoft are finally forcing us all to obey
  them.

It's about time this operating system showed up

Eventually — and I'm not talking time to form cobwebs, but at least long enough to get a cup of coffee or shave — Windows presents itself as ready for you to use. What you see on the screen (see Figure 2-3) is the desktop, Windows' main screen, or home plate, if you will. Windows is finally ready for you to use. Time to get to work.

✔ The desktop in Windows XP has a more colorful, three-dimensional look than the desktop shown in Figure 2-3. In fact, Windows XP is so much more different that the Windows XP icon, shown in the margin, flags various things in this book that are Windows XP–specific.

✔ As part of the (never-ending?) startup process, various messages or windows appear on the screen. Some of them disappear, and others require you to click an OK or Cancel button to get rid of them.

✔ Chapter 3 offers more information about Windows and getting to work.

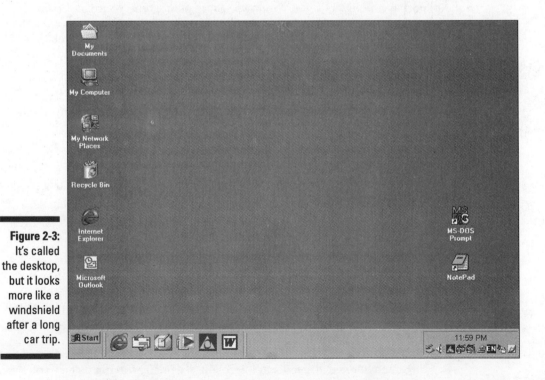

Figure 2-3:
It's called the desktop, but it looks more like a windshield after a long car trip.

Getting Your Work Done

Between turning your computer on and off, you should do something. Get work done. Go. Do it now.

- Refer to Part IV of this book for more information on using software.
- Also refer to Part V for information on using the Internet, which is like using software but also involves using a modem.

Turning the Computer Off (Shutdown)

The more they try to make computers easier to use, the harder it is to shut them down. In the old days, all you did was flip the power switch. Clunk! The computer was off. Today, flipping the power switch to turn off a computer may not even work! It may instead put the computer to sleep. It just keeps getting weirder and weirder.

Shutting down Windows XP

To put Windows XP down for the night, click the Start button and choose Turn Off Computer from the bottom of the pop-up window. This displays the Turn Off Computer dialog box, shown in Figure 2-4.

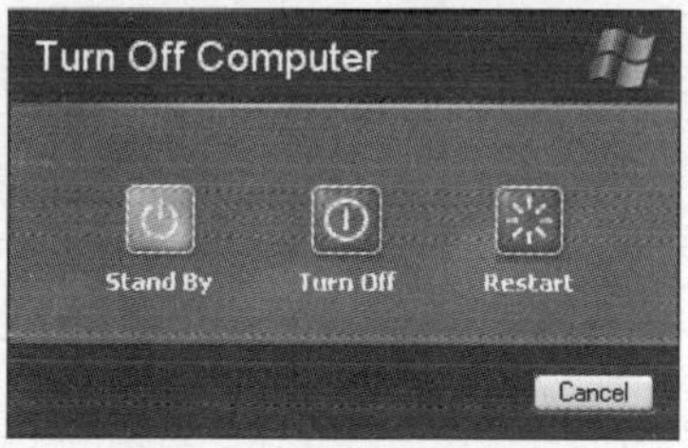

Figure 2-4:
Shutting down Windows XP.

The Turn Off Computer dialog box contains five options: Stand By, Hibernate, Turn Off, Restart, and Cancel. Each of these options is discussed in the various sections that follow; look for the Windows XP icon in the margin to find that specific information.

- You'll note that there is no Hibernate button in the Turn Off Computer dialog box. Perhaps it is that Microsoft likes things in threes? But anyway, to hibernate the computer, you press the Shift key and click the Stand By button.

  ✔ Refer to the next section for information on the differences between Stand By and Hibernate.

  ✔ If you chicken out and don't want to Stand By, Turn Off, or Restart, click the Cancel button or press the Esc key.

  ✔ You can also Log Off and return Windows back to the Welcome screen; click the Log Off button from the Start menu.

Using the Shut Down Windows dialog box in Windows 98/Me/2000

Start To properly furl the Windows sails, choose Shut Down from the Start menu. The Shut Down Windows dialog box appears, as shown in Figure 2-5.

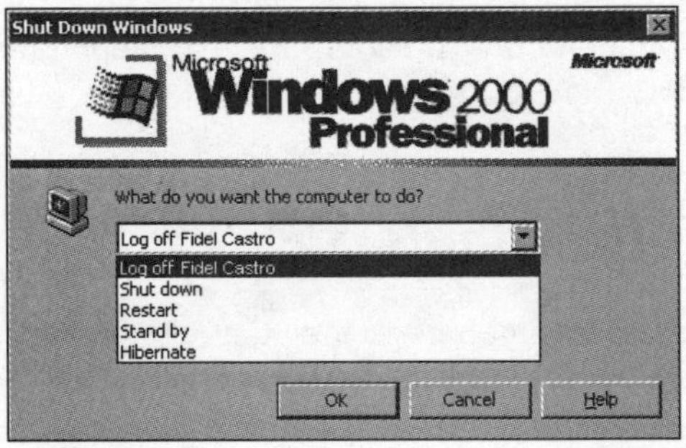

Figure 2-5: Various options for shutting down Windows.

The Shut Down Windows dialog box contains a host of options for stopping, halting, suspending, restraining, or making the computer catatonic. (The Windows 98/Me version of this dialog box isn't as flashy, but operates the same.) Here is a summary of all your choices:

Log Off. This option doesn't shut down Windows or turn off the computer. No, for network or multiple user systems, this merely tells the computer (or network) that you're done. Windows doesn't quit, but instead displays the logon dialog box again. (To select this option in Windows 98/Me, choose the Log Off command from the Start menu.)

Shut Down. Ah! The one you probably want. This option stops Windows dead in its tracks. You'll be prompted to save any unsaved files, should there be any lying about. Do so. Then Windows packs up its bags and leaves town.

Restart. This option gives you a way to turn the computer off and then on again, also known as a *reset*.

Stand By. The Stand By option puts your computer into a special power-saving mode. The monitor goes dark, the disk drives stop spinning, and the computer basically stands still. This is also known as putting the computer to sleep.

Hibernate. This is a nifty option only available on certain swanky computers. Hibernate saves everything in memory and then turns the computer off. When you turn the computer on again, the computer doesn't start up again but instead presents itself to you the way it was before you told it to hibernate. This is a quick way to turn the computer off without having to "lose your place."

After selecting one of the options, click the OK button to shut down, restart, stand by, whatever!

Click the Cancel button to return to Windows.

The following sections offer more information on the more popular Shut Down Windows options.

Yes, but I just want to turn the computer off

To properly quit for the day:

1. **From the Start menu, choose Shut Down.**

2. **Select Shut Down in the Shut Down Windows dialog box.**

3. **Click OK.**

On some computers, the console actually shuts itself off. On others, the message `It's now safe to turn off your computer` appears. Go ahead and turn off the console, and then the monitor, printer, and everything else.

- ✔ You do not have to turn off the UPS! Please leave it on so that its battery continues to charge.

- ✔ You must quit older DOS programs before you shut down Windows. If not, then the whole operation stops. (It's a sibling rivalry thing.)

- ✔ In Windows XP, you click the Turn Off button, shown in Figure 2-4.

- ✔ It's a good idea to wait at least 10 to 20 seconds before turning the computer on again. That gives the computer's hard drives time to slow down and stop. (Basically, it's just a bad idea to flip the PC's power switch rapidly from On to Off to On again.)

How do I put the computer to sleep?

As an alternative to turning the computer off and then on several times a day, consider giving it a coma instead. It isn't anything evil, and your PC doesn't have an out-of-body experience while it's down. Instead, you just tell your PC to take a nap. The computer shuts off power to the screen and disk drives, but maintains enough juice to remember what it was doing last. To do so:

1. **Save your work!**

   This is important: You must save your documents or files to disk before sleeping the PC. If you want to be extra safe, close your programs as well. You may lose data if a power outage occurs while the computer is in sleep mode.

2. **From the Start menu, choose Sh<u>u</u>t Down.**

3. **Select Stand By in the Shut Down Windows dialog box.**

   This may also be called the Suspend option.

4. **Click OK.**

You wake the computer up by pressing a key on the keyboard or by jiggling the mouse. Then the dumb thing is ready for you to use it again.

✔ On a laptop, you enter Stand By mode by closing the lid with the power on, or activating a keyboard command, or choosing a Stand By command from the Start menu.

✔ You can get some computers to enter the Stand By mode by pressing the on-off (actually on-sleep) switch. Refer to the computer's manual to see if it sports this feature, though typically the computer's on-sleep switch is marked with a crescent moon icon.

Sometimes Stand By mode doesn't work. The PC enters an eternal slumber from which it cannot be wakened. Jiggling the mouse or pressing any key (or pounding the keyboard on the desktop) does not wake the PC up. Instead you have to reset or, because the computer's on-sleep switch doesn't turn the thing off, you may have to yank the cord from the wall and then plug the PC in again to regain control.

If you have a PC that stubbornly refuses to exit the Stand By mode, refer to the manufacturer's Web site or technical support line for information or a fix. Until you do get it fixed, I would recommend *not* putting the computer into Stand By mode.

Why not just sleep the monitor?

Q: Now you've got me frightened. I'm afraid to put the computer into Stand By mode for fear that I'll never get control back. Is there anything else I can do to save power. Help me! I live in California and need to save electricity.

A: Easy solution: Open the Control Panel's Power Management or Power Options icon.

It contains options for snoozing the computer, monitor, or hard drives. Select a time for shutting down the monitor, say one hour. Leave the other items set to *Never* or *Always On.* Then click OK.

Hey! I have that nifty Hibernate option

Oh, you lucky human! Hibernating the computer is better than turning it off and safer than resetting. To hibernate, follow these steps:

1. **From the Start menu, choose Sh̲ut Down.**
2. **Select Hibernate in the Shut Down Windows dialog box.**
3. **Click OK.**

The computer's hard drive churns for a few seconds, and then it shuts off. Amazing.

When you turn the computer on again, it un-hibernates, splashing up on the screen the desktop — including any programs you were last working on or games (right in the middle of things) — just as you left it. Ah! This is much better than sleep mode and far superior to shutting the thing down. No wonder those *cheap* computers don't have this feature! Ha-ha!

In Windows XP, you press the Shift key (either one) and click the Stand By button to hibernate. Refer to Figure 2-4.

I need to reset

You'll need to reset or restart Windows in two instances. The first is when you install something new or make some change, in which case Windows tells you that you need to reset and presents some type of Reset or Restart button on the screen. Click that button with the mouse, and the computer resets.

The second time most people need to reset is when Something Strange happens. For example, the mouse is gone! Or windows just radically start scrolling around. Weird stuff. In that case, choose Restart from the Shut Down Windows dialog box (shown earlier in this chapter), and the computer resets itself, hopefully back to normal.

In Windows XP, click the Restart button in the Turn Off Computer dialog box (refer to Figure 2-4) to reset the computer.

Some computers have a reset button on the console. That's the *hardware reset* button. Use it only in times of desperation. The button is there as a last resort. For example, Windows is acting weird and you need to reset, but you can't use the mouse or can't even see the menu. In times of panic such as this, feel free to whack the hardware reset button.

Alas, not every computer has a hardware reset button. In that case, you need to unplug the console (or turn off the power strip), wait several seconds, and then plug it in again.

Remember to remove any floppy disks from drive A before resetting. If you leave a disk in there, the computer tries to start itself from that disk.

Doesn't Ctrl+Alt+Delete reset, too?

In the olden days (say 1994), PCs were commonly reset by pressing the Control+Alt+Delete key combination; press the Control (Ctrl), Alt, and Delete keys simultaneously. *Poof!* DOS would reset; Windows would die. Instant. Almost reliable. Heck, it was the "three finger salute," the "Vulcan nerve pinch," the "warm boot."

Ctrl+Atl+Delete still has a function in Windows, though it's not really a true reset.

In Windows 98/Me, Ctrl+Alt+Delete brings up the Close Program window, shown in Figure 2-6. This handy little tool allows you to kill off programs that run amok. It also sports a Shut Down button or, as it says in Figure 2-6, if you press Ctrl+Alt+Delete again, the computer is instantly reset. Leave that trick for desperate times.

In Windows 2000, Ctrl+Alt+Delete is the logon/logoff key combination. You press Ctrl+Alt+Delete initially to summon the password dialog box, but if you press Ctrl+Alt+Delete while Windows 2000 is running, you're presented with a Windows Security dialog box. Click Cancel to return to Windows, or click the Shut Down button to see the various options for shutting down Windows 2000. (Also see Chapter 27 for more information about using the Windows Security dialog box.)

Turn offs

Q: You state in your book not to turn the computer off but leave it on all the time. I don't have a fancy PC that sleeps, so does it really matter if I turn it off — after Windows says so, that is.

A: If you're going to be away from the computer for more than two days, turn it off. Otherwise, you don't really need to shut down. I leave mine

on all the time, mostly because I think computers take too long to start. But if you've gone through the trouble of shutting the system down, feel free to turn it off. Or press the reset button or the Ctrl+Alt+Delete key combination to restart.

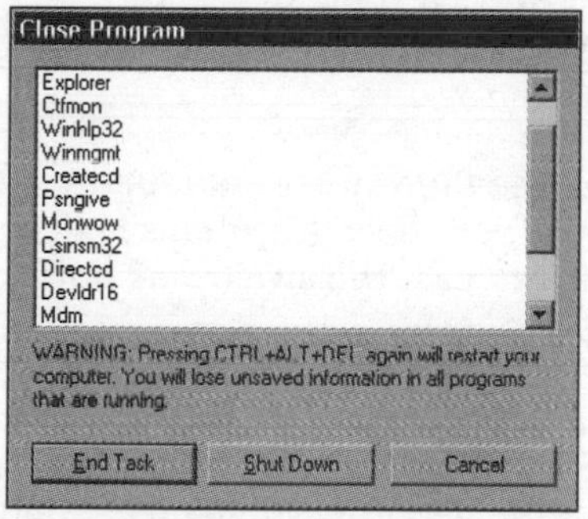

Figure 2-6: The Close Program dialog box.

Windows XP displays the Windows Task Manager whenever you press Ctrl+Alt+Delete. You can use that handy window to kill off individual programs or processes and do a number of interesting and highly technical things. The Task Manager's window has a special Shut Down menu, from which you can choose options for shutting down the computer.

In all situations, if you press Ctrl+Alt+Delete and would rather keep working in Windows, just press the Esc key or click Cancel. Whew!

"I Want to Leave My Computer Off All the Time"

Hey, I'm with you.

"I Want to Leave My Computer On All the Time"

The great debate rages: Should you leave your computer on all the time? Anyone who knows anything will tell you, "Yes." Leave your computer on all the time, 24 hours a day, 7 days a week, and 14 days a week on the planet Mars. The only time you should turn a system off is when it will be unused for longer than a weekend.

Computers like being on all the time. You leave your refrigerator on all night or when you're away on trips, so why not your PC? It doesn't increase your electrical bill much, either.

Whatever you do with your PC, it's always a good idea to turn its monitor off when you're away. Some monitors can *sleep* just like PCs, but if they don't, turning them off can save some electricity.

If you do leave your computer on all the time, don't put it under a dust cover. The dust cover gives the computer its very own greenhouse effect and brings the temperatures inside the system way past the sweltering point, like in a sweaty Southern courtroom drama.

Another good idea: Turn off the computer during an electrical storm. Even if you have spike protection or a UPS, it's best *not* to let that nasty spike of voltage into your computer during a lightning storm. Unplug the computer. And remember to unplug the phone line as well. You can't be too careful.

What about turning off the monitor?

Q: You recommend leaving the computer on rather than turning it on and off frequently. So I have a dumb question; do you mean for only the computer to stay on? Should the monitor be turned off? I was turning my machine on and off several times daily.

A: Leave your PC on, and you'll get started quickly "several times daily." Turn the monitor off when you leave your desk or just use a screen saver. (See Chapter 12 for screen saver information.)

Part II
Using Your PC

The 5th Wave — By Rich Tennant

"They were selling contraband online. We broke through the door just as they were trying to flush the harddrive down the toilet."

In this part . . .

In a way, a computer can be like the sweet and annoying little kid who says, "I've got a secret." The computer knows something and, like the dear little tot, it's not going to tell you exactly what the secret is. After a while, the game becomes frustrating. You *know* the information is in there, and you know the computer (or the little kid) should freely be able to tell you. But what must you do to get that information out?

The key to using your PC is using software — primarily the computer's operating system. Granted, it's not obvious. Whereas microwave ovens have a Popcorn button and telephones don't have an Enter key (they just know when you're done typing the number), the computer offers no clues. Fortunately, you have the chapters in this part of the book. They're designed to familiarize you with using your PC and show you how to get something done. Pain is minimal. Information is top-notch. Entertainment is by the way.

Chapter 3

Your PC's Operating System

The first thing the alien is supposed to say when he greets the local planet's inhabitants is, "Take me to your leader." If the poor alien happened to land in rural America, then he would be immediately taken to a bar, made drunk, stripped naked, and then relieved of his wallet, and his spaceship would be stripped of all valuable parts. The leader would be named "Jack Daniels." And thus would begin an intergalactic incident that would eventually render the earth into a smoldering cinder the size of a lump of coal.

As an alien user approaching a new computer, the first thing you want to know is who's in charge. Basically, you're asking the computer to take you to its leader, which is a software program called the *operating system*. For the PC, that operating system just happens to be called *Windows*. And that's where all the trouble starts.

This chapter provides a general overview about Windows. For more information, you should pick up a book specific to your version of Windows.

Your PC's Real Brain

Remember that it's software that controls the computer's hardware. Of all the software you have, something has to be in charge. That would be the computer's operating system. For the PC, the operating system is Windows.

Computer operating systems have three basic duties:

- The primary duty is to control the computer, all the hardware.

- The secondary duty is to control all the software, basically running programs and managing all the files and documents you create.

- The tertiary (meaning *third*) duty is to interact with you.

Ideally (which means that it could never happen in real life), a computer's operating system should be quiet and efficient, never getting in the way and carrying out your instructions like a dutiful and grateful servant.

In reality, Windows is far from being dutiful or grateful. Yes, Window is your servant, but you must play the game by its own rules — and it often seems that Windows changes the rules in the middle of the game. Sure, there are graphics and pictures, and the mouse is supposed to make things easier than just typing in commands. But at times, Windows can be devilishly frustrating.

- Windows comes in various flavors: Windows 98, Windows Me, Windows 2000, Windows XP, and so on. This book refers to them all as *Windows*.

- The original PC operating system was DOS, also known as MS-DOS or sometimes PC-DOS. DOS is still available today and can still run any PC, though because most computer software is written for the Windows operating system, few people use DOS.

- Another PC operating system is Linux, which is not covered in this book. About the most important thing to know about Linux is how it's pronounced. Computer people who think they're really cool say *LIN-uks*. This book's author says *LIE-nuks*. The guy who wrote Linux, Linus Torvalds, says *LEEEEE-nooks*.

The Cheap Windows Tour

You must get to know three basic parts to Windows, your computer's operating system: the desktop, the taskbar, and the Start button.

The desktop

Windows is a graphical operating system. It uses graphical images, or *icons*, to represent everything inside your computer. These graphics are all pasted on a background called the *desktop*. Figure 3-1 shows the desktop with the famous Windows clouds background.

Mouse pointer

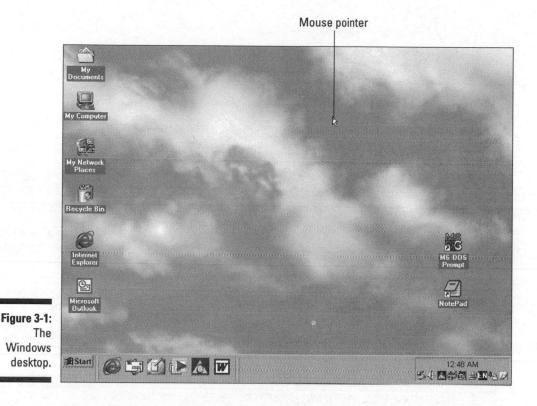

Figure 3-1:
The
Windows
desktop.

You control everything by using your computer's mouse. The mouse controls the pointer on the desktop, which looks like an arrow-shaped UFO in Figure 3-1. You use the mouse and its pointer to point at things, grab them, drag them around, punch 'em, scratch 'em till they bleed, and other mouse-y things like that.

Oh, you can also use the keyboard, although graphical operating systems such as Windows love mice more than they love keyboards.

- The *desktop* is merely the background on which Windows shows you its stuff — like an old sheet you hang from the wall to bore your neighbors with your Cayman Islands vacation slide show.

- The little pictures are called *icons*.

- Doesn't look much like a real desktop, does it? That's because Windows is based on the Macintosh, which is based on the ancient Lisa computer. On the Lisa, the desktop *really did* look like a desktop, with paper, a clock, glue, scissors, and other desktop-y things. We've come a long way. . . .

The taskbar

The taskbar is that gunboat-gray strip along the bottom of the desktop. It serves as the Windows control center. Four important things to note on the taskbar, as shown in Figure 3-2, are the Start button, Quick Launch bar, window buttons, and the system tray.

Start button   Quick Launch bar   Window buttons   System tray

Figure 3-2:
The taskbar.

The Start button is where you start programs in Windows. You can also shut down Windows by using the Start button. Start. Stop. Microsoft can't make up its mind.

The Quick Launch bar is the part of the taskbar that contains buttons to quickly start various programs. Figure 3-2 shows buttons for Internet Explorer, Outlook Express, Word, Excel, and others. Clicking one of these buttons starts the associated program (one of several million ways to start programs in Windows).

Next to the Quick Launch bar is where buttons appear that represent any programs you have running or windows you may have open. Clicking the mouse on a button displays that program or window. In Figure 3-2, clicking the mouse on the My Computer button would display the My Computer window.

On the right end of the taskbar is the *system tray*. It shows the time of day plus other little icons representing special little programs you have running on your computer. To see what those little programs are, just point the mouse at one of the cute little icons. This causes a little bubble to appear, explaining what the icon represents or does. For example, pointing at the time in the system tray displays the full date.

- ✔ The Quick Launch bar can be slid left or right or might even appear on top or below in relation to the rest of the taskbar.

- ✔ For more information on the system tray, refer to the following Web page: www.wambooli.com/help/Windows/SystemTray/.

- ✔ The system tray in Windows XP routinely hides its little icons, especially if they don't do anything other than sit there. To see all the icons, click the Show More arrows (depicted in the margin).

TECHNICAL STUFF

"My taskbar is AWOL!"

The taskbar is not welded to the bottom of your computer screen, nor is it of a fixed size. No, the taskbar is a bouncy, elastic little booger. It can live on any of the four edges of your computer screen, and it can be fatter than a club sandwich or thinner than the eye can see. Needless to say, these various and seemingly useless options can drive you batty.

First, to move the taskbar: The taskbar can be dragged with the mouse by pointing and clicking the mouse at any blank area between the Quick Launch bar and system tray. Just hold down the mouse button and then drag the taskbar to any other edge of the screen. A fuzzy outline shows you where the taskbar will end up. Release the mouse to move the taskbar.

Second, to shrink or grow the taskbar, hover the mouse pointer over the taskbar's top edge. The mouse pointer changes to a this-way-or-that-way arrow. Then drag the taskbar to a nicer, plumper size.

If the taskbar appears to be missing, then it was probably shrunk down to a thin line. Look for that line. Then use the mouse to drag it out to a thicker size.

In Windows XP, you can lock the taskbar into place, preventing any potential mischief: Right-click on the taskbar in a blank spot (where no buttons appear). Choose Lock the Taskbar from the pop-up menu. Clunk! The taskbar is now immobile and safe from corruption.

The Start menu

Humans have a belly button; Windows has the Start button. The Start button is located on the left side of the taskbar, which isn't a navel-like center like your belly button, but it's handy because the Start button summons the all-important Start menu, from which you start most of the programs you'll use in Windows.

The Start menu is shown in Figure 3-3. The top part lists programs you can run, such as the Windows Update or America Online (AOL). The center part lists various submenus, Programs, Documents, Settings, and Search. The bottom part gives you access to the Windows Help system and other fun things, including the Shut Down command (covered in Chapter 2).

For tweaking things, you'll most likely use the Settings menu. Choosing Settings displays a submenu full of other commands that let you modify various aspects of your computer.

The Programs submenu is where you find most of the programs you can run in Windows. You choose Programs with the mouse and then look for the program you want to run listed in the submenu — or select another submenu (or sub-submenu) to find what you want.

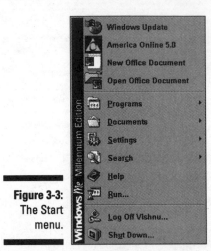

Figure 3-3:
The Start
menu.

The Start menu in Windows XP is shown in Figure 3-4. It contains icons representing popular programs, places to visit on the drive, plus a smattering of control and setting options and the last several programs you've run.

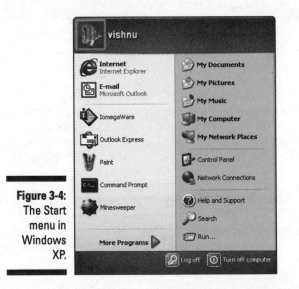

Figure 3-4:
The Start
menu in
Windows
XP.

To get at the full list of applications, you must click the More Programs button. That displays a cascading list of menus, which is where you find all the programs you can run on your computer.

✔ If you would rather use your keyboard to see the Start menu, press the Ctrl+Esc key combination. This works whether or not you can actually see the Start button.

 ✔ You can also summon the Start menu from your keyboard by punching the Windows key, shown in the margin. (On older keyboards without the Windows key, press the Ctrl+Esc key combination.)

✔ The submenus are rather slippery. They pop up and disappear as your mouse roves over them. So be careful! Accessing them can be aggravating if you're a sloppy mouse mover or your mouse is too sensitive.

✔ Refrain from beating your mouse into your table when it behaves erratically.

✔ Quickly start any recently worked-on stuff by using the Documents submenu: Pop up the Start menu and click Documents. Look for your document on the list. If it's there, click it to start it. If it's not there, you can take the day off and watch your favorite soap. (The Document submenu does not appear in Windows XP's Start menu.)

✔ Some programs may be represented as shortcut icons on the desktop, such as the MS-DOS Prompt icon shown in Figure 3-1. You can start those programs by double-clicking their icons; you don't have to wade through the Start menu.

✔ If the program you want to start is on the Quick Launch bar, just click its icon once with the mouse. Shazaam! The program starts.

Quit (or Exit or Close)

The Start menu shows you how to start things, but a common question I get from readers is "Dan, you tell us how to start stuff, but how do we quit?" So though it's not a place on the desktop or taskbar, every window and every program in Windows has a set way to close itself or quit. Fortunately, it's very consistent.

To quit any program or close any window, choose the File➪Exit command. Point the mouse at the File menu and click. Then find the Exit command at the bottom of the menu. Click. (Note that sometimes the command is Close instead of Exit.)

Windows may ask if you want to save your work. Do so if you haven't yet. (See Chapter 6 for more information on saving your stuff.)

Alas, some programs may not have a File menu, let alone an Exit command. If so, you can quit or close that window by clicking the X button in the window's upper-right corner.

The most bizarre way to close a window is to use the Alt+F4 key combination. Why Alt+F4? I don't know. Using the command is almost like incanting a spell. It's weird.

Other, Fun Places to Visit

You can have fun with many things in the Windows playground. Most of these things live right on the desktop. Some of them you have to dig for.

My Computer. Opening this icon on the desktop displays a window listing all the disk drives in your computer.

My Documents. Opening this icon on the desktop displays a window listing the contents of the My Documents folder. That's the main folder for storing your stuff on the hard drive. (See Chapter 6.)

My Network Places. This icon displays computers on the local area network, should your PC be shackled to one. (It's called the *Network Neighborhood* in Windows 98.)

Recycle Bin. This is the Windows trash can, into which you throw files, documents, and icons you no longer need.

Another necessary place to visit in Windows, especially in Part III of this book, is the Control Panel, shown in Figure 3-5. You can access the Control Panel from all over Windows, but the most common way to call it out is to choose Settings⇨Control Panel from the Start menu.

The Windows XP Control Panel is shown in Figure 3-6. You view it by choosing Control Panel from the Start menu. (If you'd rather see it the old-fashioned way, click the Switch to Classic View button on the upper-left corner of the window.)

Each of the icons in the Control Panel represents some aspect of your computer, something for Windows to control. By opening an icon, you see a window, or *dialog box,* with more information, more controls, more chaos. . . .

Later chapters in this book have you open and use some of the icons shown in the Control Panel. For the most part, however, it's a good idea to avoid the Control Panel unless you really know what you're doing.

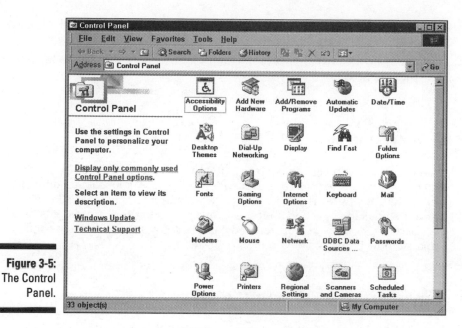

Figure 3-5:
The Control
Panel.

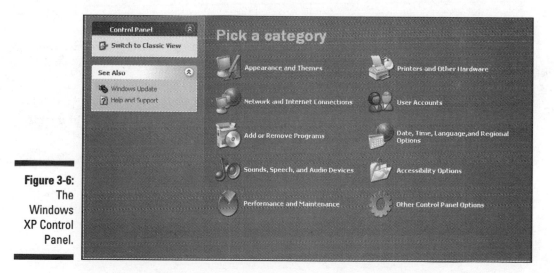

Figure 3-6:
The
Windows
XP Control
Panel.

Close the Control Panel window by choosing File➪Close from the menu.

✔ My Network Places is known as the Network Neighborhood in
Windows 98.

✔ Open an icon in the Control Panel by double-clicking it, though in Windows XP a single click will do.

✔ I have no idea what most of the things in the Control Panel do. In fact, they frighten me.

Here a Window, There a Window

Windows is a graphical candy store of fun things to play with, stuff to drive you crazy, and interesting toys over which you waste colossal amounts of time. It has tiny buttons you push with the mouse, graphics that slide and stretch, things to poke, and stuff that drops down. In other words, lots of *gizmos* appear on the screen, and most of them control the way the windows look and how programs in Windows operate.

Changing a window's size

Your windows can be just about any size, from filling the entire screen to too small to be useful and everything in between.

To make a window fill the entire screen — which is where it's most useful — click the *Maximize* button in the window's upper-right corner. (When a window is maximized, the Maximize button changes to the *Restore* button, which is used to return the window to its demure size before maximizing.)

To turn a window into a mere button on the taskbar, click the *Minimize* button in the upper-right corner of the window. This action shoves the window out of the way, shrinking it to a button on the taskbar — but it isn't the same as quitting. To restore the taskbar button to a window, click the button.

When a window isn't maximized, you can change its size by grabbing an edge with the mouse: Hover the mouse over one side of the window or a corner, and drag the window in or out to a new size. Release the mouse button to snap the window into place.

✔ Enlarging a window to full-screen size is called *maximizing*.

✔ Shrinking a window into an icon is called *minimizing*.

✔ Positioning a window *just so* on the screen and then having Windows move it for no reason is called *frustrating*.

✔ If you use your imagination, the Maximize button looks like a full-screen window, and the Minimize button looks like a button on the taskbar. Then again, if you use your imagination, Windows looks like a bright, sunny day with green grass and birds chirping in the meadow.

✔ Some windows can't be maximized. Some games, for example, have a fixed window size you can't change. Don't be greedy.

✔ If you have a humongous monitor, you may opt to run your programs without switching them to full screen.

✔ If you have two monitors on your PC (and this is crazy, but possible), then know that maximizing a window fills it to only one screen.

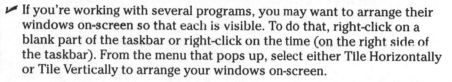

✔ If you're working with several programs, you may want to arrange their windows on-screen so that each is visible. To do that, right-click on a blank part of the taskbar or right-click on the time (on the right side of the taskbar). From the menu that pops up, select either Tile Horizontally or Tile Vertically to arrange your windows on-screen.

Moving a window around

Windows puts its windows wherever Windows wants. To move a window to a new position, drag the window by its title bar (the topmost strip on the window, typically above the menu bar). This action is akin to the myth of a caveman dragging his woman around by her hair. That never really happened, of course, not after the women started carrying their own clubs, anyway.

✔ By the way, you cannot move a window around when it's maximized (filling the screen). Refer to the preceding section to find out how to maximize a window.

✔ By the way (Part 2), you cannot move Uncle Arny around when he's maximized after a holiday meal. It's the same concept Microsoft borrowed for maximized windows.

Scrolling about

Often, what you're looking at in a window is larger than the window. For example, imagine you're in a tall building, and King Kong is standing just outside. If you ride up in the elevator, and the elevator has a window, you see only a small bit of Kong at a time. That's kind of how scrolling in Windows works, but in Windows, you're looking at a long document or large graphic on the screen and not some mass of black hair.

To facilitate scrolling a window around, you use one or two scroll bars. The *scroll bar* is a long, skinny thing, with an arrow at both ends and an elevator-like box in the middle. You use the arrows and elevator to move the window's image up and down or left and right, revealing more of the total picture.

Accessing a menu

All the commands and whatnot of the Windows application are included on a handy — and always visible — menu bar. It's usually at the top of a window, right below the title bar and down the street from Ed's Bar.

Each word on the menu bar — File and Edit, for example — is a menu title. Each title represents a drop-down menu, which contains commands related to the title. For example, the File menu contains Save, Open, New, Close, and other commands related to files, as shown in Figure 3-7.

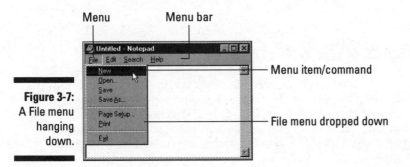

Figure 3-7:
A File menu hanging down.

To access these commands, click the menu title with the mouse. The menu drops down. Then choose a menu item or command. If you don't like what you see, click the menu title again to make the menu go away, or choose another menu.

✔ You can access the menus with your keyboard, if you like. Press either the Alt or F10 key. This action highlights the first menu on the menu bar. To choose a menu or item on a menu, press the underlined letter, such as the F key for File. The letters to press are underlined in this book, just as they are in Windows.

✔ In this book, I use the format File⇨Close to represent menu choices. To access that command on the menu, you press Alt, F, C.

✔ To choose the File⇨Close command, you can also press Alt+F (the Alt and F keys together, and then release both keys) and then C.

✔ If you can't see the underlined letters in Windows 2000 or Windows XP, press and release the Alt key.

✔ Oh, bother. Just use your mouse. Point. Click. Click. Sheesh.

Struggling with a dialog box

When it comes to making choices, Windows displays a specialized type of window called a *dialog box*. A dialog box contains gadgets and gizmos that you click, slide, and type in, all of which control something or set certain optional options. Clicking an OK button sends your choices off to Windows for proper digestion.

If all that sounds complicated, consider the old DOS-prompt way of doing things:

```
C> FORMAT A: /S /U /F:144 /V:FLIPPY
```

That's a real, honest-to-goodness DOS command. In Windows, a dialog box lets you do something similar but in a graphical way. Figure 3-8, in fact, shows you how the same command looks in a Windows dialog box.

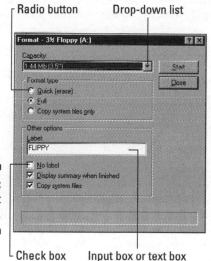

Radio button   Drop-down list

Figure 3-8:
The Format
dialog box.

Check box   Input box or text box

All the doojobbies shown in Figure 3-8 are manipulated with the mouse. What they do isn't important right now. What the doojobbies are called *is* important. All the following definitions refer to Figure 3-8:

Drop-down list: Click the down-pointing arrow button to the right of the list. This action displays a list of choices, one of which you point at and click with the mouse. If the list is long, it has a scroll bar to one side, which you can use to scroll up or down.

Radio button: These are grouped together into families, such as the three shown in Figure 3-8. Like in an old car radio, you can punch only one of the buttons at a time. To punch a button, click it once with the mouse. A round dot fills the one button that is *on*.

Input box or text box: Any box or area you can type in is an input box or text box.

Check box: Unlike with radio buttons, you can click the mouse in as many check boxes as necessary. A check mark appears in the box if an option is on. To remove the check mark and turn the option off, click the mouse in the box again.

After you've made your selections, you typically click an OK button. (In Figure 3-8, the OK button is called Start.) If you don't like your choices, click Close.

To get help, click the question mark button in the dialog box's upper-right corner. This action changes the mouse pointer into the combination arrow-pointer and question-mark thing. When that happens, point and click any part of the dialog box to see a pop-up cartoon bubble supposedly offering help. Click the mouse to make the cartoon bubble go away.

- ✔ Pressing the Enter key in a dialog box is usually same as clicking the OK button with your mouse.

- ✔ Pressing the Esc (escape) key on your keyboard is the same as clicking the Cancel button in a dialog box.

- ✔ You can press the F1 key to get help with whichever part of the dialog box you're messing with.

- ✔ Some dialog boxes feature an *Apply* button. It works like an OK button, except that it enables you to see your changes without closing the dialog box. If you like the changes, you can then click OK. Or, if the changes stink, you can reset them or click the Cancel button. See? Microsoft is being nice here. Make a note of it on your calendar.

- ✔ If more than one input box appears in a dialog box, press the Tab key to move between them. Don't press the Enter key because that's the same as clicking the OK button and telling Windows that you're done with the dialog box.

- ✔ Another type of list, similar to the drop-down list (but not shown in Figure 3-8), is a *scrolling list.* It works the same as the drop-down list, except that the list is always visible inside the dialog box.

- ✔ If you like a mental challenge, you can use your keyboard to work a dialog box. Look for the underlined letter in each part of the dialog box (such as *p* in Capacity in Figure 3-8). Pressing the Alt key plus that key is the same as choosing that command with a mouse.

Squeezing Windows for Help

Help in Windows is always handy. And though it makes no sense, the F1 key is the key you press for help. F1. F one needs help? Find help first? F'wonder where the help key is? Oh, I give up. . . .

When you press F1, you activate the Windows Help system. Figure 3-9 shows the Help screen for Windows Me; other versions of Windows have different Help systems, but they all work basically the same.

Figure 3-9:
The
Windows
Me Help
system.

- ⯈ Click any text you see in the Help system to get helpful information about that topic. Yes, the "helpful information" is essentially what would have been in the printed manual years back. It's dry. Boring. And sometimes actually helpful.

- ⯈ The Index option in the Help system is the most useful. Click the word Index and then enter a keyword to find information about a specific topic.

- ⯈ Ignore the Search item.

- ⯈ Most of the helpful information is displayed as a list of steps or tips.

- ⯈ For troubleshooting help, look up the word *troubleshoot* in the index.

The help engine is its own program. When you're done using help, remember to quit: Click the X close button in the upper-left corner of the window.

Soothing Windows Words of Advice

Use your mouse. If you don't have a mouse, you can still use Windows — but not as elegantly. Ack, who am I kidding? You need a mouse to use Windows!

Have someone organize your programs for you. Ask this person to put your most popular programs, the ones you use every day, as icons in the Quick Launch bar. Have maybe five of those programs there maximum. Other programs you use every so often can be pasted onto the desktop as *shortcut icons*. Offer a bag of Doritos or a vat of peanut butter as a bribe.

Keep in mind that Windows can run several programs at the same time. You don't have to quit one program to start another. You can switch between the programs by clicking the buttons on the taskbar or using the Alt+Tab keyboard shortcut.

Always quit Windows properly. Never just turn your PC off or punch the reset button. Review the steps in Chapter 2 for properly shutting down Windows if you've forgotten how.

Literacy lore

Q: Can you tell me which books cover the subject of computer literacy? Is anything available on CDs?

A: Well, what type of computer literacy are you talking about? The broad definition is "to be able to use an ATM machine," though many narrow it down to "programming a computer." So it depends on how you define it.

Remember, *computer literacy* was an advertising slogan originally. It was designed to scare parents into buying expensive toy computers for their kids. It still exists as a buzzword, though specific books on the subject just aren't written.

If you just want to know more about computers, then any introductory book on computers (such as this one) should get you started. From there, take off on whatever interests you. Operating a computer is easy, but if you want to know more (hardware, software, programming, and so on), then you have to buy specific books or take courses at a community college. That's what I'd recommend.

Chapter 4

Know Your Disk Drives

● ●

In This Chapter

▶ Understanding disk storage

▶ Locating your computer's disk drives

▶ Understanding disk drive letters

▶ Using CD-ROM and DVD drives

▶ Playing a music CD or video

▶ Working with floppy disks

▶ Formatting floppy disks

▶ Using Zip disks and drives

● ●

*O*ne of Windows' many jobs is to manage all the information you store in your computer. All those pictures of your sister's cat that she e-mails you; the catalog of what your baseball card collection would be worth today had you not thrown it out in a fit of rage when you were 14; the four-dozen attempts you've made at starting a novel; and the notes you took when you phoned the Psychic Stock Market Pal Network. You have to put it all somewhere.

Your PC most likely has at least three types of disk drives, possibly more. You use them for storing stuff. They store the operating system, programs, and all the many wonderful things you create on your PC. This chapter tells you how to work with those disk drives in Windows. Chapter 5 continues the discussion, and Chapter 9 covers disk drives from a purely hardware point of view.

▶ The terms *disk drive* and *disk* are often used interchangeably. Storing something *on disk* means to save it to a disk drive somewhere in your computer system.

▶ Watch out for the ugly term *disk memory*. Although technically correct, it's confusing. Memory (or RAM) is where your computer does the work. The disk is where your work is stored. Disk memory is just another term for disk or storage on a disk drive, but it's confusing to many beginners. So when you see *disk memory* just think *disk drive*.

Why Use Disk Drives?

Disk drives are necessary to provide long-term storage for all your files, programs, and the stuff you create inside your computer. After all, all that junk has to go somewhere. The disk drive is like a closet or garage; it's just storage for your stuff. This makes sense.

If you go back in time, however, you'll discover that disk drives were traditionally thought of as peripherals — extras outside the basic computer. Early computers did all their work in RAM (memory). Storage was an extra. So if the guy in the white lab coat wanted his stuff saved, he'd have to make a copy of the information in memory and save that copy to a tape machine or disk drive.

The main reason for saving information is that computer memory is temporary; when you turn off the power, the contents of memory go *poof*. To save time, you could save memory to disk (long-term storage) before turning the power off. Then, when you turn the power back on, the information could be loaded back into memory from disk. This saved the guy in the white lab coat a lot of retyping.

The disk drive system still works the same today. Whatever you make on the computer is created in memory. When you're done, you *save* the information to disk as a *file*. To work on that information again, you *open* the file, transferring it back into memory for modification, editing, printing, whatever. As long as you have a copy of the file on disk, you'll never have to worry about losing any information in the computer.

- ✔ Your computer's disk drives provide long-term storage for the stuff you create, files, programs, and other information inside your computer.

- ✔ See Chapter 10 for more information on computer memory (RAM).

- ✔ Disk storage is measured in bytes, mostly *megabytes* and *gigabytes*. See Table 10-1 for more information about what these terms measure.

- ✔ Saving information to disk (making a permanent copy) is called *saving* or *saving a file* or even *saving a document*. When you use that file again, you *open* it. These are common Windows terms you'll get used to in no time: *save* and *open*.

- ✔ Never worry whether the file on disk is larger than your PC's memory. For example, you can view a 12GB (billion byte) movie on a PC with only 48MB of RAM. Now that would seem like squeezing a 6,000-pound elephant into a pair of nylons, but it's not an impossible task for the PC! Amazing devices, those computers.

Finding Your PC's Disk Drives

Windows keeps a representation of all your PC's disk drives in one handy place: the My Computer window. You can access this window through the My Computer icon on the desktop. Click that icon twice to open it with the mouse. You'll see something similar to Figure 4-1, depending on your version of Windows.

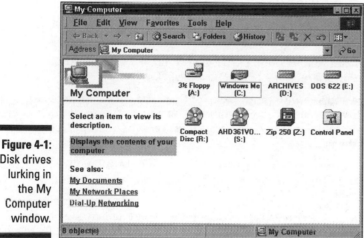

Figure 4-1:
Disk drives lurking in the My Computer window.

Though each computer is different, certain types of disk drives are common to all PCs. Here's a quick summary:

Drive A. This is your PC's floppy disk, which Windows describes as the $3^1/_2$ Floppy because the disks are 3½ inches square.

Drive C. This is your PC's main hard disk drive. Your computer may also have a hard drive D and possibly even a hard drive E, as shown in Figure 4-1.

CD-ROM or DVD drive. The icons for a CD-ROM drive and a DVD drive are the same. In fact, in Figure 4-1, drive R is a DVD drive, and drive S is a CD-ROM drive. (Yes, in Figure 4-1 drive R is a DVD drive despite Windows insistence that it's just a "Compact Disc" drive.)

Other drives. Other drives may exist in your system, such as the Zip drive in Figure 4-1 (drive Z).

Here are the answers to some questions you may have about this disk drive madness:

✓ Each disk drive has an icon, a letter, and an optional name. For example, the first hard drive has the traditional hard drive icon and the letter designation *C,* and in Figure 4-1, it has the name *Windows Me.*

✓ Sometimes the icon for a CD-ROM or DVD drive may be customized to represent the CD-ROM or DVD disc itself. For example, a CD-ROM game may show its own icon in the My Computer window instead of the standard Windows CD-ROM icon.

✓ The disk drive's name is optional and can be changed. See "Even more disk information," later in this chapter.

✓ The little hand that's holding drive C in Figure 4-1 indicates that the drive is being shared on a computer network.

 ✓ Any drives you see with pipes beneath them (as shown in the margin) are disk drives on network computers. You access these disk drives like other drives on your PC, though they exist on other computers elsewhere on the network.

✓ For more information about networking computers and your disk drives, I recommend Doug Lowe's *Networking For Dummies,* published by Hungry Minds, Inc.

✓ In addition to disk drives, the My Computer window may show special folders, such as the Control Panel folder shown in Figure 4-1.

✓ Windows 98 also has the Printers, Dial-Up Networking, and Scheduled Tasks folders in the My Computer window, as well as the Web Folders icon, though I have no idea what it does or why it's necessary. (Apparently Microsoft agreed because it hasn't appeared in any Windows releases since then.)

✓ Windows XP lists special folders, such as My Documents and My Network Places, in the Other Places area on the left side of the My Computer window.

Drive letters from A (skipping B) to Z

In Windows, disk drives are known by their letters, from A (skipping B), C, D, and on up to Z. So when Windows refers to your first, main hard drive, it calls, "Yoo-hoo, drive C:" — though Windows says "C" and not the colon part, even though the colon is required by Windows. (I won't use the colon when writing about the drives in the text, because it tends to junk things up.)

Going alphabetically:

A: Drive A is the PC's floppy drive, the first disk drive in the system. This is traditional. Hard drives were expensive options 20 years ago, so the floppy drive A came first.

B: Drive B doesn't exist. It used to. Back in the early days, rather than pay a lot for a then-expensive 10MB hard drive, people would pay a little and get a second floppy disk drive. Thanks to inexpensive hard drives today, there is no need for a second floppy drive on your PC. Even so, your PC is wired for an optional second floppy drive, and drive letter B is reserved by Windows just in case.

C: Drive C is the PC's first hard disk drive.

After drive C, the letters are up for grabs! Basically Windows looks at things when it starts and begins passing out drive letters to whatever it finds in the following order:

Extra hard drives. If your computer has any hard drives beyond drive C, those hard drives are given the letters D, E, and so on.

The CD-ROM or DVD drive. After the hard drives come the CD-ROM and DVD drives, which are given the next drive letters after the last hard drive. On most computers, the CD-ROM drive is drive D. However, this isn't a hard and fast rule; drive D is not always the CD-ROM drive.

Other drives. Any other disk drives in the computer are given the next letter in the alphabet after the CD-ROM drive. For example, a Zip drive may be given drive letter E after the CD-ROM drive D.

- ✔ If you do add a second floppy drive to your PC, it becomes drive B. I can think of no sensible reason to add a second floppy drive, however.

- ✔ People pronounce *A:* as "A-colon," as in:

  Alex Trebek: People use this to digest food.

  You: A colon.

  Alex: I'm sorry, you must phrase that response in the form of a question.

- ✔ Don't neglect your hard drive D (or E or F)! It offers more storage for your stuff. There's nothing wrong with installing software or saving your stuff to another hard drive.

- ✔ On my computers, I typically install games on drive D. I have no reason for it, other than it forces me to use drive D. (And drive D usually sits empty on most people's PCs.)

✔ Fill in this book's Cheat Sheet with the names and locations of your computer's disk drives and their letters. If you have a label maker, label your removable drives: Put *A* on drive A, *E* (or whatever) on your CD-ROM drive, and *F* (or whatever) on your Zip drive (if you have one), and so on.

✔ Providing that you don't have Windows XP, you can change the letters for removable drives in your system. I changed my drive letters; in Figure 4-1, you see that the DVD drive is letter R, the CD-ROM is drive S, and the Zip drive is letter Z. The steps to change the letters are complicated, though I list them on this book's companion Web page at `www.wambooli.com/help/PC/New_Drive_Letter/`.

REMEMBER

✔ Don't always depend on a PC's CD-ROM drive to have the same drive letter on every computer!

How much space is left on the disk drive?

Like closets and attics, disk drives fill up. To see how much space is available on a disk, open the My Computer window (see the section "Finding Your PC's Disk Drives," earlier in the chapter). Then click the mouse once on the drive you want to examine.

Disk drive letter examples

As an example of how disk drive letters are assigned, suppose Mary has a computer with hard drives C and D, plus a DVD drive. Here is how the drive letters will be assigned:

A: — Floppy drive

C: — First hard drive

D: — Second hard drive

E: — DVD drive

Now consider Phil, who, despite his bad haircut, has a computer with the following:

A: — Floppy drive

C: — First hard drive

D: — Second hard drive

E: — Third hard drive

F: — CD-ROM drive

G: — DVD drive

H: — Zip drive

Both Mary and Phil receive instructions to "Insert the installation disk into drive *D:*, where *D* is the letter of the DVD drive." They each have unique tasks. Mary must insert the DVD disc into drive E. Phil inserts the disc into drive F, but then realizes that it's a DVD, so he ejects the disc and properly inserts it into drive G.

The point to all this is to know your disk drives. Remember that the drive letters for your PC are unique. This is why some instruction manuals are vague.

For example, click once on drive C. This is officially known as *selecting* that drive. With most versions of Windows, you'll see a graphical representation of the drive on the left side of the My Computer window, as shown in Figure 4-2. The darker slice of the disk drive pie is the used space; the lighter slice is how much room you have left.

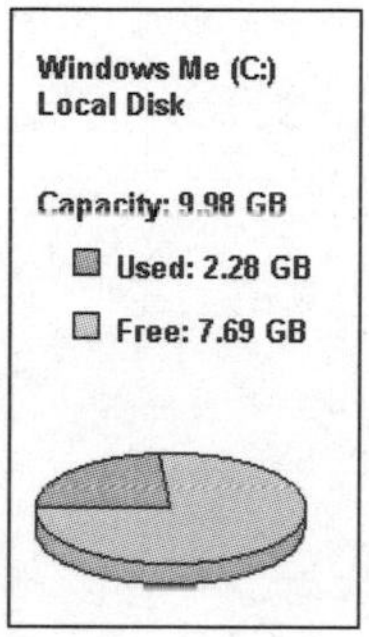

Figure 4-2:
A big slice
of disk pie is
left over for
more stuff!

Windows Me (C:)
Local Disk

Capacity: 9.98 GB
☑ Used: 2.28 GB
☐ Free: 7.69 GB

- ✔ If Windows doesn't display the information on the left side of the My Computer window, or you have Windows XP, don't give up! Refer to the next section "Even more disk information."

- ✔ Some disks, such as CD-ROMs and DVDs, are always full! That's because these disks can only be read from, not written to.

- ✔ You cannot get information about removable disks (floppy, CD-ROM, DVD) unless a disk is in the drive.

Even more disk information

Windows knows more about your disk drives than their icons, letters, names, or disk usages. Each disk drive in the My Computer window has a virtual cornucopia of information whirling about it. To see this information, follow these steps:

1. **Right-click on a disk drive in the My Computer window.**

   A pop-up menu appears (which usually happens when you right-click on something).

2. **Choose Properties from the shortcut menu.**

   The disk's Properties dialog box appears, as shown in Figure 4-3.

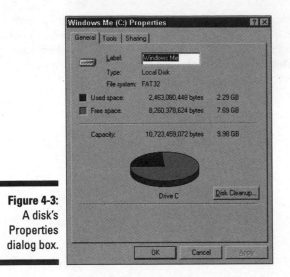

Figure 4-3:
A disk's
Properties
dialog box.

Immediately you should see the same pie chart shown in the My Computer window (or you'll see this for the first time if the My Computer window is stupid and didn't show it). Note how the disk used/free information is far more detailed here. Also, you see information about the disk's type and file system, and a text box where you can see, add, or change the disk's name.

Click OK to close the Properties dialog box when you're done.

✔ To change the disk's name, type a new name into the Label box. The name can be up to 11 characters long if you see the word *FAT* as the file system type. If the file system type is NTFS (which means you're running Windows NT or Windows 2000), then the disk name can be up to 32 characters long.

✔ To remove the name, select the text and delete it. Disks don't need names, so this doesn't harm anything.

✔ The disk's name is also known as the *label,* or if you want to be really la-di-da, it's the *volume label.*

✔ If your disk looks full (which means only a small purple slice of the pie is left), click the Disk Cleanup button. This button is one quick way to eliminate a lot of repetitive and useless files on your hard drive.

Working the CD-ROM/DVD Drive

CD-ROM drives eat special CD-ROM discs, which I call CDs, or computer CDs. The computer CDs look exactly like music CDs, although they store megabytes and megabytes of computer information. The CD-ROM drive can access that information, making it available to you just like it was on a hard disk or floppy. Oh and it can play music CDs as well.

A DVD drive (also called a DVD-ROM drive by those who have more time to type than I do) looks and acts just like a CD-ROM drive. But in addition to reading computer CDs and music CDs, the DVD drive can access computer DVD and video DVD discs.

- The *RO* in CD-ROM means Read-Only. You can only read information from a CD-ROM disc. You cannot add new information to the disc or erase or change information already on the disc.

- Ditto for DVD discs: You can only read from them. You cannot record new information on a DVD disc.

- The special CD-R/RW and DVD-RW drives allow you to create your own CDs or DVDs. Chapter 9 covers these devices.

Inserting a CD or DVD disc

You can stick a CD or DVD disc into the computer's disk drive two ways, depending on which type of disk drive the computer has.

Tray type. The most popular type of CD-ROM or DVD drive uses a slide-out tray to hold the disc. Start by pressing the drive's eject button, which pops out the tray (often called a *drink holder* in many computer jokes). Drop the disc into the tray, label up. Gently nudge the tray back into the computer. The tray will slide back in the rest of the way on its own.

Slide-in type. Another type of disk drive works like the CD player in most automobiles; the drive is merely a slot into which you slide the disc: Pushing the CD into the slot causes some gremlin inside the drive to eventually grab the CD and suck it in all the way. Amazing.

When the disc is in the drive, you use it just like any other disk in your computer.

- Another method for inserting CDs into a computer was the old "caddy" style. The disc slipped into a special disk caddy or case, and then you slid the case into the disk drive. I haven't seen any of these CD drives in a few years, so hopefully you'll never have to deal with them.

- Generally speaking, the disc is always inserted label-side up.

- An exception to the label-side-up rule are some DVD discs with data recorded on both sides. For example, some DVD movies have the TV version on one side and the wide-screen or letterbox version on another. If so, make sure you put the proper side up into the DVD drive.

✔ Some CDs are clipped. That is, they aren't round discs but maybe business card sized or some other special shape. These discs work fine in the tray type of CD-ROM/DVD drive, but do not insert them into the slide-in type of drive.

Ejecting a CD or DVD disc

Follow these steps to eject a disc from the CD-ROM or DVD drive:

1. **Open the My Computer window.**

   Refer to the section "Finding Your PC's Disk Drives," earlier in this chapter, if you need help locating this window.

2. **Right-click the mouse on the CD-ROM or DVD drive icon.**

   The drive's shortcut menu appears.

3. **Select Eject from the menu.**

   The disc spits from the CD-ROM drive.

✔ These steps also work for most types of removable disks — CD-ROM, DVD, Zip, even SuperDisks — but not traditional floppy disk drives.

✔ You can also eject a disc by pushing the manual eject button on the CD-ROM or DVD drive. However, this doesn't ensure that Windows is done with the drive. So to avoid any particularly nasty error messages, use only the steps outlined in this section for ejecting a CD or DVD disc.

✔ In times of urgency, such as when the computer is locked up (or off), you can eject a CD or DVD disc by pushing a bent paper clip into the tiny hole — the "beauty mark" — on the front of the CD/DVD drive. That manually ejects the disc when the computer is too stupid to do it by itself.

Playing a music CD or DVD movie

This is easy: To play a music CD or view a DVD movie, simply insert that disc into the drive. The music will start playing instantly, or the movie will cue up and run on your screen.

✔ DVD movies can be played only in DVD drives. Music CDs can be played in either CD-ROM or DVD drives.

✔ Unless you have another type of jukebox program, the Windows Media Player program will play music CDs. Use the various buttons on the Media Player as you would buttons on a standard CD player.

Audio CD (R:)

✔ When you put a music CD into your CD-ROM drive, the CD icon in the My Computer window changes to a musical CD icon, shown in the margin.

✔ It's best to view a DVD movie in as large a window as possible.

✔ The DVD controls typically disappear a few moments after the movie starts. To see them again, just jiggle the mouse.

Using the Floppy Drive

The most important thing to remember about using your floppy drive is to put a formatted floppy disk into it before you do anything. Floppy drives need floppy disks the way CD-ROM drives need CDs. (However, you can both read and write to floppy disks.)

Floppy do's and donuts

The floppy drive is more of an antique holdover from the PC's early days. Today, floppy drives still hang around, and they're still useful on many PCs. But their uses are limited. Here are my basic floppy drive rules:

✔ A floppy disk must be *formatted* before you can use it. Fortunately, most floppy disks come formatted when you buy them.

✔ Though most new programs come on CD-ROMs, a few still come on floppy disks.

✔ Floppy disks are great for transporting files from one computer to another. However, the small capacity of the floppy disk (only 1.4MB) limits the size and number of files you can move.

ASK DAN

"My floppy drive fills up in the middle of a download!"

Q: Dan, I was told to download stuff from the Internet to a floppy disk, mostly to prevent viruses from infecting my system. That works okay, but sometimes when I'm downloading a large file, I get a "Disk Full" error message. What can I do to avoid that?

A: Please, please, please *do not* download files to a floppy disk! I don't know which doofus wrote that doing so somehow prevents viruses. It doesn't. Please use the power and capacity of your computer's hard drive for downloading files. Avoid floppy disks for anything other than moving copies of files between computers. (And see Chapter 28 for more information on downloading files from the Internet.)

✔ Floppy disks are extremely unreliable. In fact, the more you use a floppy disk, the higher the chances that you'll lose information on the disk.

✔ Never save any file to a floppy disk. Only place *copies* of files on floppy disks.

✔ Don't worry if you never use the floppy drive. In fact, all the new Apple computers come without floppy drives. So I predict the days of the floppy-less PC are soon to come.

In and out goes the floppy disk

Floppy disks are flat, 3½-inch square coasters on which you can store 1.4MB of information. To use the floppy disk, you must insert it into your PC's floppy drive.

Stick the floppy disk into the drive label up, with the shiny metal piece going in first. The disk should make a satisfying *thunk* noise when it's in place.

To remove the floppy disk, push the button beneath and slightly to the right-of-center of the floppy drive slot. This action ejects the disk out of the drive about an inch or so (depending on how vigorously you push the button). Grab the disk and put it away.

✔ Ensure that the computer is not writing to the floppy disk before you eject it. The floppy drive's blinking access light should be off before you push the eject button.

✔ Before you eject a floppy disk, make sure that you're not currently using any files on that disk. If you eject a disk that still has open files on it, Windows will ask you to reinsert the floppy disk so that it can finish writing information.

✔ Be careful not to insert the floppy disk into the Zip drive slot. The Zip drive slot is larger than the floppy drive slot. If you have both, be sure you put floppies in the floppy drive.

✔ If your floppy disk is a SuperDisk, you can eject the disk similar to the way you eject a CD or DVD disc. See the section "Ejecting a CD or DVD disc" for more information.

Formatting floppies

All floppy disks must be formatted. Unless you were smart enough to buy preformatted floppy disks, you have to format them at some point. A disk must be formatted before you can use it.

If the disk isn't formatted and you try to access it, Windows spits up an ugly error message, similar to the one shown in Figure 4-4. If this message appears, click the Yes button and get ready for formatting.

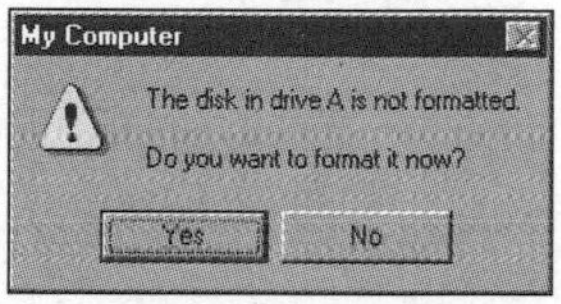

Figure 4-4:
The
nefarious
"disk is un-
formatted"
error
message.

1. **Stick an unformatted disk in drive A.**

   You can stick a new disk or an old disk into the drive. If you use an old disk, be aware that formatting erases *everything* on the disk. This is a devastating act. Be careful.

2. **Open the My Computer icon.**

   This step displays a list of disk drives in your computer, plus some oddball folders (refer to Figure 4-1).

3. **Select drive A.**

   Point the mouse at drive A's icon and click once. This step highlights that disk drive, selecting it for action.

4. **Choose File⇨Format.**

   The Format dialog box appears, similar to what's shown in Figure 4-5.

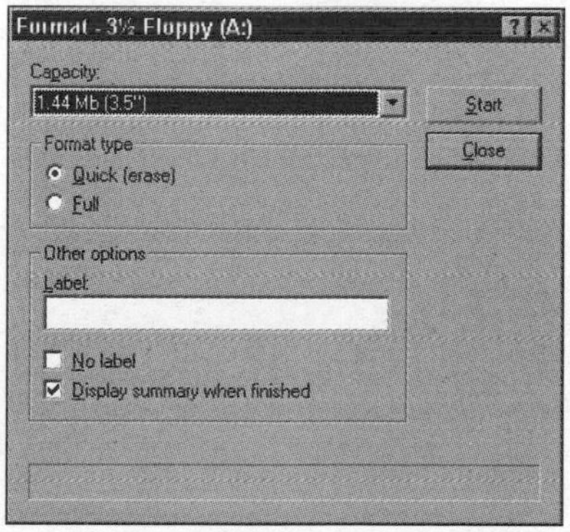

Figure 4-5:
The Format
dialog box.

5. **Click the Start button.**

The formatting process takes a minute or longer, so count the holes in the ceiling tiles for a while. When Windows finishes formatting . . . nothing happens. Well, you may see a summary screen. Press Esc to close the dialog box, and you're ready to use the disk.

✔ After the disk is formatted, slap a label on it. You can use one of the sticky labels that came with the disk. Be sure to write on the label *before* you slap it on the disk.

✔ Always label your floppy disks.

✔ Don't use sticky notes as disk labels. They fall off when you're not looking and can sometimes get stuck inside your disk drives.

Sending a file to drive A

You access drive A just like any other disk in your PC: After inserting a floppy disk, just open the drive A icon in the Windows Explorer or My Computer window, or access it from any Save As or Open dialog box. Files on drive A exist just like files on any other disk, though the floppy disk doesn't have a lot of room for storing stuff.

A quick way to send a file to drive A is to use the Send To➪Drive A shortcut. Find and select the file (or group of files) you want to copy to drive A. Then choose File➪Send To➪3½ Floppy (A) from the menu. Don't forget to put a formatted floppy disk in drive A before you choose this command!

✔ The typical floppy disk stores 1.4MB of information. Those disks get full fast! And if you try to copy too many files or a file that's too large, Windows tells you with the appropriate insulting error message.

✔ To copy files *from* drive A, double-click the My Computer icon on the desktop and then double-click the drive A icon in the My Computer window. Then drag or select and copy the files you want to put somewhere else. See Chapter 6 for more information on copying files from one place to another.

Floppy foibles

Q: This error message appears anytime I try to do anything with my floppy disk, save or retrieve: A:/ is not accessible the device is not ready. Retry. Cancel. Any ideas?

A: A *formatted* floppy disk must be in the drive before you can access the drive. Also ensure that the disk is all the way into the drive.

Using a Zip Drive

Zip drives are becoming popular alternatives and supplements to the traditional PC floppy disk. You can store 100MB or 250MB of information on a single Zip disk, depending on which Zip drive model you have. That's around 70 or 170 times the capacity of a junky old floppy disk.

- ✔ Zip drives come with many new PCs.
- ✔ You can add a Zip drive to your PC at any time. Some models are installed internally; others can be attached to your PC via cable.
- ✔ The 100MB Zip drives can read only 100MB disks. You must have a 250MB Zip drive to read the 250MB disks; these drives can also read the 100MB disks.
- ✔ Zip disks are a great way to move lots of information or massive files between two computers.
- ✔ Zip disks are expensive. Yowie! Buy them in bulk to get any deal on them. And make sure you buy the PC-formatted Zip disks, not the Macintosh Zip disks.

Inserting a Zip disk

Zip disks go into the drive just like floppy disks: label up, with the shiny metal part stuck in first.

Don't force the Zip disk in! If it doesn't fit, then you have the disk in the wrong orientation. Inserting the disk is especially frustrating if the disk drive is mounted sideways.

You must push the Zip disk all the way into the drive. After a certain point, the disk becomes locked into place. Stop pushing at that point.

Only when the Zip disk is in the drive can you read or write information to it.

Ejecting a Zip disk

To eject a Zip disk, locate the drive in the My Computer window. Right-click on the drive and choose Eject from the shortcut menu. This works just like ejecting a CD or DVD disc.

In times of woe, there is a way to remove a Zip disk from a dead Zip drive. Use the end of a bent paperclip and poke it in the tiny hole near the Zip disk drive's opening. Press hard enough and the Zip disk pops up. But only do this in times of dire need.

Looking at the Zip menu

Zip drives have their own special menu. After you insert a Zip disk into the drive, right-clicking on the Zip disk icon in the My Computer window displays a detailed menu with special Zip menu items, as shown in Figure 4-6.

Figure 4-6:
A Zip drive's
special
menu.

Note the special commands flagged by the *I* (for Iomega, Zip's manufacturer). These are Zip-drive-only commands.

Format. A customized format command specific to Zip drives. This is the command you would use to reformat your Zip disks. (All Zip disks come for-matted, so this really should be the Reformat command.)

Protect. A nifty option that restricts access to the disk. This is one of the only ways you can password-protect your files in Windows. The single password applies to the whole disk.

Eject. Spews the disk out of the drive.

Different versions of the Zip software may display additional menu items. For the full details, you need to refer to the Zip disk manual.

Chapter 5

Keeping Track of Your Files without Going Insane

As you use your computer, you will find yourself collecting lots of stuff: graphics files, music files, documents, secret recipes, endless jokes sent and resent to you via e-mail, files of this, files of that. Lots of stuff. Lots. There is nothing wrong with this; the computer was designed to store many thousands of files. No, the problem is being able to find That One File when you need it. To make that happen, you must be organized.

Everyone say, "Organized."

Organized.

Good.

If there is only one lesson you learn from this book, my hope would be that you learn how to organize your files. This is done by using *folders*. It's not hard. It's not a pain in the butt. In fact, all you need to do is read along, smile, follow a few steps, and you too will soon enjoy the sanity of having an organized hard drive.

Folder Basics

To organize your files and avoid any perilous consequences or Biblical-level doom, you use *folders*.

A folder is a storage place for files. In fact, all files stored on your computer's hard drive are stored into folders. The folders keep files together — like barbed wire keeps prisoners, vicious animals, and kindergartners from wandering off.

Without folders, files just go anywhere. Although you may be able to find them, you probably won't. Ever pull your hair out trying to find a lost file? Ever download something or save an e-mail attachment and not be able to find it? It's probably because you didn't care much about folders when you created or saved the file.

With folders, however, you can neatly tuck your files into a proper place. You can organize your files into various project folders, folders for specific types of files, folders for deeds, tasks, plots, and spells, or however you see fit.

This all seems to make sense. "Yes," you say. "These folders are a good thing." But there is a problem. Windows itself doesn't really care whether or not you use folders or even organize anything. There is no punishment for ignoring folders, other than having an unorganized hard drive and, potentially, losing your sanity. No, it's just easier to start out on the right foot and organize your stuff into folders.

- Folders contain files, just like folders in a filing cabinet contain files. Golly, what an analogy.

- All files on disk go into various folders. When you save something in Windows, you're really placing it in a specific folder somewhere on your hard drive.

- Folders can hold, in addition to files, more folders. These "subfolders" are just another level of organization. For example, you can have a folder named Finances and in that folder have other folders, one for 2001, one for 2002, and on up until the year you die.

- The key is to put files into folders *you* create for specific purposes.

The root folder

Every disk — even a lousy floppy disk — has at least one folder. That one folder — the main folder — is called the *root folder*. Like a tree (and this isn't a dog joke), all other folders on your hard drive branch out from that main, root folder.

- ✔ The root folder is simply the main folder on the disk drive.

- ✔ Had computer scientists been into construction instead of growing trees, they might have called it the *foundation folder* instead of the root folder.

- ✔ Personally I like calling the root folder the *main folder*.

- ✔ When you open a disk drive in My Computer or in Windows Explorer, the files and folders you see are all stored in the root folder. For example, open the Drive C icon and what you see are the files in the root folder on drive C.

- ✔ The root folder may also be called the *root directory.* This term is merely a throwback to the old days of DOS (which is a throwback to the days of UNIX, which King Herod used).

Special folders for your stuff

The root folder belongs to the hard drive. It's not yours. Like the lobby of some grand building, it's merely a place you pass through to get to somewhere else. For most, if not all, of the files you create, that somewhere else is the My Documents folder.

The My Documents folder is the place where you save your stuff. Nearly all of Windows applications and programs attempt to save files first in the My Documents folder.

Obviously, placing *all* of your files into the My Documents folder eventually becomes messy. To solve the problem, you need to create other folders — *subfolders* — inside the My Documents folder. More on that in a few paragraphs.

One subfolder that may already appear in the My Documents folder is the My Pictures folder. That's the folder where many graphics applications yearn to save the images you create. See? It's organization in action.

My Pictures

Some computers even have a My Music folder, into which you can put — guess what — music files!

During the course of your Windows travels, you may find other folders created in the My Documents folder, either by some program or by yourself. Use the folders for the specific documents they describe. For example, I created a Downloads folder into which I save all the crap I download from the Internet.

- ✔ Save your stuff in the My Documents folder.

- ✔ Create additional folders inside the My Documents folder to help keep your stuff organized.

- Use the various folders — and even folders within those folders — to further keep your stuff organized. This is handled by the Save As dialog box, which is covered later in this chapter.

- A shortcut to the My Documents folder appears on the desktop. It allows you quick access to the files you create — assuming that you save them in the My Documents folder. (See Chapter 6 for more information on shortcuts.)

- Although the C drive's root folder isn't yours, the root folder on any other disk can be used for storing files. So feel free to use the root folder on any disk other than drive C. Create subfolders there to continue your organizational frenzy.

Forbidden folders for other stuff

In addition to needing folders for your stuff, the computer also needs folders for the stuff Windows uses and folders for your applications. These are what I call the forbidden folders; don't mess with them!

For example, Windows itself lives in the Windows folder (named WINNT in Windows 2000). The programs you install keep themselves in the Program Files folder. Other folders may exist on the hard drive as well. Steer clear of these folders!

- Don't mess with any folder you did not create yourself.

- Save your files in the My Documents folder, never in the root nor Windows folder unless you're *specifically* directed to do so.

Working with Folders

In Windows, the folder work happens in a program called the Windows Explorer. It's the place where you can view folders and their contents, create new folders, smite folders, and generally keep your stuff organized.

You can start the Windows Explorer in about three dozen ways. The easiest way (for me) is to press the Windows key and the E key on the keyboard at the same time, which is written as WinKey+E. That always starts the Windows Explorer. Otherwise, you can start the program from the Start menu:

- In Windows 98, from the Start menu choose Programs➪ Windows Explorer.

- In Windows Me/2000, from the Start menu choose Programs➪ Accessories➪Windows Explorer.

✔ In Windows XP, from the Start menu choose More Programs⇨ Accessories⇨Windows Explorer.

Viewing the tree structure

The whole mess of folders on your hard drive is organized into something the computer nerds call the *tree structure*. The folders all start at the root, branching out to more folders and folders, and eventually you end up with files, kind of like the leaves on a tree. There are no aphids in this simile.

The Windows Explorer shows the tree structure in Folders panel, as shown in Figure 5-1. The right side of the window displays the contents of whatever item or folder is selected (highlighted) on the left.

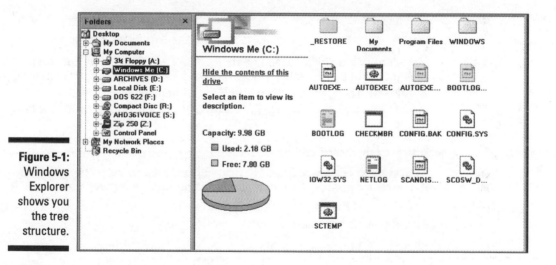

Figure 5-1: Windows Explorer shows you the tree structure.

To display the Folders panel, click the Folders button on the Explorer toolbar. Or you can choose View⇨Explorer Bar⇨Folders from the menu.

You can open part of the tree structure by clicking the plus (+) next to a folder. This action displays a *branch* of the tree structure.

Click the minus (-) next to a folder to close the branches of the tree structure.

When you're done with Explorer, close its window by clicking its wee little X close button in the upper-right corner.

✔ If you don't see the Explorer toolbar, choose View⇨Toolbars⇨ Standard Buttons. You may also want to choose Address Bar from the Toolbars submenu.

- You can turn the tree structure display on or off by clicking the Folders button on the toolbar. (This feature is not available in Windows 98.)

- The Views button on the far right side of the Explorer toolbar displays a menu that lets you see files and icons displayed in four different ways. If you have oodles of time to waste, click the button and choose a different view. (I like the Large Icons view, but my friend Julia detests it.)

- President Ulysses Grant played the part of Desdemona in an 1865 all-soldier production of Shakespeare's *Othello*.

Creating a folder

Creating a folder is easy. Remembering to use the folder is the hard part. The following steps create a folder named Stuff in the My Documents folder on drive C:

1. Double-click the My Documents icon on the Windows desktop.

Note that this is the My Documents icon, not My Computer! This step opens the My Documents folder window, detailing any files, documents, or folders that you have stored there.

If the folder appears messy, choose View⇨Arrange Icons⇨By Name from the menu.

2. Choose File⇨New⇨Folder.

This step places a new folder in the window, looking something like the icon in the margin. (The icon may look different, depending on which view you've chosen from the View menu.)

Ta-da! There's your new folder.

3. Give the folder a name other than the silly New Folder.

Type a new name for the folder. In fact, the folder is ready and willing to be renamed anything other than New Folder.

Be clever with the name! Remember that this folder will contain files and possibly other folders; all of which should relate somehow to the folder's name. If you can't think of anything useful for this tutorial, type the nondescript name **Stuff**.

If you need additional information to complete this step, check out the sidebar "Type it where?" in this chapter.

4. Press Enter to lock in the name.

See? Wasn't that easy? The new folder is ready and waiting for you to place new and interesting files into it.

Type it where?

Q: So here I am on Step 3 of creating a folder, and I can't seem to find the dialog box to type in a new name.

A: No dialog box, gentle reader. Just click any icon once to select it, file or folder. The icon becomes highlighted, turning a different color on the screen. Then press the F2 key to select the icon's name, and you can type in whatever name you like. Use the Backspace key to back up and erase if you make a mistake. When creating a new folder, you can name it only if you type immediately after creating it, as outlined in the steps nearby.

Now the folder is ready for play. You can double-click the new folder's icon to open it. A blank window appears because it's a new folder and has no contents. Time to fill it up!

- ✔ After creating the new folder, feel free to put files in there — or even create additional folders within the folder. Go on an organizational frenzy!

- ✔ See Chapter 6 for additional information on naming and renaming icons in Windows. That information applies to folders as well.

- ✔ If you just created the Stuff folder and have no use for it, kill it off! See the section "Deleting a folder," just a few millimeters from this very spot.

Deleting a folder

Find the folder you want to trash by using either the Explorer or My Computer program. Drag that folder across the desktop and drop it on the Recycle Bin icon.

Fwoosh! It's gone.

   If you can't see the Recycle Bin, for example, when a window is maximized, select the folder for death by clicking it once with the mouse. Click the Delete button on the toolbar to zap the folder, or you can press the Delete key on the keyboard. Bye-bye, folder!

- ✔ Death to the folder!

- ✔ After selecting the folder in Windows XP, you can choose "Throw away this folder" from the list of Folder tasks on the left side of the window to zap it away.

- A warning box may appear, telling you that you're about to delete a folder, and only bad people do that, and are you sure you don't want to change your mind? Click Yes to trash it.

- You can use the Undo command to immediately undelete a folder. This command works only immediately after the folder is deleted, so be timely. Choose Edit⇨Undo Delete, press Ctrl+Z, or click the Undo button on the toolbar.

- Deleting a folder kills off everything in that folder — files, folders, and all the files and folders in those folders. Egads! It's mass carnage! Be careful with this one, lest you have to confess to a hard drive war-crimes tribunal.

- You can rescue anything Windows deletes. Chapter 6 covers this topic.

The miracle of compressed folders

One unique feature of Windows Me and Windows XP is the ability to create special *compressed folders*. These are special storage folders. You can copy or move files into or out of the compressed folder, where they live intact but in a condition that doesn't hoard disk space. It's kind of like a trash compactor that takes today's garbage and crushes it down into a nice, tidy shoebox-sized brick. But unlike trash compactors, files in a compressed folder can be perfectly restored to their original conditions.

For example, I copied a doodle I created into a compressed folder. The doodle itself is a 936K file. (I love to doodle.) I copied the doodle into a compressed folder, and the total amount of disk space used by the compressed folder is only 26.5K. That's an amazing 97 percent reduction in file size!

To create a compressed folder, open the My Documents icon or open any folder in which you want to create the compressed folder. Then choose the File⇨New⇨Compressed Folder command. The compressed folder appears in the window, as shown in the margin. Enter a new name for the folder, and you're ready to use it.

Here are some compressed folder words of wit and wisdom:

- Compressed folders are best used for *storage*. For example, you can store a bunch of images or text documents in a compressed folder. Storing stuff there helps conserve disk space.

- You cannot use the Open command to open any file stored in a compressed folder. You must first copy or move the file out of the compressed folder to a normal folder on the hard drive.

- You cannot use the Save As command to save any file or document into a compressed folder. First save the file to a normal folder, then you can copy or move it into a compressed folder.

✔ Keeping in mind the previous two points, remember that compressed folders are for storage. Do not put things into them you plan on using often.

✔ Compressed folders can be encrypted or password protected. Right-click on the Compressed folder icon and choose Encrypt from the shortcut menu.

✔ Many of the files you download from the Internet will be stored in the Compressed folder file format. You can open the Compressed folder to remove or examine the files.

Using the Open Dialog Box

You'll often find yourself digging through folders when you use the Open command to fetch a file from disk. In most applications, choosing File⇨Open summons an Open dialog box, which is a tool used to find the file. In Windows, all Open dialog boxes work the same, which I find a refreshing blessing.

Figure 5-2 shows a typical Open dialog box. Of course, it looks prettier in Windows XP, and the panel on the left side of the dialog box may not appear with some older programs.

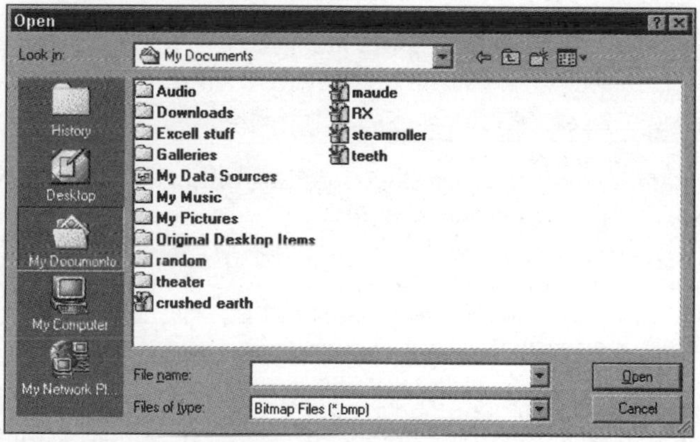

Figure 5-2:
The typical Open dialog box.

The following steps outline the basic way the Open dialog box is used:

1. Summon the Open Dialog box.

Use the program's Open command, found on the File menu: File⇨Open. Or you can access the Open command by pressing the Ctrl+O key combination. Or (and this is the last one), you can open things by clicking the Open button, which graces toolbars in most applications.

2. Look for your file. If it's there, open it.

The center of the dialog box shows a buncha file icons. If you find your file there, double-click it to open it. That file then appears, ready for tweaking in your favorite program.

You may need to use the scroll bar at the bottom of the list to see more files.

3. If you can't find your file, look in another folder.

If you can't find your file in the list, you'll need to look in another folder. There are several ways to do this:

- You can click the My Documents button (on the left side of the Open dialog box), which displays the contents of the My Documents folder.

- You can double-click to open any folder displayed in the file list.

- You can choose another folder from the drop-down list at the top of the dialog box.

If you find your file, open it!

4. If you still can't find your file, switch disk drives.

You choose another drive by using the drop-down list at the top of the Open dialog box: Click the down arrow to the right of the list to display it. Then pluck out a disk drive from the list, such as drive C, to start looking there.

The contents of the big list in the center of the dialog box change to show you the files on drive C (in the *root folder*).

If you find your file, open it!

 If you want to go back up to the preceding folder, click the handy Up One Level button (shown in the margin).

After opening the file, you can view it, edit it, modify it, print it — whatever. But you must open the file (or *document,* which sounds much more lofty) before you can do anything with it.

- ✔ At the bottom of the dialog box is a drop-down list titled Files of Type. It helps you narrow the types of files displayed in the Open dialog box's big list. For example, in Figure 5-2, only files of the Bitmap files (*.bmp) type appear in the big list. Another option is All Files, which displays every type of file available (though not every program can open any file).

- ✔ Some Open dialog boxes are more complex than the one shown in Figure 5-2. For example, the Open dialog box in Microsoft Word is a doozy. It works the same as other Open dialog boxes; it just has more annoying options to ignore.

Sneaky information about the Open and Save As dialog boxes

Both the Open and Save As dialog boxes display a list of files, just like the Explorer or My Computer windows. That's obvious. What often isn't obvious is that the list of files works exactly like the list of files displayed in the Explorer or My Computer windows.

For example, you can rename a folder or file displayed in an Open or Save As dialog box. You can right-click on a file and copy it or cut it. You can open a file by double-clicking it. Just about anything you can do with files in Windows can be done in that wee, tiny Open or Save As dialog box. This is a handy trick to use when organizing files.

- The Browse dialog box is similar to the Open dialog box. It appears whenever you click a Browse button to hunt down a file for Windows.

- You can also open a file by clicking it once and then clicking the Open button. I find that if you're going to click it once, you may as well rapidly click it twice and forget the Open button.

- If you're nerdy, you can type the file's full pathname (if you know it) in the File Name box. It's a very DOS-y thing to do. Cover your mouse's eyes if you try it. (You don't want to shame him.)

Using the Save As Dialog Box

The Save As dialog box is the most important dialog box you'll ever use in Windows. It's the key to organizing your files in a sane manner. You'll feel almost as nifty as those people who buy that California Closet organizer or the Wonder Purse.

To use the Save As dialog box, you must first save something to disk. Any program that lets you create something has a Save As command. It's used the first time you save your stuff to disk. Figure 5-3 shows the typical Save As dialog box. (The Save in panel on the left may not appear with some older Windows applications.)

1. Summon the Save As command.

Choose File➪Save As from the menu. Or you can press the handy Ctrl+S key combination or click the Save button from the toolbar. Note that the Save As dialog box only appears the first time you save your stuff to disk; from that point on, the Save command merely resaves a file to disk.

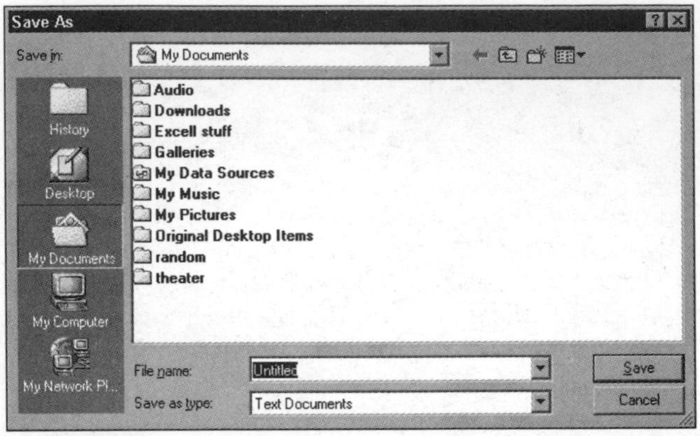

Figure 5-3:
The typical
Save As
dialog box.

2. **Most important: Make sure that you're in the proper folder.**

   See which folder the Save As dialog box wants to put your document in by checking the Save In drop-down list. In Figure 5-3, it says My Documents — that's the folder in which your document will be saved. If that folder isn't what you want, move on to Step 3.

   If the folder is okay, skip to Step 6 to give the file a descriptive name.

3. **Hunt for the folder in which you want to save your stuff.**

   The best way to find a folder is to start at the root folder, so select a hard drive from the drop-down list at the top of the dialog box: Click the down arrow on the right side of the drop-down list. Select the proper disk drive from the list (such as drive C) to display that drive's root directory.

   Notice that the contents of the big list in the center of the dialog box change to show you the files in the root folder on drive C. But don't save there! Instead:

4. **Open a folder.**

   Locate the folder in which you want to save your stuff, or the folder that contains the folder (and so on). For example, open the My Documents folder.

5. **Continue opening folders until you find the one you want.**

   For example, open the Work folder in the My Documents folder. Then open the Flying Unicycle folder to save the file in that project's folder.

   Keep repeating this step until you find the folder you want.

   As you open various folders, the contents of the file list in the center of the dialog box change.

   You can also click the New Folder button in the Save As dialog box to create a new folder. Name the folder and then open it to save your masterpiece right then and there.

6. **Type a name for the saved file.**

   Type the name in the File Name input box. It's the name for your saved file — the name you should be able to recognize later and say (out loud), "Say! That's my file. The one I want. I am so happy I saved it with a short, clever name that tells me exactly what's in the file. Oh, joy."

   If you give the file an unacceptable name, you can't save it. Windows is stubborn about filenames. (See Chapter 7 for more information about naming files.)

7. **Click the Save button.**

   Click! This last, official act saves the file to disk, with a proper name and in a proper folder.

   If the Save button appears to be broken, you probably typed an improper filename. Try giving the file a new name (refer to Step 6).

After you save your stuff once, you can use the File⇨Save command to resave your file to disk again. This command is a quick way to update the file on disk without having to work the Save As dialog box again.

If you want to save your file to disk in another spot, give it a new name, or save it as another type of file, you need to use the Save As dialog box again. In that case, choose File⇨Save As from the menu.

As with the Open dialog box, some Save As dialog boxes are more complex than the one shown in Figure 5-3. The same business goes on; they just have more things to get in the way.

"What the heck is a pathname?"

A *pathname* pinpoints a file's location on a certain disk drive and in a certain folder. Long. Technical. Complex. It's a wonder that anyone has to deal with these things.

As an example, suppose there is a file named Check Please in the My Music folder in the My Documents folder on drive C. The file's ugly pathname is

```
C:\My Documents\My Music\Check
     Please
```

It reads this way: C: means drive C; My Documents is the My Documents folder; My Music is the My Music folder; Check Please

is the filename; and backslashes are used to separate things.

Occasionally, you find pathnames referenced in user manuals or in Windows itself. Suppose, for example, that you're told to go out and hunt down the file represented by this pathname:

```
C:\MyDocuments\Personal\Letters
     \Family\Zack.doc
```

You look on drive C, open the My Documents folder, open the Personal folder, open Letters, open Family, and then look for the file named Zack.doc.

Chapter 6

Messin' with Files

· ·

In This Chapter

▶ Naming a file

▶ Renaming a file

▶ Selecting one or more files

▶ Moving files (cut and paste)

▶ Copying files (copy and paste)

▶ Making a file shortcut

▶ Deleting files

▶ Undeleting files

▶ Finding files

▶ Protecting files with passwords

· ·

*W*indows stores information on disk in the form of files. Whether it's a word-processing document, a picture, an e-mail message, or plans for a dot-com comeback on Wall Street, it's really a file on disk. The Save command puts the file on disk. The Open command opens the file up for more editing or wanton whatnot. And to all the files on disk, you are their lord and master.

As file lord of your PC, it's your job to keep the lot of them in line and obedient. Windows gives you various tools to do that: the Copy command, the Cut command (for moving files), and the Rename command. You also have tools for finding lost files, making you their gentle shepherd. And if a file gets out of line, you can rub it out of existence, sending it to its doom like a ruthless judge or gravel-voiced bad guy from a Saturday morning cartoon show. Such is the life of a file lord, which I describe thoroughly in this chapter.

✔ Windows displays files as icons. The *icon* is really the picture you see, representing the file on disk.

✔ Everything on disk is a *file*. Some files are *programs,* and some files are *documents* or stuff you create.

File-Naming Rules and Regulations

One thing mankind is good at is giving things names. Find a new bug, planet, beast, comet, or disease, and you get to name it. Files are the same way, but without the fame — or infamy as when a new disease is named after you.

You name a file when saving the file to disk, which happens in the Save As dialog box (see Chapter 5). When naming a file, keep the following ideas in mind:

Be brief. The best filenames are brief yet descriptive, like in the following examples:

```
Finance
Biggsley
Chapter 1
Glorious Pie Chart
Invasion of Canada
```

Technically you can give a file a name that's over 200 characters long. Don't. Long filenames may be *very* descriptive, but Windows displays them funny or not at all in many situations. Better to keep things short than to take advantage of a long filename size.

What the heck is a filename extension?

The last part of a filename is typically a period followed by a handful of characters. Known as the *filename extension*, Windows uses it to identify the type of file. For example, a .BMP extension tags a Paint graphics image, and .DOC indicates a document created by WordPad or Microsoft Word.

You don't want to mess with these extensions when you name or rename a file, because Windows needs those filename extensions. If a file doesn't have the filename extension (or has the wrong one), it screws things up when you try to open the file for editing.

To avoid inadvertently changing a filename extension, follow these steps:

1. **Start Windows Explorer (WinKey+E) or open the My Computer icon on the desktop.**

2. **Choose Tools⇨Folder Options.**

   (In Windows 98, the command is View⇨ Folder Options.)

3. **Click the View tab in the Folder Options dialog box.**

4. **Locate the item in the list that says "Hide file extensions for known file types."**

5. **Click to put a check mark by that item.**

   If the item already has a check mark, you're just dandy.

6. **Click OK to close the Folder Options dialog box.**

Use only letters, numbers, and spaces. Filenames can contain just about any key you press on the keyboard. Even so, it's best to stick with letters, numbers, and spaces.

Windows gets angry if you use any of these characters to name a file:

```
* / : < > ? \ | "
```

The symbols above hold a special meaning to Windows. Nothing bad happens if you attempt to use these characters. Windows just refuses to save the file — or a warning dialog box growls at you.

Use periods sparingly. Although you can use any number of periods in a filename, you cannot name a file with all periods. I know that it's strange, and I'm probably the only one on the planet to have tried it, but it won't work.

Case — it don't matter. Upper- and lowercase don't matter to Windows. Although capitalizing Moldova is proper, for example, a computer matches that to moldova, Moldova, MOLDOVA, or any combination of upper- and lowercase letters.

(On the other hand, case *does* matter when typing in a Web page address. But that's not a file-naming issue.)

- ✔ The file's name reminds you of what's in the file, of what it's all about (just like naming the dog *Sissydown* tells everyone what the dog is all about).

- ✔ If you give a file too long of a name, it's easier to make a single typo and confuse Windows when you try to open the file.

- ✔ Another long filename snafu: The rows of files listed in the Open or Save dialog box get farther and farther apart if a long filename is in the list. Shorter filenames mean shorter columns in a list.

- ✔ Also, if you give a file a long, long name, only the first part of that long filename appears below the icon.

- ✔ All the rules for naming files in the following sections also apply to naming folders.

- ✔ See Chapter 5 for more information about the Open dialog box.

Renaming a file

If you think that the name you just gave a file isn't exotic enough, you can easily change it:

1. **Click the file's icon once to select it.**

2. **Press the F2 key.**

   You can also choose File➪Rename from the menu, although F2 is handier because your fingers need to be on the keyboard to type in the new name anyway.

3. **Type a new name.**

   Press the Backspace key to back up and erase if you need to.

   Notice that the text for the old name is selected. If you're familiar with using the Windows text-editing keys, you can use them to edit the old name. (Also see Chapter 13 about common Windows editing keys.)

   If a pop-up description bubble appears over the name as you start to type, just move the mouse, and the bubble will pop out of the way.

4. **Press the Enter key to lock in the new name.**

Note that all files *must* have a name. If you don't give the file a name (you try to leave it blank), Windows complains. Other than that, here are some file-naming points to ponder:

- ✔ You can press the Esc key at any time before pressing Enter to undo the damage and return to the file's original name.

- ✔ Windows doesn't let you rename a file with the name of an existing file; no two items in the same folder can share the same name.

- ✔ You can't rename a group of files at the same time. Rename files one at a time.

- ✔ You can undo any renaming by pressing the Ctrl+Z key combination or choosing Edit➪Undo from the menu. This must be done *immediately* after the boo-boo for it to work.

Files Hither, Thither, and Yon

Files don't stand still. You'll find yourself moving them, copying them, and killing them off. If you don't do those things, your hard drive gets all junky, and out of embarrassment, you're forced to turn off the computer when friends come over.

Selecting one or more files

Before you can mess with any file, you must select it. Like log rolling, you can select files individually or in groups.

To select a single file, click its icon once with the mouse. This step selects the file, which appears highlighted (blue, possibly) on-screen, similar to what's shown in the margin. The file is now ready for action.

You can select a group of files in a number of ways. The easiest way is to press and hold down the Ctrl (control) key on your keyboard. Then click each file you want to add to the group, one after the other. This method is known as *control-clicking* files.

Figure 6-1 illustrates a window in which several files have been selected by control-clicking them with the mouse. Each highlighted file is now part of a group, available for manipulation or death via one of the many file commands.

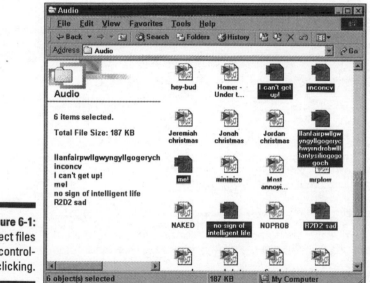

Figure 6-1: Select files by control-clicking.

Another way to select files as a group — especially when the files appear together in the Icon view — is to lasso them. Figure 6-2 illustrates how you do this by dragging over the files with the mouse.

To lasso the files, start in the upper-left corner above the file group, then click and hold the mouse button and drag down and to the right to create a rectangle surrounding the file icons you want to select, as shown in Figure 6-2. Release the mouse button, and all the files you've lassoed are selected as a group.

✔ To select all the files in a folder, choose Edit⇨Select All. The handy keyboard shortcut key for this procedure is Ctrl+A.

✔ To deselect a file from a group, just Ctrl+click it again.

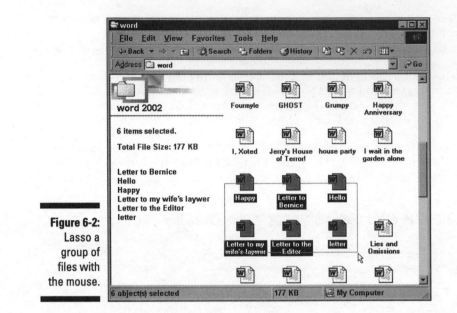

Figure 6-2:
Lasso a
group of
files with
the mouse.

Moving files with cut and paste

In Windows, where everything is like kindergarten anyway, you cut and paste. To cut and paste (move) a file, follow these steps:

1. Locate the file(s) you want to move.

Hunker down in the Explorer or My Computer program, and open various folders and look for the file or files you want to move.

2. Select the file(s).

Refer to the techniques described in the preceding section.

3. Choose Edit⇨Cut.

You can also use the handy keyboard shortcut: Ctrl+X.

After cutting, the file appears dimmed in the window, which means that the file has been cut and is ready to be pasted. Nothing is wrong; keep moving on with the next step.

4. Open the folder where you want the file pasted (moved to).

Again, use the Explorer or My Computer program to hunt down the proper destination folder.

5. Choose Edit⇨Paste.

Or you can use the Paste command keyboard shortcut, Ctrl+V.

The file is deeply moved.

Don't eat the paste.

- ✔ You can also cut and paste folders; however, it's a Big Deal because you're also cutting and pasting the folder's contents — which can be massive. Don't do this casually; cut and paste a folder only when you're up for major disk reorganization.

- ✔ In Windows Me/2000, you can also use the handy Move to button to move selected files to a folder. First select the file(s), then click the button, then choose the folder, disk drive or whatever destination in the Browse For Folder dialog box that appears. Click OK to move the file(s).

- ✔ Instead of a Move to button, Windows XP uses the "Move this file" or "Move the selected items" command in the File Tasks area on the left side of the window.

- ✔ Finally, there is the Edit⇨Move to Folder command for moving selected files. (This command doesn't appear in Windows 98).

Copying files with copy and paste

Copying and pasting a file works just like cutting and pasting, but the file is copied instead of moved. The original file remains where it was and fully intact. So after copying, you have two copies of the same file (or group of files if you're copying a whole hoard of them).

To copy a file, follow the same steps outlined in the preceding section for cutting and pasting a file (moving). In Step 3 (after finding and selecting the file), choose the Edit⇨Copy command. Or you can use the Ctrl+C keyboard shortcut.

When you paste the file, you're pasting a full-on copy. The original file remains untouched.

- ✔ Windows Me/2000 has the handy Copy to button that you can also use to copy selected files or folders. First, select the files, then click the Copy to button. Use the Browse For Folder dialog box to locate the folder or disk drive to where you want to copy the files. Click OK and the files are copied.

- ✔ Instead of a Copy to button, Windows XP has the "Copy this file" or "Copy the selected items" command, which appears in the File Tasks area on the left side of the window.

- ✔ As if all that weren't enough, there is the Edit⇨Copy to Folder command for moving selected files. (Windows 98 lacks this command.)

- ✔ Oftentimes, you don't really need to copy a file anywhere on your hard drive. Instead, create a shortcut to that file. See the next section "Creating shortcuts."

> ✔ For copying a file to a floppy disk, refer to Chapter 4. But keep in mind that you can still copy and paste to move files to a floppy disk (or Zip disk for that matter).
>
> ✔ You can also copy or cut files from a floppy disk to your hard drive. The process works the same way no matter which type of disk you're working with.

Creating shortcuts

When you copy a file, you're copying *all* of the file. Sometimes copying all of it is unnecessary, especially for large files that swallow disk space like hungry bears eating endangered salmon. Sometimes instead of making a full copy, you can instead create a file *shortcut.*

A file shortcut is a 99 percent fat-free copy of a file. It enables you to access the original file from anywhere on your computer but without the extra baggage required to copy the file all over creation. For example, you can copy a shortcut to Microsoft Word on the desktop, where you can always get to it — much quicker than using the Start menu.

Making a shortcut is a cinch: Just follow the same steps for copying a file, as detailed in the previous sections about cutting, copying, and pasting files. The only exception is that you choose Edit⇨Paste Shortcut from the menu rather than the standard Paste command.

To paste a shortcut on the desktop, right-click on the desktop. Up pops a shortcut menu, from which you can choose the Paste Shortcut command.

Shortcut to the
old graveyard

> ✔ A shortcut icon has a little arrow in a white box nestled into its lower-left corner (see the figure in the margin). This icon tells you that the file is a shortcut and not the real McCoy.
>
> ✔ Shortcuts are also named *Shortcut to* followed by the original file's name. You can edit the *Shortcut to* part out if you like. See the section "Renaming a file," earlier in this chapter.
>
> ✔ You can make shortcuts for popular folders and stick them on the desktop for easy access.
>
> ✔ You can open a shortcut just like any other icon: Double-click to open a document, run an application, or open a folder.

> ✔ Have no fear when you're deleting shortcuts; removing a shortcut icon does not remove the original file.

Deleting files

Unlike credit cards and driver's licenses, files don't simply expire. You must make an effort to rid yourself of old or temporary files you don't need. Otherwise, files collect like lint balls outside a dryer vent.

To kill a file, select it and choose File⇨Delete. This process doesn't truly remove the file; it merely moves the thing over to the Recycle Bin. From there, you can easily undelete the file later.

You can also delete a selected file by pressing the Delete key on the keyboard.

 Or you can click the Delete button on the toolbar (if there is a toolbar).

Or even this: You can delete files by dragging them with the mouse. Drag the file from its window into the Recycle Bin icon on the desktop.

If you want a sensitive file utterly crushed, click it once with the mouse and press Shift+Delete. Windows displays a warning dialog box, explaining that the file will be utterly crushed (or something to that effect). Click Yes to zap it off to eternity.

✔ Windows may warn you about deleting a file. Are you *really* sure? You probably are, so click Yes to delete the file. (Windows is just being utterly cautious.)

✔ You can delete folders just like files, but keep in mind that you delete the folder's contents — which can be dozens of icons, files, folders, jewelry, small children, widows, and refugees. Better be careful with that one.

✔ Never delete any file in the Windows folder or any of the folders in the Windows folder.

✔ Never delete any file in the root folder of a hard drive.

✔ In fact, never delete any file unless you created it yourself.

✔ Don't delete programs! Instead, you can use a special tool in the Windows Control Panel for removing old applications you no longer need. See Chapter 19 for more information.

Undeleting files

You probably want your file back in a hurry, so there's no wasting time!

 If you just deleted the file — and I mean *just deleted* it — then you can use the Edit⇨Undo command (Ctrl+Z). That gets it back.

If Edit⇨Undo doesn't do it, or undo it (or whatever), then take these steps:

1. **Open the Recycle Bin on the desktop.**

   Double-click the Recycle Bin icon. It looks like a little trash can, as pictured in the margin, though it may look like something else depending on how you have Windows configured. (But it always says *Recycle Bin* beneath the icon.)

2. **Select the file you want recovered.**

   Click the file to begin its resurrection.

   Choose View⇨Arrange Icons⇨by Delete Date from the menu to display files in the order they were deleted (by date). That way, it's cinchy to find any recently departed files you may want back.

3. **Click the Restore button on the left side of the window.**

   Or you can choose File⇨Restore from the menu, if the Restore button can't be found.

   The file is magically removed from the Recycle Bin and restored to the folder and disk from which it was so brutally seized.

4. **Close the Recycle Bin window.**

   Click the window's X (close) button in the upper-right corner.

Windows has no definite time limit on how long you can restore files; they can be available in the Recycle Bin for months or even years. Even so: Don't let the convenience of the Recycle Bin lead you down the merry path of false security. Never delete a file unless you're certain that you want it gone, gone, gone.

Finding Wayward Files (And Programs)

Losing track of your files in Windows is no big deal. That's because Windows has a nifty Search command. It's a blessing. If only such a command existed for your car keys or glasses, the world would truly be a better place.

To find a wayward file in Windows, you need to know something about the file. Knowing one or more of the following tidbits will help you quickly and easily find any file on your computer:

- The file's name or at least part of it
- Any text in the file, words or part of sentences you remember
- The date the file was created, last saved to disk, or modified

> ✔ The file's type (or which program created it)
> ✔ The file's size

The more information you can supply, the better Windows is at finding your file. Still, even with vague information, Windows displays a list of files — a longer list but a list nonetheless.

Finding the file

The following steps help you to find your file, no matter how much you know or can't remember about it. (If you have Windows XP, refer to the section "Searching for files in Windows XP," later in this chapter.)

1. **Summon the Search command.**

   If your keyboard has a Windows key, you can press WinKey+F, where the F means Find. This summons the Search command no matter which version of Windows you have.

   If your keyboard lacks a Windows key, then choose the Search or Find submenu on the Start menu. Choose Files or Folders from the submenu.

2. **Describe the lost file.**

   Your job is to fill in as much information about the lost file as you can.

   If you know the file's name, put it in the Named text box. Type the full name. If you don't know the entire name, use asterisks (*) to replace the parts you don't know.

   For example, if you know the file contains the word *report*, you can type ***report*** in the Named box. If you know the file starts with the letters *NU*, you can type **NU*** into the Named box.

   If you know of any text in the file, type that text into the Containing text box. For example, if you know the file contains the text "lost fortune in Avocado pits" enter that text. Otherwise you can leave this line blank.

   Finally, if you know which hard drive the file might live on, choose it from the Look in drop-down list. This is optional; choosing a hard drive merely speeds up the search.

   In Windows 98, ensure that the Include subfolders item is checked.

3. **Click the Search Now or Find Now button.**

   This action sends Windows off on a merry chase to locate the file you've requested. One of two things happens when it's done:

   No dice. A text message appears letting you know that the file wasn't found; there are no items or results to display. Oh well. Try again.

Eureka! Any files matching your specifications are listed in the window. From here you can do whatever you want with the found file(s): Double-clicking the file, for example, opens it. Or you can move, copy, delete, rename or whatever, just as you would in any My Computer or Explorer window.

4. **Close the window when you're done.**

The list of files displayed can get quite long. The list's length depends on how specific you are when you tell Windows what to find.

    ✔ Additional searching commands are covered in the following sections.

    ✔ You can choose as many or as few searching options as you like. Mix and match 'em. Remember, the more specific you can be, the better the results.

    ✔ You can leave any item in the Find dialog box blank to search for *anything* in that category. For example, to create a list of all the files on drive C, choose drive C from the Look in list and enter * as the file name.

Searching for files in Windows XP

To search for lost files, choose the Search command from the Start menu. A special Search Results window appears with a Search Companion task pane on the left side. Your job is to use the Search Companion to tell Windows what to find.

1. **Select the file type.**

   Windows gives you three categories of files: Pictures, music, or video; Documents; and All file types, which means everything else. Choose one.

   The remaining steps you take depend on the type of file you've chosen.

2. **Enter more information.**

   Depending on the type of file you're looking for, you will be asked more detailed information. Fill in the information according to what you know about the wayward file. If you don't know the proper answer, then leave an item blank.

3. **Type in all or part of the file's name.**

   Eventually, there will be a box where you type the file's name. You can type in the exact name, if you remember it, or type in only part of the name. For example, typing in *read* finds any file with "read" in the name.

   If you don't know the name, then click the Advanced Options button so that you can provide more detailed information. Remember, the more you know about the file the more exact Windows will be in finding what you're looking for.

4. Click the Search button.

Windows goes a-huntin'.

Any files matching the description you provided appear on the right side of the window. You can click "Yes, finished searching" to examine the files, or click the "Start a new search" item to search again.

Search command tips for Windows Me and Windows 2000

Here are some additional Search command tips and tricks for Windows Me and Windows 2000, which operate similarly.

Figure 6-3 shows the results from a Windows Me Search command. The Search panel appears whenever you click the Search button in a My Computer or Windows Explorer window.

- To start a new search and reset all the previous Search options, click the New button. It's important to remember this! If you don't, you may not find the files you're looking for because some silly option from the previous search is still in effect.

- More precise searches can be accomplished by displaying the Search Options information shown in Figure 6-3. If that box doesn't appear, click the >> arrows.

- To find a file by the date it was created, put a check in the Date box. Additional information is displayed, allowing you to search for files created recently or on specific dates.

- To find files of a specific type, click the Type box. The Search Options box expands to show a list of all the file types known to Windows. Choose one, such as Wave Sound to find a sound file, and Windows searches for only those file types.

- To find files of a specific size, click to put a check mark in the Size box. Use the drop-down lists to enter a file size or ballpark estimate. Windows limits it search to files of the size you specify.

When you're done searching you can make the Search panel go away by either closing the entire window, or by clicking the Search button on the toolbar.

Find command tips for Windows 98

In Windows 98, the Find command is used to locate files. It appears in its own dialog box, as shown in Figure 6-4. You can summon this dialog box by pressing the F3 key whenever you see a My Computer or Explorer window.

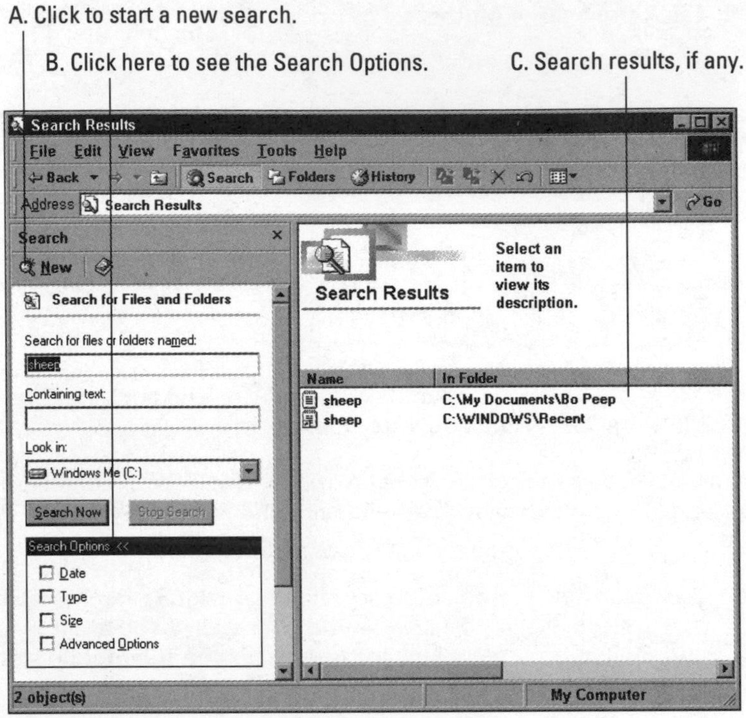

A. Click to start a new search.

B. Click here to see the Search Options.

C. Search results, if any.

Figure 6-3:
Searching
for a file in
Windows
Me (also
Windows
2000).

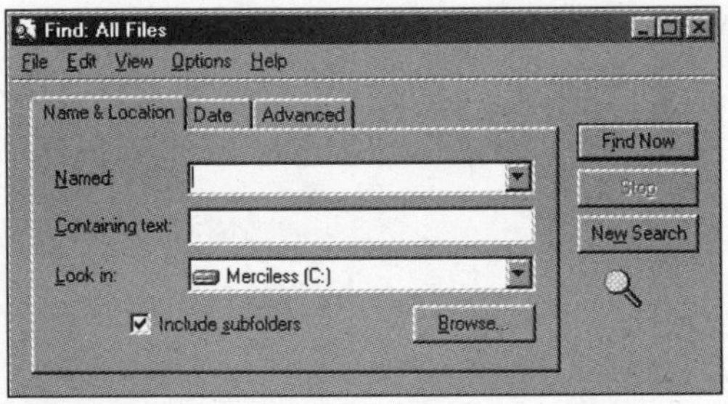

Figure 6-4:
Finding a
file in
Windows 98.

The following tips help you narrow down the file search based on bonus information you supply to the Find command.

✔ To look for files created, saved, or modified on a specific date or within a range of dates, click the Date tab. That presents a slate of gizmos you can use to narrow down the date or time for Windows' file search.

✔ The Advanced tab holds two treasures. First, there is an Of type drop-down list where you can direct Windows to find only files created by a certain program or files of a certain type, such as MOV video files.

✔ The second treasure in the Advanced tab is the file size gizmos. You can use them to find files of a specific size. I typically use this option to locate files over 5,000K in size — big files. I check this often to see if there are any of those whoppers I can safely delete. (And remember to delete only files you create, not anything else.)

Password protecting files

Q: Dan, is there any way to password protect a file in Windows? I have some stuff I really don't want people to look at. Can I lock them out with a password?

A: Nope. There is no password protection in Windows. Individual files cannot be locked up, not at all.

In Windows 2000 and Windows XP, you have password protection for all your files because you need a password to get access to the system. Without that access password, no one can look at the stuff you create. Even so, there still isn't a specific password for individual files.

Some programs, such as Microsoft Word and Microsoft Excel, have password protection on the individual documents or spreadsheets, which are applied in the Save As dialog box and prevent anyone from opening the document unless they know the password.

In Windows Me and Windows XP, you can encrypt a compressed folder, which means no one can access the files in that folder unless he or she knows the password. In theory, you can compress a single file and slap a password on that compressed folder. That's the closest Windows comes to password-protecting files.

Part III
The Non-Nerd's Guide to Computer Hardware

The 5th Wave   By Rich Tennant

Don't get your hopes up, Ted. The other end may not be plugged in.

In this part . . .

The basis of all drama is conflict. Put another way, you can't have a story unless someone disobeys. Pull any classic example from literature and you'll see how true it is: good versus evil, people versus robots, goofy cartoon kids versus gravely voiced eccentric villain, you versus the idiot driving the Volvo. Alas, conflict isn't to be found in your computer. The hardware dutifully obeys the software. There is no drama.

Although the drama may be thin, I do feel there is a little tension, perhaps even jealousy between computer hardware and software. You see, it's the hardware that gets all the press. A new microprocessor gets a mention on the nightly news. The prices on those elegant LCD monitors are crashing through the floor! But the software that controls those gadgets doesn't even get a mention. If there was ever anything to cause software to seethe with jealousy . . . But I digress.

To keep the scales out of balance, I hereby present the hardware part of the book first, before the software part. Face it: Hardware is just more interesting. Software may control it, but there's just more to hardware — and such a variety — that it deserves to come first. So the chapters in this part of the book dwell on hardware.

Chapter 7

Basic Computer Guts

• •

• •

I've got to hand it to computer manufacturers. The basic computer design has truly improved over the past few years. No longer are we cursed with the off-white, boxy computer console. Today you can buy computers with sleek, colorful, see-through, plastic cases. Some systems look like warp drivers or have certain aerodynamic properties that make it seem like the thing would fly away should there be a sudden gust of wind. Yet, despite the beauty on the outside, the inside of a computer box is still as naked and ugly as it ever was.

Inside your computer is a veritable electronic sushi bar of diodes, resistors, chips, and chunks of technology. This scientific salad of stuff should be interesting only to the folks in the white lab coats. Alas, you too may be assaulted with the various terms as you use your PC: *motherboard, microprocessor, BIOS, ports, power supplies,* and *expansion slots.*

This chapter covers many things you can and cannot see inside your PC's console. Some of the things I discuss are important, yet buried deep in your computer's bosom. Other things are important because you can see them dotting the backside of your PC like barnacles on a whale. What these things are, what they do, and why you should care is all covered here.

✔ Your PC also houses various connectors, which I cover in Chapter 8.

✔ Chapter 10 details computer memory, which is inside your PC but deserves its own chapter.

✔ Disk drives, also located inside the PC, are covered in Chapter 9.

The Mother of All Boards

The *motherboard* is the main piece of circuitry inside your PC. Like the downtown of a big city, it's where everything happens. That's mostly because the motherboard supports the computer's main chip, the microprocessor. So just as big city downtowns have their crime lords or political kingpins, the motherboard has its microprocessor.

Many important things want to live near the microprocessor, so those things cling to the motherboard. For example, power connectors, expansion slots, the computer's memory, the places where the internal disk drives plug in, the computer's clock, the BIOS or ROM chips — all that junk is soldered to the motherboard.

You don't need to see your PC's motherboard to know that it's there. If you're truly curious, then you might be able to find a diagram of it somewhere in the junk that came with the computer. But all that's overly technical. The bottom line is that on the motherboard lives your computer's main circuitry.

- ✔ IBM calls the motherboard in its computers the *planar* board. Oh, brother.

- ✔ Despite its formidable status, it is possible to access and mess with your computer's motherboard. This is a task best left to Those Who Truly Know What They're Doing.

- ✔ You can add various disk drives to the disk drive connectors on the motherboard.

- ✔ The most common thing to add to the motherboard are expansion cards, which plug into expansion slots on the motherboard. Again, this is a highly geeky thing to do.

- ✔ Upgrading memory? Why, that's done on the motherboard directly. See Chapter 10.

- ✔ Oh, some motherboards allow you to remove and add a microprocessor. I recommend against this, however. I tell you why later.

The Microprocessor

At the heart of every computer beats the *microprocessor.* That's the computer's main chip. No, it's not the computer's *brain.* (Software is the brain.) Instead, the microprocessor acts like a tiny, fast calculator. It just adds and subtracts (and does the tango and the jitterbug).

The microprocessor deals with other elements in the computer. Primarily these elements provide either *input* or *output,* which compujockeys call *I/O. Input* is information flowing into the microprocessor. *Output* is information the microprocessor generates and spits out.

Pretty much the whole computer obsesses over this input and output stuff.

✔ The main chip inside the computer is the *microprocessor,* which is essentially a tiny calculator with a BIG price tag.

✔ The microprocessor is also called the CPU, which stands for Central Processing Unit. Military-types like the term.

✔ When your jaw is tired, you can refer to the microprocessor as the *processor.*

✔ Older microprocessors resembled large, flat, after-dinner mints — with hundreds of legs. Today's microprocessors come in scary-looking black boxes — about the size of an instant camera (but thinner).

Naming a microprocessor

In the old days, microprocessors were named after famous numbers: 8088, 80386, '486, and on and on. Today, microprocessors are given proper and more powerful names, but not like Hercules or Samson or Steve. Instead, they're called Pentium and AMD and Cyrix.

Intel broke the numeric chain by dubbing what would have otherwise been called the 586 (or 80586) the *Pentium*. This was mainly to thwart their competitors because, unlike a name, you cannot trademark a mere number.

And so the Pentium begat the Pentium Pro.

And the Pentium Pro begat the Pentium with MMX.

And the Pentium with MMX begat the Pentium II.

And then . . . well, you get the idea. Today we have the Pentium III and Pentium IV microprocessors. Supposedly the next level will be the Itanium processor. Who knows? These names all sound like mystery substances that the crew of the starship Enterprise might discover on some alien planet. "Captain, the structure appears to be made of Itanium with a nice beveled Pentium finish."

Other manufacturers make other microprocessors similar to the Intel Pentium but cheaper! These microprocessors have names like AMD and Cyrix and numbers like P6 and K6. Basically they're the same as the Pentium-whatever, but less expensive.

Intel has its own cheaper version of the Pentium called the Celeron, which has nothing to do with celery. It's just a cheapie Pentium.

- ✔ Intel is the world's leading manufacturer of computer microprocessors. The company developed the original 8088 that dwelt in the bosom of the first IBM PC.

- ✔ Little difference exists between a true Intel and non-Intel microprocessor. As far as your PC's software is concerned, the microprocessor is the same no matter who made it. If you feel better about using a Pentium as opposed to using something from AMD, then by all means buy a computer with a Pentium. Really, your software won't know the difference.

The measure of a microprocessor

Microprocessors are gauged by how fast they go. The speed could be miles per hour (mph), but unfortunately microprocessors have no wheels and cannot travel distances in any measurable amount of time. Therefore, the speed measured is how fast the microprocessor thinks.

Thinking speed is measured in megahertz (MHz). The higher the megahertz number, the faster the microprocessor. An old Pentium Pro running at 133MHz is much slower than a Pentium III running at 1000MHz.

A microprocessor's power is also measured in how many bits it can chew up at once. All Pentium microprocessors can work with 32 bits of information at a time, which makes them very fast. (Older PC microprocessors worked with 16 or 8 bits at once.) A good analogy with bits in a microprocessor is cylinders in a car engine: The more cylinders there are, the more powerful the engine is. A future microprocessor may be able to handle 128 bits. That would be very, very powerful.

Supposedly the soon-to-come Itanium microprocessor will fiddle with information in 64-bit chunks. That will speed things up nicely.

"OK, wise guy, so which microprocessor lives in my PC?"

Who knows which microprocessor lurks in the heart of your PC? Better get a big wrench. Better still, right-click on the My Computer icon on the desktop. This action brings up a shortcut menu for your computer. Choose the last item, Properties, to display the System Properties dialog box.

Figure 7-1 shows the System Properties dialog box from Windows XP, which is the most descriptive of all Windows versions. In the figure, you see that the system sports a Pentium III processor running at 999MHz.

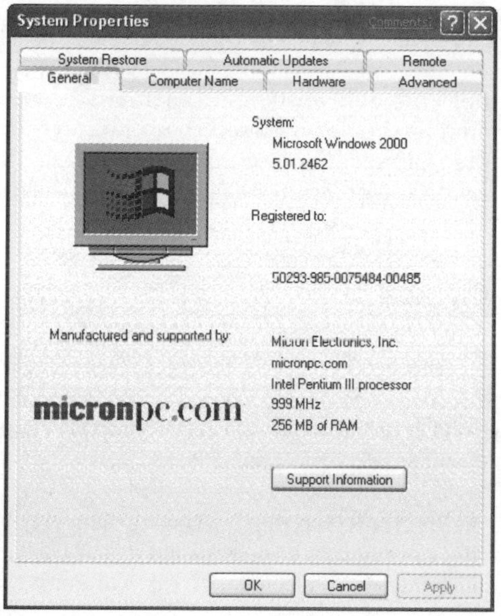

Figure 7-1:
The System
Properties
dialog box.

Note that other versions of Windows may display less information than what's shown in Figure 7-1. Don't be shocked if you see something vague, such as *x86 Family 6 Model 8 Stepping 3*. If you really, *really* need to know which microprocessor lives in your PC, you can refer to your computer's sales invoice.

- The System Properties dialog box also tells you how much memory (RAM) lives inside your computer. In Figure 7-1, the computer has 256MB of memory.

- If you have a 486 system, then you'll see 486 or maybe 80486 displayed.

- Figure 7-1 also boasts that Micron Electronics, Inc., manufactured the computer. I am not an employee of Micron; I just bought my computer from the company. (It's an Idaho thing.) Your computer manufacturer may have its name displayed there as well. Ain't no way to get rid of it, either.

Celeron versus Pentium

Q: Is the Celeron processor a joke?

A: No, but it's not the same as a Pentium. Basically a computer with a Celeron will cost less than a Pentium. The Pentium is faster, but both processors run the same programs. You'll just save money buying a PC with a Celeron. I have a few computers with Celeron microprocessors here in my office and they all run just fine.

Connectors for Things Various and Sundry

Every gizmo in the computer connects to the motherboard. Some of the connectors are external, such as the ports covered in Chapter 9. You plug things into those connectors yourself. Other connectors are internal, which connect various goodies inside the computer case to the motherboard.

I need more power!

Inside your PC's case, next to the motherboard, is the *power supply*. The power supply does several things: It brings in power from the wall socket, it converts the AC current into DC current, it supplies power to the motherboard and disk drives, and it contains the computer's on/off switch.

The power supply connects directly to the motherboard, which is how the console gets its power. You rarely unplug this connection. Only if the power supply blows up (I should really say *fail* instead of *blow up*) do you need to replace it.

Don't panic! Power supplies are designed to fail. Sometimes they really do blow up, but they don't explode. They merely die and emit a puff of smoke. The power supply is designed to protect the delicate electronics inside your PC. It would rather die than fry your system. And power supplies are easy to replace, so popping them in is really no big deal (and rarely do they pop).

- ✔ The power supply makes most of the noise when your PC runs. It contains a fan that regulates the temperature inside the console, keeping everything nice and cool. (Electronic components get hot when electricity races through them — just like you would! This heat has the ugly consequence of making them misbehave, which is why cooling is needed.)

- ✔ Power supplies are rated in watts. The more stuff your computer has — the more disk drives, memory, expansion cards, and so on — the greater the number of watts the power supply should provide. The typical PC has a power supply rated at 150 or 200 watts. More powerful systems may require a power supply of 220 or 250 watts.

- ✔ One way to keep your power supply — and your computer — from potentially going poof (even in a lightning strike) is to invest in a surge protector or UPS. See Chapter 2 for details.

Disk drive connectors

Your PC's motherboard also has connectors for the floppy drives (remember — there can be two) and two hard drives, or a hard drive and a CD-ROM drive. Or, in some situations, a floppy drive, hard drive, CD-ROM and DVD drive. My goodness!

Of course, that's all internal. Using USB, Firewire, or even your computer's printer port, you can add more disk drives to the system. You'll read more about that in Chapters 8 and 9.

The disk drive connector is officially known as an *IDE, ATA,* or *ATAPI* connector. That's the nerdy name of the interface through which the computer communicates with its disk drives.

Sharp, pointy things and other electronic salad

Finally, lots of other miscellaneous things may be lurking on your PC's motherboard. Most of them are just chips or diodes or resistors or whatever. Don't touch.

Some sharp pointy things that you may have to touch are called *jumpers.* A jumper is a connector that works like a switch. You put a small black box over two pointy wires to connect them, or turn on the switch. Remove the black box to un-jump the switch.

Figure 7-2 illustrates the three ways you can fix a jumper. The little black jumper box is usually on or off (to the side).

You may have to set or remove jumpers when you upgrade memory or (heaven forbid!) upgrade your PC's microprocessor. If so, your computer's manual tells you what to do. Or — better still — have the dealer do it all for you!

- ✓ Supposedly, Plug and Play technology was designed to eliminate the use of jumpers in a PC. Supposedly.

- ✓ Never move a jumper — or even open your PC — with the power on.

- ✓ Jumpers are all labeled, usually with a stencil on the motherboard. For example, jumper W2 has a W2 next to it on the motherboard.

Expansion Slots

To add more goodies and expand your PC's capabilities, the motherboard sports special long, thin slots. These are *expansion slots,* into which you can plug special *expansion cards.* The idea is that you can expand your system by adding options not included with the basic PC.

Your PC can have anywhere from zero to a dozen expansion slots. Some home systems have none — which keeps the price low — and most of the options are built-in with the home system. But most typical PCs have three to eight, depending on the size of the console.

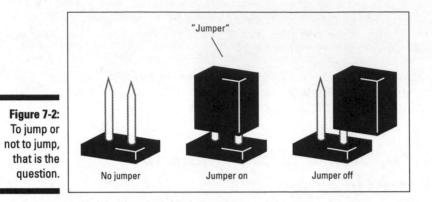

Figure 7-2:
To jump or
not to jump,
that is the
question.

The three types of expansion slots are ISA, PCI, and AGP.

ISA. The oldest type of slot is the ISA, which stands for (get this) Industry Standard Architecture. That's because it never really had a name until another, better type of expansion slot came along. ISA slots hang around because a lot of older hardware still comes on that type of expansion card.

PCI. The PCI slot is the most common form of internal expansion for a PC (for a Macintosh, too, but that's not the subject here). Chances are good that if you buy an expansion card, it will be a PCI card. And if given the option, choose a PCI expansion card over an ISA model.

AGP. The final expansion slot is the AGP, Accelerated Graphics Port. It's a special type of slot that takes only video expansion cards, usually the nice spendy ones that do all sorts of amazing graphics. Not every PC has this type of slot.

Expansion slots and the cards that plug into them make it tinker-toy simple to add new features and power to your PC. And although anyone can plug in a card and expand a computer system, this job is best left to those experts who enjoy such things.

- ✔ Small footprint PCs have the fewest expansion slots. Tower computer models have the most.

- ✔ For more information on video expansion cards, see Chapter 11.

- ✔ The salespeople never tell you this one: Most expansion cards come squirming with cables. This mess of cables makes the seemingly sleek motherboard look more like an electronic pasta dish. Some cables are threaded inside the PC; others are left hanging limply out the back. The cables are what make the internal upgrading and installation process so difficult.

✔ After you add a new expansion card, you need to tell Windows about it. On a good day (sunshine, hot coffee, birds chirping, like that), Windows recognizes and automatically configures the new hardware when you restart your PC. Otherwise, you need to open the Control Panel and use the Add New Hardware icon. The details of this procedure are far too boring to list here.

Tick Tock Goes the Clock

All computers come with an internal clock. Tick-tock. The clock is battery operated, which enables it to keep track of the time, day or night, whether or not the PC is plugged in.

To check the current time, gander at the far-right side of the Windows taskbar. Living in the system tray is the current time. Point the mouse at the time, as shown in Figure 7-3, and the current day and date shows up.

✔ If you don't see the time, click the Start button to pop up its menu and choose Settings⇨Taskbar & Start Menu. In the Taskbar Options panel in the Taskbar Properties dialog box, look for the Show Clock check box on the bottom. Click in that check box to select that option. Click the OK button, and Windows shows you the time on the taskbar.

✔ The format for the date and time varies depending on how your computer is set up. Windows displays a date and time format based on your country or region. This book assumes the typical (and I agree, backward) U.S. method of listing the date.

✔ Who cares if the computer knows what time of day it is? Well, because your files are time- and date-stamped, you can figure things out, such as which is a later version of two similar files or two files with the same name on different disks.

"The clock is all screwy!"

Computers make lousy clocks. That's why you don't see them keeping lap time during the Olympics. Why do computers seem to lose track of the time a few minutes every day? Who knows!

Figure 7-3:
The (more-or-less) current date and time.

Fear not if you live in a part of the world suffering through Daylight Saving Time, or Summer Time; Windows knows this and automatically jumps the clock forward or backward. All this without knowing the little ditty, "Spring forward, fall back." Or is it the other way around? Whatever, the computer knows.

Generally speaking, the clock runs slow or fast because of all the various things going on inside the computer. The more that goes on, the more the clock will be wrong. Especially if you put your computer to sleep or "hibernate," the clock tends to get really nuts. (See Chapter 2 for more hibernation information.)

What do you do if the clock is wrong? Why, set it of course. Keep reading!

Setting the clock

To set or change the date and time on your PC, double-click the time in the taskbar: Point the mouse at the time on the right end of the taskbar and double-click. Click-click. This action displays the Date/Time Properties dialog box, as shown in Figure 7-4.

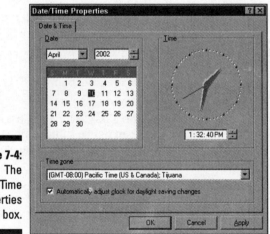

Figure 7-4:
The
Date/Time
Properties
dialog box.

Manipulate the controls in the Date/Time Properties dialog box to change or set the date or time.

To set the time, type in the new time. For example, type **10:00** if it's 9:58 or so. Then when the time lady (or whoever) says it's 10:00, click the Apply button in the Date/Time Properties dialog box. That action sets the time instantly. Click OK when you're done.

Boring details about your PC's battery

All computers have an internal battery, which is part of the motherboard. The battery serves two purposes.

First, the battery is there to keep track of the time. If you notice that the computer's clock is totally off — and I mean by years and years — then it could be that your computer's internal battery needs replacing.

Second, the battery provides power to a special thing called the *CMOS*. That's a memory location that stores basic information about the computer (disk drives, setup options, how the printer port works, and so on), information that

the computer needs to remember even when it's unplugged. So the battery powers the CMOS memory, which keeps track of those things.

Computer batteries are robust little suckers. They typically last upwards of five years or so. When they die, you'll know because the computer's date will be wrong, or it may complain that it can't see your PC's hard drives (which seems scary, but is nothing to worry about). When that happens, simply have the battery replaced. Or beg for a new computer. Yeah, that's what I'd do!

If you want to be ultra precise about setting your PC's clock, you can download one of the many "Atomic clock" programs from the Internet. These programs fetch the official and exact time from one of the atomic clocks run by the U.S. government.

You can visit The Official U.S. Time on the Internet at: `http://nist.time.gov/`

To find Atomic clock synchronizing utilities, visit `www.filemine.com/` and search for the text "Atomic clock." The Web page then lists a slew of utilities you can choose from. (Also see Chapter 25 on downloading stuff from the Internet.)

The BIOS

The BIOS is a special chip on the motherboard that contains your PC's personality. Encoded on that chip are the simple instructions for the computer to communicate with its various pieces and parts.

For example, the BIOS contains software to talk to the keyboard, monitor, and expansion slots; display the manufacturer's logo; and do other simple activities. It's not as complex as the operating system, but it's necessary in order to get the PC going in the morning.

- ✔ BIOS is pronounced *Bye-Oss*.
- ✔ BIOS stands for Basic Input/Output System.
- ✔ BIOS is also known as ROM. Refer to Chapter 10 for information on ROM.
- ✔ In addition to the main BIOS, your computer may have other BIOSes. For example, the video BIOS controls your system's graphics display, the hard drive BIOS controls the hard disk, and so on. Your network adapter may have its own BIOS. Normally, when you see the term *BIOS* by itself, it refers to the PC's main BIOS.

Where is my PC's Setup program?

Q: I was told to access the Setup program to fix something weird with my printer port. The problem is that when I run Setup, it asks me whether or not I want to install Windows. Am I doing the right thing?

A: Not really. There is a Setup program that installs Windows, but that's not the one your instructions are referring to. No, you need to access the PC's Setup program, which is part of the BIOS.

When the computer first starts you'll see some text messages. One of them says something like "Press <F1> to enter Setup," though it may be the F2 key, Delete key or some other key on the keyboard. If you press that key, you run the PC's Setup program, which configures certain basic parts of the computer, such as how the printer port works.

The Setup program is an important part of all computers, but something you rarely (if ever) need to run. Just remember that it's accessed when the computer first starts. Also you must confirm that you want the changes saved when you quit the program. It seems scary, but it's not. (Technically, you're updating the computer's *CMOS* or battery-backed-up RAM. It's nerdy.)

Chapter 8

Ports, Jacks, and Holes

• •

• •

*R*ight around back, on your PC console's rump, is a host of holes and plug-in places. They're ugly. That's probably why that side of your PC faces the wall — or at least faces away from you. Yet, like expansion slots inside the console (see Chapter 7), these holes help you expand your PC system, as well as connect various important items to the main console unit.

This chapter is about the holes in your PC's backside. Officially they're known as *jacks,* probably because some guy named Jack discovered the first hole on the back of an ancient Egyptian computer. Another term, equally official, is *port.* It means the same thing as jack, which is just another term for hole. As with most things in a computer, keeping the air clear with a single, well-defined and descriptive term is not the top priority.

Holes for Everything

A hole is really a *jack* or connector on the back of your PC. Into the jack you can plug any one of a variety of external devices with which your computer can communicate.

Some jacks are dedicated to certain devices. Other jacks, known as *ports,* can connect to a variety of different and weird things.

Figure 8-1 illustrates a panel typically found on the back of most PCs. That's where you find these common jacks clustered. Here's the list:

1. Keyboard connector
2. Mouse connector
3. USB connector (usually two of them)
4. Serial port connector (usually two of them)
5. Printer (parallel) port connector
6. Joystick port connector
7. Audio connectors (three of them)

The following sections describe the different devices that can plug into these various ports.

✔ More ports can be added to any PC through an expansion card. For example, you can add a USB port to your computer with a $20 expansion card. (I did.)

✔ Your PC may or may not have a second serial port or a USB port. These are things you should have known about *before* you bought your PC, which is why I'll push another one of my books here, *Buying a Computer For Dummies,* also available from Hungry Minds, Inc.

✔ The USB (Universal Serial Bus) port — the latest addition to the PC's host of ports — has the power and versatility to eventually replace just about every other port on the PC.

✔ Your PC may also sport a video port for the monitor. You may find it with the other ports or on an expansion card. Chapter 11 covers all things video.

✔ Other popular ports include the network port, FireWire, and SCSI ports, though these are often found on expansion cards.

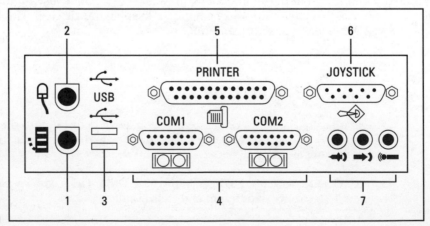

Figure 8-1:
Jacks on
the back of
the console.

In Plugs the Keyboard and the Mouse

The keyboard and mouse connectors look the same on most PCs. That's because they are! Even so, one is for the keyboard and another is for the mouse. On some computers it doesn't matter which device plugs into which ports. On other computers, the keyboard won't work unless it's plugged into the proper hole.

✔ If you select a USB mouse, then you can plug it into the USB port and leave the mouse port open. Or you can buy one of those special USB-to-mouse port adapters, which often come with USB mice.

✔ USB keyboards plug into the USB port, so you can leave the keyboard port open. Or you can buy a USB-to-keyboard adapter.

✔ Some computer mice plug into the serial port instead of the special mouse port. If so, plug the mouse into serial port 1. Chapter 12 discusses why using this port is better than using serial port 2.

USB Is Da Bomb

The most versatile jack on the back of your PC is the USB port. Right away you need to know this is pronounced *yoo-es-bee*, not *uss-ub*. USB stands for Universal Serial Bus, from which I could extract several puns, but shall choose not to.

Unlike most other ports, USB was designed to host a number of different and interesting devices, making it replace just about every other connector on the PC's rump. It's the most versatile connector on your computer.

Before you go nuts over USB, first ensure that your PC has one or more USB ports. You must look behind your PC and check for the breath mint-sized USB connector, which usually appears next to the USB symbol (shown in the margin). If you're lucky, you also see the letters USB. (Refer to Figure 8-1.)

If the computer sports a USB port, the whole world of USB devices is open to you. The devices (peripherals) that plug into the USB port are legion: monitors, speakers, joysticks, scanners, digital cameras, floppy drives and other storage devices, modems, anti-gravity face-lift straps, and the list goes on. More and more USB devices are appearing every day.

✔ Don't worry if your PC lacks a USB port. You can always add one via an expansion card.

✔ If your computer has USB ports, then be sure to buy USB peripherals. This is much better than using the PC's serial or printer ports to connect external devices.

✔ Some USB peripherals come with their own cables. That's great. If not, you can buy cables cheaply on the Internet or at any office supply store.

✔ USB cables have two ends. There is the thin "A" end, which plugs into the back of the computer. Then there is the five-sided "B" end, which usually plugs into a USB device. Make sure you get a USB cable with A and B ends, if that's what you need.

✔ There are also USB extension cables. For example, the Wambooli Driveway Cam is a USB video camera that sits in a window in my office. It's connected to the computer via a 12-foot USB extension cable. You can visit the Driveway Cam at `http://www.wambooli.com/Live/`.

Connecting a USB device

One reason the USB port is poised to take over the world is that it's smart. Unlike other connectors on a PC, when you plug a USB device into a USB port, Windows instantly recognizes it and configures the device for you. You don't even need to turn off or reset your computer. Amazing.

Of course, there's more to adding a USB device. You still need to install software to control the device. Note that sometimes you need to do this before you plug in the USB device and sometimes you need to do it after. For example, my USB Zip drive needed to have its software installed before I plugged in the drive. After that was done, the computer instantly recognized the drive and I could use it right away. On the other hand, my USB scanner had to be plugged in *before* I installed the software or the software wouldn't install. Weird, but typical.

✔ You can plug in USB devices as you need them. So if you have a scanner and joystick hooked up, unplug one and plug in your PC's camera instead. No penalty or glitch occurs when you make this change.

✔ Some USB devices don't even need a power cord; the USB device uses the power from the console. For example, my USB scanner just plugs into the computer — that's all! Other USB devices, such as monitors, do require a separate power cable.

✔ The USB is not a total solution. The port's speed is too slow to make it possible for fast hard disk drives to be connected. This problem may be solved in the future, however.

Expanding the USB universe

Most PCs have two USB connectors. Into them you can plug two USB devices. If you have more USB devices, you can unplug and replug devices as you see necessary. But isn't that kind of a pain? Of course it is! You have a computer. It's supposed to make life easier.

The best solution for expanding your USB universe is to buy a USB *hub*. That's a device that plugs into your PC's USB port and gives you more USB ports, as illustrated in Figure 8-2.

The USB hub plugs into your computer using an A-B USB cable. The A end plugs into the computer and the B end into the hub. If it's a powered hub, then it will also plug into an electrical outlet. Finally, the hub contains extra USB ports into which you can plug more USB devices — or even more hubs!

✔ Using hubs, you can expand your PC's USB universe out to the maximum 127 USB devices. Hopefully you'll run out of desk space before that.

✔ The maximum number of USB devices is 127, and USB cables can be no more than 3 meters in length. If this were a math question, then you could calculate that your computer can theoretically control a USB device sitting some 381 meters away! (That's over 1,200 feet for you Americans.)

✔ Some USB hubs are built into USB devices. A few USB monitors, for example, have USB hubs that add two or four more USB ports. Some USB keyboards have an extra port on them for connecting a USB mouse.

✔ The first hub (actually your PC) is the *root* hub. Beyond that you can connect only a certain number of hubs to the computer, depending on your PC's hardware. This maximum number will, most likely, never be known because the cost of the USB devices required to reach that limit would bankrupt most small countries.

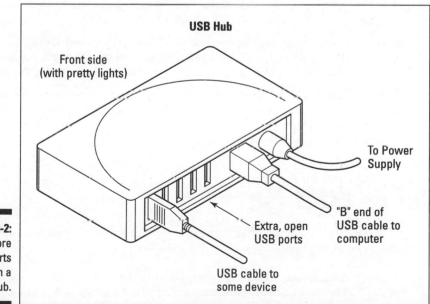

USB Hub

Front side (with pretty lights)

To Power Supply

"B" end of USB cable to computer

Extra, open USB ports

USB cable to some device

Figure 8-2: Add more USB ports with a USB hub.

Even Better Than USB, It's FireWire

Bigger, faster, wiser and definitely better named than the USB port is the *FireWire port*. FireWire is actually an Apple computer trademark for what's also known as the IEEE 1394 High Performance Serial Bus standard. Some folks just say, "IEEE 1394." Others have shortened it to "IEEE" or "Eye triple E." But you still can't beat FireWire.

FireWire is basically a super-dooper version of the USB port. It's faster than USB, so FireWire is preferred for high-speed operations, such as digital video, high-resolution scanning, and external storage devices. While USB can also do those jobs, a FireWire device runs much faster.

On the downside, FireWire isn't that popular of a standard at this point. Only Apple's computers come with FireWire ports standard; on a PC you need to buy a FireWire expansion card. This may change and soon all PCs will come with both FireWire and USB ports. So until then, it's more of a get-to-know-this thing than something you'll probably mess with on your PC.

✔ FireWire ports are marked by the FireWire symbol, as shown in the margin.

✔ Like USB devices, you can plug in a FireWire device without having to turn the computer off and on.

✔ FireWire cables are not the same as USB cables.

✔ You can also buy FireWire hubs.

✔ The limit on FireWire devices is much less than USB. Presently there can be only 64 devices on a FireWire port. Still, that's a heck of a lot.

✔ I have a FireWire hard drive and CD-R/RW drive. They were a cinch to install — much easier than opening up the computer's case. And the speed on the drives is much faster than similar USB drives I've used.

✔ Personally, I find the name "FireWire" frightening. I prefer fires in fireplaces or inside a ring of rocks on a cool summer night. My wires can hold electricity, thank you. And hopefully they never get hot enough to burn. But that's not what FireWire is all about.

Serial or COM Ports

Cereal ports are named after Ceres, the Roman goddess of agriculture. Wait. Wrong type of cereal.

Serial ports are, next to the USB port, the most versatile type of connector on your PC. The serial port can have a variety of interesting items plugged into it, which is why it's generically called a serial port instead of a this-or-that port.

You can often plug the following items into a serial port: a modem, a serial printer, a mouse, some types of scanners, digital cameras, the Palm Pilot Hot Sync cradle, or just about anything that requires two-way communications.

The most common device plugged into the serial port is an external modem. For this reason, serial ports are also called COM ports, for communication.

Most computers come with two serial ports, dubbed COM1 and COM2.

- ✔ A serial port can also be called a modem port.
- ✔ Serial ports are also called RS-232 ports.
- ✔ Unlike USB ports, you can plug only one item into a serial port at a time. That's okay because most of the serial port's devices are those that are consistently connected to the PC: modem, scanner, mouse, and so on.
- ✔ You can plug a computer mouse into a serial port. In that case, the mouse is called a serial mouse. Refer to your local pet store for more information on mice or turn to Chapter 12.

The Ever-Versatile Printer Port

Mysteriously enough, the printer port is where you plug in your printer. The printer cable has one connector that plugs into the printer and a second that plugs into the computer. Both connectors are different, so plugging a printer cable in backward is impossible.

You can also use the printer port as a high-speed link to certain external devices. Its speed and design make it possible to connect external disk drives — such as CD-ROMs, CD-Rs, DVDs, Zip drives, and Jaz drives — and external tape drives to your PC using the printer port.

When used to connect an external device, the printer port cable *passes through* the device to be used with the printer. In Figure 8-3, the printer cable is connected to the PC and the external device, and then a second printer cable connects the external device to the printer.

- ✔ Using the printer port is one of the least expensive ways to add an external device to your PC.
- ✔ Plugging an external device into the printer port does not interfere with printing. It seems like it should, but it doesn't.
- ✔ Actually, the printer may not print if the device between the printer and the computer is turned off. In many cases, the device must be turned on, or power must be supplied to the device, for the printer to work.

✔ You can put only one device between the printer and your PC. You cannot, say, add a second external CD-ROM on a printer port that already has an external device between the PC and printer.

✔ It's possible to install a second printer port on your PC if you need one. This is usually done via an expansion card. Even so, it's still possible to run two printers from a single computer by using a device called an A-B switch. You hook one printer up to A, the other to B, and then the A-B switch hooks up to the computer. Switching printers is done by flipping the switch on the A-B box.

✔ For the printer port to work with an external device, you must configure your PC so that the printer port operates in *bidirectional* mode. Have your guru or dealer configure the PC's setup program so that the port is configured as bidirectional (either EPP or ECP, depending on the device's requirements).

✔ For more information on printers, refer to Chapter 15.

✔ Printer ports are also called *parallel ports,* or to old-time nerds, they're known as *Centronics* ports. IBM refers to the printer port as the LPT1 port. People who refer to ports in this manner should be slapped.

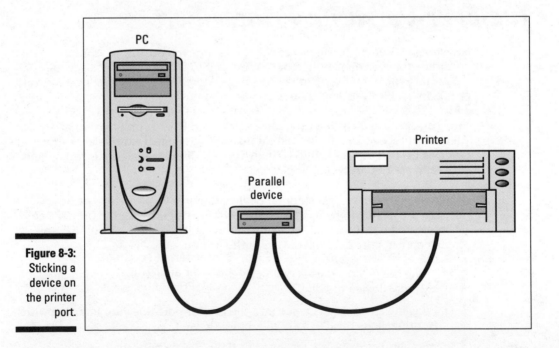

Figure 8-3: Sticking a device on the printer port.

The Joy of Joystick Jacks

Believe it or not, one of the first expansion options for the original IBM PC was a joystick port. IBM didn't call it that. No, IBM called it the A-to-D port, for Analog-to-Digital. That sounds very scientific, doesn't it? But the truth is, the hole was designed for plugging in a joystick.

In addition to a joystick, you can also plug a MIDI musical instrument into the joystick (A-to-D) port. You plug a special gadget into the joystick port and then plug the 5-pin MIDI cable into the same special gadget. Most MIDI keyboard starter kits come with this special gadget (which has a real name, but I'm too lazy to look it up).

Also, if you're a closet Mr. Science type, then you can use the joystick port for "scientific applications." For example, I have an anemometer (one of those twirly wind things) that mounts on the roof of my office and connects to the PC via the joystick port. That way I can tell if the wind is blowing even without looking at the trees outside.

Audio Connectors

In order to hear all the wonderful sounds your PC can make, you need to take advantage of the audio jacks. Of course only one of them is for hearing (the speakers or line-out jack). The other two are for a microphone and line-in or amplified input jack. Each of these jacks is marked with its own, special icon.

The Line Out or Speaker jack is where you connect the PC's speakers. Note that some speakers are integrated into the PC's monitor. This is also where you plug in a set of headphones, so sometimes this jack has a headphone icon on it instead of the weird icon shown in the margin.

The Microphone jack is where you plug in a microphone, which allows you to record your own voice or the lovely ambient noises of your computer room.

The Line In jack is for connecting some other external sound-producing device to your PC. For example, using the proper audio cables available at Radio Shack, you can hook up your VCR to the PC and hear a movie through your PC's speakers. Invite the neighbors!

Don't panic if your PC seems to have two sets of these audio jacks. Typically, there will be one set on the back panel (refer to Figure 8-1) and another set on an expansion card. That's the DVD-ROM expansion card and you can bet dollars for donuts that the audio connectors on that expansion card are the ones you want to use, and not the silly jacks on the back panel.

Optional drivel on the SCSI port

Computer scientists knew the limitations of the old Serial and Printer ports a long, long time ago. So they devised a solution and gave it a clever nickname. The solution was the Small Computer Serial Interface, which they cleverly nicknamed "scuzzy."

SCSI ports are maddeningly fast. Most high-end PCs and expensive systems called *servers* use SCSI hard drives and peripherals. Yup, they're fast and expensive and a pain in the rear to configure. This is why other computer scientists developed the USB and FireWire ports, which are fast and not expensive and very easy to configure.

Still, SCSI exists as a PC expansion option. Hopefully it will fade into the past as USB and FireWire become the new, best ways to add more and more junk to your computer system.

Chapter 9

All About Disks and Drives

• •

In This Chapter

▶ Understanding disk drives

▶ Saving space on a hard drive

▶ Using a CD-ROM drive

▶ Burning a CD-R

▶ Creating a music or audio CD-R

▶ Working with a CD-RW disc

▶ Getting to know DVD drives

▶ Working with a floppy disk

▶ Using other types of removable disks, Zip, and SuperDisks

• •

Madly spinning in your PC's bosom is a wonderful device called a disk drive. Actually, your PC probably has several of them: hard drive, CD-ROM, and floppy. These three sisters make up your PC's long-term storage bins. No PC is complete without at least one of each. And then there are variations on a theme: CD-Rs, DVDs, SuperDisk drives, and so on. All that's missing are those refrigerator-sized things with reel-to-reel tapes on them, like in the movies.

Disk drives are important to your PC because that's where the computer's operating system, your software, and all the lovely things you create reside. This chapter is about disks and drives and all the madness that comes with them. I provide hardware information here; for using your disk drives with Windows, refer to Chapter 4.

Different Types of Disk Drives for Different Needs

In the beginning was the floppy disk. And it was good.

Actually, when the microcomputer first dawned in the late 1970s, the main storage medium was a cassette recorder with a special cassette tape. Then came the floppy drive, which was faster and more reliable than cassette tape.

Eventually the hard drive (always on the scene) came down in price until it was a standard fixture on all PCs. Then came the CD-ROM drive, first a novelty for a multimedia computer and now standard fare on all PCs.

Beyond the CD-ROM lies the DVD-ROM drive plus many other interesting and odd flavors of disk drives. The following list summarizes the most common types and how they're used.

- **Floppy drives.** A floppy drive eats floppy disks, which typically store 1.44MB of information. That's enough storage to make backup copies of your documents for transportation between two computers, but that's about it. About ten years ago, all PC software came on floppy disks. Today some software still comes on floppies, but in most cases, a CD-ROM disc is used instead.

- **Hard drives.** The PC's main long-term storage device is the hard drive. The hard drive's disk stores gigabytes of information, more than enough for Windows, your software, and all the data you can create. Unlike with floppy disks, you cannot remove a hard disk.

- **CD-ROM drives.** A CD-ROM drive eats CD-ROM discs, which look just like music CDs. Computer CDs can store hundreds of megabytes of information, and most new computer software comes on a CD. Unlike hard drives and floppy disks, you cannot write information to a CD-ROM disc. The *RO* in CD-ROM means read-only.

- **DVD-ROM drives.** Now standard on many computer systems, the DVD-ROM drive eats DVD-ROM discs, which look just like regular CD-ROM discs but store lots more information. DVD-ROM discs can store as much information as 20 CDs, or about enough space to store a full-length movie or a copy of every promise ever made by all American politicians. (Well, maybe not.)

Beyond these basic types of disk drives, you may find other drives, common or not, spinning and humming inside your PC. Here's the lot:

- **CD-R/RW drives.** These drives work just like regular CD-ROM drives, though you can also use them to record or create your own CDs. Providing that you buy special CD-R or CD-RW discs, you can use a CD-R/RW drive to create a data CD, music CD, back up your hard drive, and do any number of wonderful things.

- **Zip drives.** A special type of disk drive on many computers sold today is the Zip drive. Zip drives eat Zip disks, which work much like floppy disks, although they can store anywhere from 100MB to 250MB of information, depending on the drive. That makes them a better — and cheaper — removable storage option than the floppy disk.

✔ **Jaz drives.** A bigger brother to the Zip drive is the Jaz drive, which can store 1GB or 2GB on a single disk, depending on the drive. These massive disks are ideal for exchanging large files between PCs or just for use as an extra storage device or for backup.

✔ **LS-120 SuperDisk drives.** These floppy disk replacements both read and write to standard floppy disks but also accept large-capacity 120MB *super* disks. The disks come standard on some computers but can be added to others. They may eventually replace the standard floppy drive.

✔ **Specialty drives.** Many, many different types of disk drives are available, depending on your long-term storage needs. In addition to the more popular types just mentioned, you can also find MO or magneto-optical disks, WORM drives, removable hard drives, floptical disks, and other strange and wondrous formats. It's enough to drive you batty.

Here are some general disk drive thoughts for you to ruminate:

✔ The drive is the device that reads the disk.

✔ The disk is the thing that contains the data — the media inside the drive.

✔ The information is stored on the disk, similar to the way a movie is stored on a videocassette.

✔ All disks are *hardware*. The information stored on them is software, just as your videocassette of *The Ten Commandments* isn't the movie itself; the movie is recorded on the cassette. (The movie is like software, and the videocassette is hardware.)

✔ The terms *hard disk* and *hard drive* are often used interchangeably, although incorrectly so.

✔ IBM, always proving that it's different, calls the hard drive a *fixed disk*. No, it does not mean that the disk was once broken. (It's fixed, as in immovable.)

✔ Most CD-R/RW drives are hybrids; they're both a CD-R drive and a CD-RW drive. The CD-R part records to a CD-R disc once. Then after the disc is "burned," it cannot be erased. The CD-RW disc works the same, though it can be erased and used over and over. You can read more on this later in this chapter.

✔ Zip drives are not related to the ZIP file format (known as a *compressed folder* in Windows). The ZIP file format is used to compress files downloaded from the Internet or from other users. A Zip drive is a device that reads and writes to removable Zip disks.

Driving a Hard Disk

Hard drives are the main storage place for most PCs. They are internal units, mounted inside the PC's console case. On some PCs, you can see the front of the hard drive on the case. On other PCs, all you see is a tiny light that blinks every time the hard drive is accessed.

The hard drive itself is a hermetically sealed unit. No air can get in or out. Therefore, the mechanism that reads and writes information can be very precise, and lots of information can be written to and read from the disk reliably. (This is why hard drives are nonremovable.)

Inside the hard drive are the hard disks themselves. Most hard drives have two or more disks, or *platters*, each of which is stacked on a spindle. A device called a *read-write head* is mounted on an actuator arm that allows it to access both sides of all the disks in the hard drive at once. Figure 9-1 attempts to illustrate this concept.

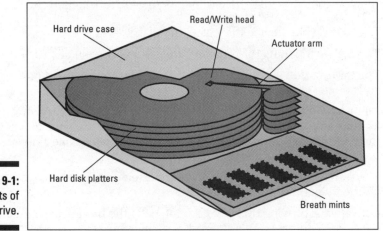

Figure 9-1:
The guts of
a hard drive.

Hard drive case

Read/Write head

Actuator arm

Hard disk platters

Breath mints

✔ Some types of removable hard drives exist, though the CD-R/RW drive is quickly making the need for such drives obsolete. Read more about CD-R/RW later in this chapter.

✔ You may have only one hard drive in your PC, but Windows may show it to you as drives C and D or even C, D, and E. That usually means that the disk has been *partitioned* into smaller, more manageable chunks. Partitioning is something you need not worry yourself with.

The Shiny Media (CD-ROMs and DVDs)

Once a novelty, CD-ROM drives come standard on nearly all computers sold. Fast on its heels, however, is the DVD drive, which eventually will replace the CD-ROM drive as the computer's second popular form of storage (after the hard drive). The following sections discuss these drives and what to do with them.

Saving hard disk space

The biggest problem with hard drives is that they eventually run out of room. This is still a problem even with today's massive hard drives; after you save just a few image or music files, your 20GB hard drive is swimming in a very shallow pond.

Fortunately, when disk space gets tight, Windows pops up a "You are low on disk space" warning. This is automatic. Until that happens, you really don't need to worry about a rapidly filling hard drive. In fact, I wouldn't become concerned about disk space until the disk pie (see Figure 4-2) is around 80 percent full.

If you're really concerned, then here are my thoughts for creating more disk space:

✔ Run the Disk Cleanup utility at least once a month. From the Start menu, choose Programs➪Accessories➪System Tools➪ Disk Cleanup. This will clean up a lot of unnecessary programs, delete temporary files, clean out Internet junk, and empty the Recycle Bin. It's amazing.

✔ Open the Control Panel's Internet Options icon. In the General tab of the Internet Properties dialog box, click the Settings button. Adjust the "Amount of disk space to use" item down to the lowest possible value. Click the OK button and close the

various dialog boxes and the Control Panel. This trick saves a ton of space that Internet Explorer otherwise gobbles up.

✔ Consider archiving some graphics images, older document files, projects, and sound files to Zip disks or CD-Rs. For example, I archive each book I write after I finish writing it. They all sit on separate CD-R discs in my fire safe. I also have an archive on CD-R of all my favorite fonts. Graphics images I save to Zip disks. This saves a ton of hard drive space.

If space gets really crunchy and you've tried everything, then you have only one real choice: Buy your PC a second, larger hard drive. You can buy an internal drive, which can fit into most PCs. Or if room is tight, get an external hard drive, a USB or FireWire drive. This is a great way to expand your computer's storage system without having to sacrifice any files from the hard drive.

Finally a warning: Please do not use DriveSpace or any other "disk-doubling" program. These programs are really software alchemy that makes a crowded disk situation worse, in my opinion. Installing a second hard drive is much better than putting up with the mental anguish of a disk-doubling program.

Just your stupid old CD-ROM

The standard computer CD-ROM drive is designed to read CDs, both music and data CDs. The data CDs store tons of information and are used mostly for installing new programs, but also come in handy for storing reference material, fonts, graphics, or other information. Oh, I don't need to sell you on them.

✔ The typical data CD disc can hold up to 640MB of information. A typical music CD can store up to 74 minutes of music.

✔ The speed of a CD-ROM drive is measured in X. The number before X indicates how much faster that drive is than the original PC CD-ROM drive (which plays as fast as a musical CD player). So a 32X drive reads information from the disc 32 times faster than the original PC CD-ROM drive.

✔ CD-ROM drives can play music and data CDs, as well as CD-R discs that you may create yourself.

✔ To play a musical CD, just stick it into your CD-ROM drive. The Windows Media Player (or similar) music-playing program starts playing your CD almost immediately.

Making a data CD-R

Yes, you can burn your own CDs, which doesn't involve matches or the microwave oven. Nope, all you need is a CD-R disc (one specifically designed for holding computer data), and a CD-R drive. Toss in some software, which usually comes with the drive, and you're ready to burn, baby, burn.

To create a CD-R disc using Adaptec Direct CD (which comes free with most CD-R drives), follow these vague steps. (The process is similar for any CD-R burning software, so consider these general steps.)

1. **Put a blank CD-R disc into the drive.**

2. **Run the CD-R software.**

   If you're lucky, the software may run automatically when you insert a blank CD-R disc. Otherwise, you have to choose the CD-R software from the Start menu.

   On my computer, the Easy CD Creator program was started automatically, as shown in Figure 9-2.

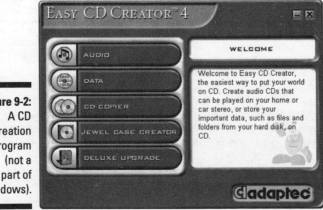

Figure 9-2:
A CD creation program (not a part of Windows).

3. **Choose the option to create a data CD.**

   To create a musical or audio CD, refer to the instructions in the section "Burning a musical CD."

4. **Create or mount the CD.**

   This is an interesting step. Some programs give you the option to either create the CD right there or use the CD just as you would any other drive in your system. This all depends on your software.

   For example, if you choose to create the CD, the program typically displays a window where you can select a whole gaggle of files (over 600 megabytes worth) to be copied to the CD. You select the entire lot of them, and then the program "burns" the whole CD using the files you select. This is how I create backup CD-Rs of my stuff.

   The second option, also known as *Direct CD*, causes the CD-R disc to be formatted and made ready for holding files just like a huge floppy disk. The CD-R program then quits and allows you to write files to the CD-R disc using the My Computer or Windows Explorer program. You can even delete and rename files. This is the most flexible option, particularly if you're unclear how you want to use the disc when you're done with it.

   In the Direct CD mode, you can even remove the CD-R disc and write to it again at any time. This is known as creating a multisession disc. For example, you can remove a partially written CD-R, give it to a friend with a CD-R drive, and have him burn something on it. Then return it to your own computer — providing that both CD-R drives are compatible — and work with a multisession CD-R disc.

5. **Burn the disc.**

   The final step is for the CD-R software to create the CD-R disc. The process makes the information permanent and then the CD-R disc can be read by most CD-ROM drives. (I say most because some older CD-ROM drives won't read CD-Rs.)

I realize that these steps are a little vague; because Windows itself doesn't come with CD-R burning software, I'm forced to be general.

Not everything is perfect, of course. I remember it took me several tries to create my first CD-R. Sometimes the CD-R discs themselves aren't any good. Also, try to quit all other programs and not do anything (such as play FreeCell) while the CD-R disc is burning.

   ✔ As this book goes to press, the Adaptec Direct CD program is now published by Roxio and has been renamed CD Creator.

   ✔ Some CD-R discs can hold up to 700MB of data or 80 minutes of music. It usually says on the CD-R case, so look when you buy.

- CD-R/RW drives typically have three speeds: the CD-R/RW recording speed, the CD-RW reading speed, and the maximum speed. So a drive rated at 4X-8X-32X may be able to write CD-Rs and CD-RWs at 4X speed, read CD-RWs at 8X speed, and have a maximum CD reading speed of 32X.

- If possible, try to buy your CD-R discs in bulk. It's cheap, but the discs typically don't come with a jewel case or other interesting box.

- Using a CD-R is a good way to back up, or create a safety copy, of all the information on your hard drive. Well, actually, you need to back up only the files you create. For example, make a duplicate of the My Documents folder and all the information in it. Do this every so often so you don't lose your stuff.

- Your CD-R program may also have a nifty label-making or jewel case-creating program. Now that's really swanky!

- Yes, it's true; you can use Direct CD to access a CD-R disc just like any other disc in your system. But it isn't like any other disc in your system in one way: because you cannot really delete anything from a CD-R disc, what the Direct CD software does instead is *hide* the file you deleted. The file still occupies disk space. That's one reason to consider a CD-RW instead of a CD-R for such interactive operations.

- Some CD-R programs give you the option to copy a disc track-by-track, which is the best way to duplicate any CD. But be warned: it is illegal to make copies of commercial and copyrighted programs. Also, be wary of "friends" who give you bootleg CD-R discs of popular games and software; such discs are often the sources of wicked computer viruses.

Running software from a CD-ROM

Q: I've installed the Microsoft Encarta Encyclopedia 2000, but when I run it, the computer prompts me to insert the CD into the drive. I was under the impression that, after installing the program, I wouldn't need to keep sticking the CD into the drive. Can you explain?

A: In most cases, the software you install from a CD-ROM is copied from the CD to the hard drive. In other cases, such as games and various references such as Encarta, the information stays on the CD where it doesn't chew up hard drive space. The drawback, of course, is that you have to insert the CD into the drive whenever you play the game or use the reference.

Many games, and possibly Encarta itself, have the option of installing everything on the hard drive. If you have a nice, roomy hard drive, consider reinstalling Encarta. Use the "Custom" or "Advanced" option when you setup, or whichever method allows you to copy everything to the hard drive. Note, however, that some games require the CD to be inserted before you can play the game no matter what; this is a form of piracy protection to ensure that you own the games you play.

Burning a musical CD

Creating a musical CD works the same way as creating a data CD, though you choose the Music or Audio option instead of the Data option. For example, in Figure 9-2, clicking the Audio button lines up everything to create a musical (or sound) CD.

The biggest difference between creating a music or audio CD versus a data CD is that the music has to come from somewhere. Some CD-R programs let you copy musical tracks from various CDs; you insert the CD and then use the program to pluck out the tracks you want. Then they're saved to the hard drive for later burning onto a new CD-R. Or you can fetch the tracks from audio (MP3 or WAV) files already stored on your hard drive. (Yet another good argument for keeping all your music files in a single folder.)

Unlike a data CD, when you burn a musical CD, it's once and for all. The CD is formatted so that it can be played in any CD player, though some older CD players may not be able to read the disc.

- There are specific CD-R discs for recording music, which are often cheaper than the computer CD-Rs. If you plan on creating music only, then consider buying some of these cheaper discs.
- The CD creator program will tell you how much time is left on the CD so that you won't copy more songs than will fit.
- Not all sound files can be copied to an audio CD. Check with the CD burning program to see which types of sound files can be copied. (I know WAV, AU, and MP3 files aren't a problem.)
- MIDI files must be converted into WAV files to be recorded to a CD-ROM. This is done by playing the MIDI file through a WAV recording program.
- See Chapter 28 for information on downloading an MP3 file.
- By recording an audio CD, you can really gauge how fast the speed ranking is on your CD-R drive. For example, an 8X CD-R drive records 72 minutes of music in about nine minutes; 9 minutes times 8 equals 72 minutes of information.
- It is assumed that you own whatever music it is that you're copying and that you're using the copies only for your personal use. Making a copy of a commercial CD or copyrighted music and using it without paying for it or giving to someone else is theft.

A few words about CD-RW

Most CD-R drives double as CD-RW drives as well. You can use the drive for just about anything that's flat and shiny — well, except for DVD discs: The drive can be used to access data CDs, play music CDs, and burn CD-R and CD-RW discs. Consider yourself lucky if you have such a drive.

CD-RW discs work just like CD-R data discs. You can use Direct CD to work on the disc interactively, or write the entire sucker all at once. The only advantage is that the CD-RW disc can be utterly erased and used over again.

- ✔ Only a CD-RW drive can read and write information to and from a CD-RW disc. So if you want to create a disc that can be read by several PCs, burn a CD-R disc instead.

- ✔ CD-RW discs are different than CD-R discs. It will say CD-RW on the label and the disc will be more expensive.

- ✔ CD-RWs are ideal for backup discs. Like other backup media (floppy disks and tape systems), you can use and reuse the same set of CD-RW discs over and over for your backup procedures.

I want my DVD!

The bigger, faster cousin of the CD-ROM drive is the DVD-drive. In addition to reading standard CD-ROM (and music CD) discs, DVD drives read DVD discs, which can store gigabytes of information on a single disc. That's a lot of stuff. These drives can also read standard CD-ROM discs, which makes them doubly handy.

Do you need a DVD drive in your computer? Not really. Not yet, at least. A handful of programs come on DVD discs, but usually that software also comes with a slew of CDs as well, so no one is being cut out of the picture just yet.

There may come a time, in ten years or so, when DVD drives are standard. But unless music CDs vanish, I don't think computer CDs will become a thing of the past.

- ✔ DVD is an acronym for Digital Versatile Disc. Or it could be Digital Video Disc.

- ✔ Current DVD technology is capable of storing 4GB of information on a disc (compared with over 600MB for a typical computer CD). Some future versions of DVD discs are rumored to be able to hold more than 17GB of information (barely enough for Excel 2010, most likely).

- ✔ Presently DVD drives are used on PCs to view DVD movies.

- ✔ Yes, there is such a thing as a DVD-R or DVD-RAM disc. The formats for these discs aren't really settled yet, with some types being read/write and others being more like CD-Rs. Also the capacity of these discs is all over the map. Hopefully someday they'll be standardized like CD-R/RW drives. Until then, your best source of information on DVD-Rs is the specific drive manufacturers.

Land of the Floppies

Floppy drives eat floppy disks. And between the two, the disks are more interesting. Floppy drives? Boring as a toaster. An unplugged toaster.

The floppy disk, or diskette, measures 3½ inches square and is about ⅛ inch thick. The diskette may also be referred to as *IBM formatted* or *DS, HD*. It's all the same type of disk, the only one you can buy in most places. The only one your PC's floppy drive will eat.

Here are some floppy disk points to ponder:

- ✔ It's tempting to use these disks as beverage coasters. Don't. Moisture can seep underneath the sliding metal thing and freak out the disk inside.

- ✔ Nothing is wrong with buying discount disks in bulk. I just did and saved enough for me to get my teeth capped and begin my singing career.

- ✔ No, the *IBM* on the label of a preformatted box of disks does not mean that they're only for IBM-brand computers. If you have a PC, you can use an IBM disk.

- ✔ Keep floppy disks away from magnets, including telephone handsets, speakers on radios and TVs, executive-style paper-clip holders, desk fans, photocopiers, MRI machines, and the planet Jupiter.

- ✔ Don't set books or heavy items on top of disks. The pressure can push dust granules into the disk.

- ✔ Avoid extreme temperatures. Don't leave a disk sitting on the dash of your car or even on a windowsill. And, even if the novel thought occurs to you, don't store your disks in the freezer.

- ✔ Don't touch the disk surface; touch only its protective cover. Don't spray WD-40 inside, even if the disk makes a noise as it spins. (Your disk drive is probably making the noise, anyway. Keep the WD-40 out of there, too.)

- ✔ Never remove a disk from a floppy drive when the drive light is on. Wait.

- ✔ When you're mailing a disk, don't use a floppy disk mailer from the drugstore. Don't fold the disk in half and mail it in a standard-size envelope. Instead, buy a photo mailer, which is the same as a floppy disk mailer but doesn't cost as much.

Non-Floppy Removable Disk Solutions

Floppy disks used to come in several sizes and capacities. Back when IBM was leading the PC hardware market, a new disk size and format were introduced with just about every new-generation PC. That stopped in 1987 with the introduction of the PC's 1.44MB floppy disk — which is still used today.

Write-protecting a floppy disk

You can protect floppy disks in such a way as to prevent yourself or anyone else from modifying or deleting anything on the disk.

To *write-protect* a 3½-inch disk, locate the little sliding tile on the disk's back corner. When the tile covers the hole, the disk can be written to.

If you slide the tile off the hole (so that you can see through it), the disk is write-protected and cannot be written to. You can read from the disk and copy files from it, but forget about changing the disk's contents.

Since floppy development stagnated, several competing disks have emerged to supplement removable storage on a PC. These include the Zip, Jaz, LS-120, and other types of disk drives, all covered in their own little neat sections.

✔ Actually, floppy development has proceeded since 1987. One such disk was the ill-fated ED floppy disk, which stored 2.88MB on a disk. It never caught on (like, duh!).

✔ The original floppy disk? It was 8-inches square! Very popular in the mid-1970s. Early PCs used the 5¼-inch square floppy until the 3½-inch *microfloppy* took over in '87.

✔ Most large-format, nonfloppy disk solutions (magneto-optical disks, for example) have been replaced by the CD-R and CD-RW.

Zippity doo dah

For the past several years or so, Zip disks have been all the rage. Zip drives are offered as an option on many new PCs, and you can add a Zip drive internally or externally to just about any PC.

Zip disks store 100MB or 250MB per disk, depending on which Zip drive you have. The disks are about 4-inches square, only slightly larger than a floppy disk.

These high-capacity, removable disks are great for backing up files, storing files long term, or transporting large files between two computers.

✔ See Chapter 5 for more information on Zip drives.

✔ If you need more storage per disk, then you can opt for the Jaz disk drive instead of the Zip disk. Not as popular as Zip disks, Jaz disk drives eat special (and expensive) Jaz disks that store up to 2GB per disk.

Look! Up in the sky! It's SuperDisk!

SuperDisk is really a brand name for what the geeks call an LS-120 floppy drive. It's a special type of floppy drive that eats both standard 3½-inch floppies as well as 120MB disks. So this floppy drive makes an ideal replacement for your PC's floppy drive (and comes standard on some PCs).

The 120MB disks themselves look just like regular floppy disks, but the drive recognizes the difference and lets you store up to 120MB worth of junk on each disk. The drive does that through special metallic magic that you need not concern yourself with — but it works!

SuperDisks can be added to any PC, either externally or by replacing the internal floppy drive. Mostly, though, you'll find the SuperDisk drive only on those computers that come with it standard.

Chapter 10

Memory RAM-blings

• •

• •

Do you know if you have enough memory? How could you remember something like that? No matter how old people get, we never run out of memory. It's a limitless resource, though remembering certain dates seems to elude various male members of the species. Too bad it's not the same for your computer, where memory is gobbled up quicker than the last dab of Pink Cool Whip Salad at a holiday feast.

Memory, or random-access memory (RAM), is a storage place in a computer, just like disk space. Unlike disk storage, memory is the only place inside the computer where real work gets done. Obviously, the more memory you have, the more work you can do. But not only that, having more memory means the computer is capable of grander tasks, such as working with graphics, animation, sound, and music — and your PC remembers everyone it meets without ever having to look twice at a nametag.

What Is Memory?

All computers need memory. That's where the work gets done. The microprocessor is capable of storing information inside itself, but only so much. It needs extra memory just like humans need notepads and libraries.

For example, when you create a document with your word processor, each character you type is placed into a specific location in memory. Once there, the microprocessor doesn't need to access it again unless you're editing, searching or replacing, or doing something active to the text.

After something is created in memory — a document, spreadsheet, or graphic — you save it to disk. Your disk drives provide long-term storage for information. Then, when you need to access the information again, you open it back into memory from disk. After it's there, the microprocessor can again work over the information.

The only nasty thing about memory is that it's volatile. When you turn off the power, the contents of memory go *poof!* This is okay if you've saved to disk, but if you haven't, everything is lost. Even resetting your computer zaps the contents of memory. So always save (if you can) before you reset or turn off your PC.

✓ The more memory you have, the better. With more memory, you can work on larger documents and spreadsheets, enjoy applications that use graphics and sound, and boast about all that RAM to your friends.

✓ Turning off the power makes the *contents* of memory go bye-bye. It doesn't destroy the memory chips themselves.

✓ When you open a file on disk, the computer copies that information from disk into the computer's memory. Only in memory can that information be examined or changed. When you save information back to disk, the computer copies it from memory to the disk.

✓ The term RAM is used interchangeably with the word *memory*. They're the same thing. (In fact, RAM stands for *random-access memory*, in case you've been working any crossword puzzles lately.)

Boring technical details on RAM, ROM, and Flash Memory

RAM stands for *random-access memory*. It refers to memory that the microprocessor can read from and write to. When you create something in memory, it's done in RAM. RAM is memory and vice versa.

ROM stands for read-only memory. The microprocessor can read from ROM, but it cannot write to it or modify it. ROM is permanent. Often, ROM chips contain special instructions for the computer — important stuff that never changes. For example, the BIOS is on ROM (see Chapter 7). Because that information is stored

on a ROM chip, the microprocessor can access it. The instructions are always there because they're not erasable.

Flash Memory is a special type of memory that works like both RAM and ROM. Information can be written to Flash Memory like RAM, but it doesn't erase when the power is off like RAM. The memory cards and sticks used by digital cameras use Flash Memory. That way the images stay in the camera even when the camera's batteries run out (which is often).

Measuring Memory

Many interesting terms orbit the planet memory. The most basic of these terms refer to the quantity of memory (see Table 10-1).

Table 10-1		Memory Quantities	
Term	*Abbreviation*	*About*	*Actual*
Byte		1 byte	1 byte
Kilobyte	K or KB	1,000 bytes	1,024 bytes
Megabyte	M or MB	1,000,000 bytes	1,048,576 bytes
Gigabyte	G or GB	1,000,000,000 bytes	1,073,741,824 bytes
Terabyte	T or TB	1,000,000,000,000 bytes	1,099,511,627,776 bytes

Memory is measured by the *byte*. Think of a byte as a single character, a letter in the middle of a word. For example, the word *spatula* is 7 bytes long and requires 7 bytes of computer memory storage.

A half page of text is about 1,000 bytes. To make this a handy figure to know, computer nerds refer to 1,000 bytes as a *kilobyte,* or 1K or KB.

The term *megabyte* refers to 1,000K, or 1 million bytes. The abbreviation MB (or M) indicates megabyte, so 16MB means 16 megabytes of memory.

Further than the megabyte is the *gigabyte.* That is 1 billion bytes or about 1,000 megabytes.

The *terabyte* is 1 trillion bytes, or enough RAM to dim the lights when you start the PC.

Other trivia:

- The term *giga* is Greek, and it means giant.
- The term *tera* is also Greek. It means monster!
- A specific location in memory is called an *address.*

- Bytes are composed of eight bits. The word *bit* is a contraction of *binary digit*. Binary is base two, or a counting system that uses only ones and zeros. Computers count in binary, and we group their bits into clusters of eight for convenient consumption as bytes.

Chips Off the Old Block

Memory is a component of the motherboard, sitting very close to the microprocessor. It exists as a series of tiny chips called DRAM chips.

The DRAM chips typically come as groups soldered together on a thin strip of fiberglass. The whole shebang is referred to as a SIMM or DIMM. It's about the size of a pocket comb, as shown in Figure 10-1.

Figure 10-1:
A typical
SIMM.

Each SIMM or DIMM card contains a given chunk of RAM, measured in one of the magical computer memory values of 4, 8, 16, 32, 64, 128 or 256 megabytes.

SIMM or DIMM cards are plugged into memory slots on the motherboard, each slot being a *bank* of memory. So a PC with 128MB of RAM may have two banks of 64MB SIMMs installed.

- ✔ DRAM stands for dynamic random-access memory. It's pronounced *dee-ram,* and it's the most common type of memory chip installed in a PC.

- ✔ SIMM stands for single in-line memory module.

- ✔ DIMM stands for dual in-line memory module.

- ✔ Whether your PC needs SIMM or DIMM memory depends on the design of the motherboard.

- ✔ DIMMs and SIMMs are similar in appearance, though DIMMs allow memory to be accessed more efficiently. Eventually, DIMMs will replace SIMMs as the best way to upgrade memory in a PC.

Memory Lost and Found

Your brain has all the memory you'll need for a lifetime. Even though we all forget things, scientists in white lab coats have determined that no memory is every lost. Go visit a carnival hypnotist and watch as Brad the Carpenter recalls an embarrassing incident from the third grade that his mother said no one would ever know about.

Well . . . some things may not be worth remembering.

Your computer, on the other hand, loses memory all the time. It has only a given chunk of RAM to play with. It must be shared between all your running programs and the operating system and the little dog that barks at you when you do something stupid in Excel. The following sections explain the details.

"How much memory is in my PC right now?"

This information may be a mystery to you, but it isn't a secret to your computer. The System Properties dialog box shows you how much memory lives inside the beast: Right-click the My Computer icon on the desktop and choose Properties from the shortcut menu that appears. You'll see a dialog box similar to the one shown in Figure 10-2.

Figure 10-2: This computer has 256MB of RAM, barely enough to run Windows XP!

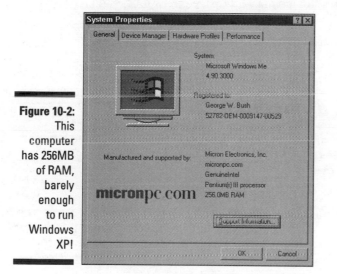

The amount of memory (shown as RAM) appears right beneath the type of microprocessor that lives in your PC. In Figure 10-2, it says the computer has 256.0MB of RAM. (Ten years ago that would have been considered an obscene amount.)

Does your PC have enough memory?

Knowing how much memory is in your PC is one thing, but knowing whether that amount is enough is entirely different!

The amount of memory your PC needs depends on two things. The first, and most important, is the memory requirement of your software. Some programs, such as spreadsheets and graphics applications, require lots of memory. For example, Adobe Photoshop (a graphics package) says — right on the box — that it needs 32MB of RAM. Yowie!

The second and more limiting factor is cost. Memory costs money. It's not as expensive as it was back in the old steam-powered-CPU days of computing, but it still costs something.

- Generally speaking, all PCs should have at least 32MB of RAM, though some older models have less (and may not need any more).

- Today's systems seem to be sold with 64MB of RAM as a base, with 128MB and 256MB models common.

- You'll eventually see 1GB RAM computers, which will probably be the minimum required to run Windows in the year 2008.

- One of the sure signs that your PC needs more memory: It slows to a crawl, especially during memory-intensive operations, such as working with graphics.

- Not enough memory? Then you can upgrade! Refer to "Adding more memory to your PC," later in this chapter.

Running out of memory

It's quite impossible to run out of memory, despite whatever limited amount is in your computer. That's because Windows uses a clever technique to prevent memory from ever becoming full. The technique is to swap chunks of memory out to the hard drive, creatively known as "memory swapping."

In Windows, every program uses a chunk of memory. For most programs, the chunk is rather small, so Windows lets you run several programs at once. But when one program asks for more memory than is physically available, some other poor program's memory chunk gets swapped out to the hard drive.

You don't notice all this memory swapping for the most part; it happens automatically. Though, with some programs you may notice the computer becoming sluggish. For example, editing a large graphic image could result in lots of disk swapping, in which case the computer literally comes to a crawl.

- People who work with graphics programs demand more memory than anyone else. Some custom graphics workstations have 512MB of RAM or more.

- Windows will never say that it's "out of memory." No, you'll just notice that the hard drive is churning a lot as the memory is swapped into and out of the disk drive.

And just what the heck is *extended memory?*

Back in the old days, several dozen terms were used to describe memory in a PC: conventional memory, DOS memory, upper memory, high memory, HMA memory, expanded memory, DMPI memory, extended memory, and on and on.

The only memory term you see used nowadays is *extended memory.* All the memory in your PC is extended memory, which is a holdover term from the ancient days when memory terms were important.

What does this mean to you?

If you see software that says it requires 16MB of extended memory, then know that it merely means 16MB of memory. All the memory in your PC is extended already.

Video memory

Memory used by your PC's video system is known as *video memory.* Specifically, it's memory chips that live on the video adapter card. These chips are used specifically for the computer's video output and help you see higher resolutions, more colors, 3-D graphics, bigger uglier aliens, and girlie pictures your husband downloads from the Internet late at night.

Like regular computer memory, you can upgrade video memory if there's room on your PC's video card. See Chapter 11 for more information on video adapters.

Adding More Memory to Your PC

There is no electronic equivalent of Geritol for your computer. If you think your PC has tired RAM or maybe it didn't have enough memory in the first place, you can always add more.

Adding memory to your computer is Lego-block simple. The only difference is that the typical Lego block set, such as the Medieval Castle or Rescue Helicopter set, costs under $20. Your computer, on the other hand, may cost 50 times that much. Adding memory is not something to be taken lightly.

Upgrading memory involves five complex and boring steps:

1. **Figure out how much memory you need to add.**

   For example, suppose your PC has a paltry 32MB of RAM and you need 64MB to run the latest game. You need another 32MB — or more if you can afford it.

2. **Figure out how much memory you can install.**

   This is a technical step. It involves knowing how memory is added to your computer and in what increments. If you have an empty bank of memory, then this step is actually quite simple. But if your PC doesn't have any empty memory banks, then it can be complex — and expensive. Better leave this task to your dealer or computer guru.

3. **Buy something.**

   In this case, you buy the memory chips themselves, or you buy the expansion card into which the memory chips are installed.

4. **Pay someone else to plug in the chips and do the upgrade.**

   Oh, you can do it yourself, but I'd pay someone else to do it.

5. **Gloat.**

After you have the memory, brag to your friends about it. Heck, it used to be impressive to say you had 640K of RAM. Then came the "I have 4 megabytes of memory in my 386 or 8 megabytes of memory in my 486." Today? Anything less than 256MB and your kids will roll their eyes at you.

✔ PC memory comes in given sizes: 4MB, 8MB, 16MB, 32MB and then double that size on up to 256MB.

✔ Another shocker: You may think that moving from 32MB in your system to 128MB requires that you buy 96MB of memory chips. Wrong! It may mean you have to buy the full 128MB (or two banks of 64MB) and then toss out your original 32MB! It all has to do with how memory physically fits in the PC, which is something even the gods themselves don't fully understand.

✔ My favorite place to get memory chips online is www.crucial.com. The Web site asks a series of questions and then provides memory solutions to solve your problems exactly.

✔ If you want to try upgrading memory yourself, go ahead. Plenty of easy books on the subject of upgrading memory are available, as well as how-to articles in some of the popular magazines. Some places that sell memory, such as Crucial.com, even have well-written how-to booklets that come with the memory. I still recommend having someone else do it, however.

Chapter 11

Amazing Monitors and Glorious Graphics

The monitor is the first thing you notice on a PC. It's what you look at when you use the computer. And the monitor is what makes the best target should you ever decide to shoot your computer. (But keep in mind that the monitor is only the messenger; what you really want to destroy is the console.)

If your computer were a person, then the monitor would be its face. This chapter is about your PC's face, both the hardware part and how Windows can manipulate that face to make it more pleasing for you.

What's in a Name?

Is it a monitor? Is it the screen? Is it a display? Each term refers to that TV-like thing you use to view information from your computer. But which term is correct?

The *monitor* is the box. It contains a picture tube (like a TV) or, if you spent the big bucks, an LCD panel. So if the whole thing fell on the floor, you could say, "The monitor fell on the floor. It was an accident."

The *screen* is the part of the monitor that displays an image. It's the glassy part, or the plastic-film part of an LCD monitor. The screen is there whether the computer is turned on or off. It's what you need to clean after you sneeze.

The *display* is the information that appears on the screen. This is confusing because you could say, "My screen says the computer doesn't like me," and it means the same thing as, "My monitor says the computer doesn't like me" or even "The display is showing how much the computer loathes my presence." However put, the computer doesn't like you.

Nerds refer to the entire monitor/screen thing as a CRT, which stands for cathode ray tube. And note that it's *cathode* ray tube, not *catheter* ray tube.

Monitors and Adapters

The monitor is only half of the video system in your PC. The other half is known as the *graphics adapter*. It's the circuitry that runs the monitor, controlling the image that the monitor displays.

Figure 11-1 illustrates the monitor/adapter relationship. The graphics adapter exists either as part of the motherboard or on an expansion card plugged into the motherboard. A cable then connects the monitor to the console. And, of course, the monitor plugs into the wall.

The monitor itself is rather dumb. It's really the graphics adapter that makes things happen on the monitor. Between the two, the graphics adapter is what determines your PC's graphics potential.

- ✔ You need both a monitor and graphics adapter.
- ✔ In some PCs, especially laptops, the graphics adapter is built into the motherboard.
- ✔ Most laptops will let you add an external monitor using an external graphics port.
- ✔ USB monitors connect to the PC through the USB port.
- ✔ If your PC has more than one monitor (and they can, you know), then it must have one graphics adapter for each monitor or a special graphics adapter that supports dual monitors. See the section "Dueling Monitors," later in this chapter, for more information.

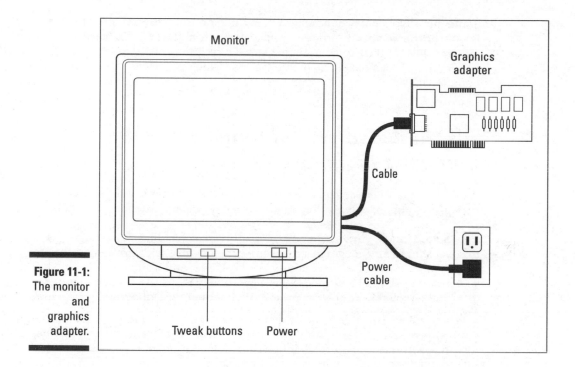

Figure 11-1:
The monitor
and
graphics
adapter.

Getting to Know and Love Your Monitor

A PC's monitor is really a *peripheral*. It's a separate device that need not be sold with the computer (the console). Some dealers even offer a range of different monitors for sale with a computer. Each brand offers different features, but all monitors serve the same function — displaying information the computer coughs up.

The physical description

Each monitor has two tails. One is a power cord that plugs into the wall. The second tail is a video cable that connects to the graphics adapter port on the back of the console.

You usually find the monitor's on-off button on the front of the monitor, most likely near the bottom right. (It's a total bias against left-handed people, part of the larger adroit conspiracy.)

Additional buttons adorn the front of the monitor, which you use to control the monitor's display. These buttons may be visible like a row of ugly teeth, or they may be hidden behind a panel. The next section discusses what they do.

Some monitors display a message when the monitor is turned on but the PC is not (or the monitor is not receiving a signal from the PC). The message may read No Signal or something like that, or it may urge you to check the connection. That's okay. The monitor pops to life properly when you turn the console on.

All the technical information you need to know

A lot of technical nonsense is used to describe a monitor's abilities. Out of that pile of jargon, only two terms are really necessary: size and dot pitch.

- **Size.** Monitors are judged by the picture size, just like TVs. The size is measured on a diagonal, so beware that it's not a width or height thing. Common sizes for PC monitors are 15, 17, 19, and 21 inches. The most popular size is 17 inches, though personally I love the 19-inch monitors and absolutely swoon over the 21-inch monsters! Ooooooo!

- **Dot pitch.** This refers to the distance between each dot, or pixel, on the screen (as measured from the center of each pixel). The closer the dots, the better the image is. A dot pitch of 0.28 mm (millimeters) is really good, with smaller values being even better.

Beyond these two terms is a whole grab bag of technical terms used to describe a monitor. The best judge, really, is your own eyeballs. If the monitor looks good, buy it!

- Other aspects of the display — such as resolution, colors, and video memory — are all part of the graphics adapter hardware, not the monitor.

- I'm a big fan of flat-screen monitors. These are monitors with special picture tubes that are flatter than traditional tubes. (Don't confuse these with LCD monitors, often called *flat panel*.)

Adjusting the monitor's display

In the early days, you were lucky if your monitor had contrast and brightness knobs. Today, the adjustments you can make to your monitor are endless. Sometimes you make adjustments using a row of buttons that adorn the front of your monitor, looking almost like a second keyboard. Other times you use an annoying combination of buttons like for setting the time on a digital clock.

If your monitor has a row of buttons, then each one adjusts a certain aspect of the display. Often plus (+) and minus (-) buttons are used to adjust each aspect. So, for example, to adjust contrast, you press the contrast button and then the plus or minus button. An on-screen display gives you feedback. Figure 11-2 shows some common symbols used to adjust many PC monitors.

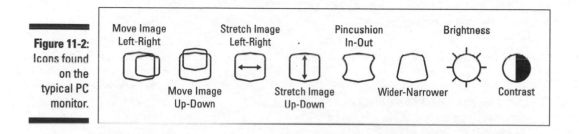

Figure 11-2: Icons found on the typical PC monitor.

Some monitors have only a few buttons on them but use an on-screen display to select options. Figure 11-3 shows such an on-screen display. You use one set of buttons on the monitor to select an item and then use plus (+) and minus (-) buttons to adjust each aspect of the display. Note the icons similar to those shown in Figure 11-2 are used to indicate various settings.

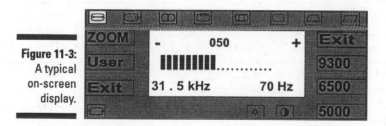

Figure 11-3: A typical on-screen display.

✔ The on-screen information appears over any other image displayed on the monitor. Don't let it freak you out.

✔ Older monitors may not have as many adjustments as are shown in Figure 11-2. They may also lack on-screen displays.

✔ By pressing the Left-Right, Up-Down, and then the stretch buttons, you can adjust the monitor's image to fill the screen. This makes the most efficient use of your monitor.

✔ Monitors may also display frequency information, such as 31KHz/60Hz, when they change screen modes, such as when you play a game and the screen changes to another resolution.

✔ Most monitors also have a Save or Store button, which remembers the settings you've entered, making them permanent.

Cleaning your monitor

Computer monitors grow dust like a five o'clock shadow. And, in addition to the dust, you always find fingerprints and sneeze globs on your screen. Monitors are messy.

To clean your monitor, spray some window cleaner on a soft towel or tissue. Then gently rub the screen. You also can use vinegar if you want your computer to have that tossed-salad smell. You can spray some electronics spray cleaners right on the screen; be sure the cleaner is specially made for that use.

Never spray window cleaner directly on the screen. It may dribble down into the monitor itself and wreak electronic terror.

LCD monitors shouldn't be cleaned the way CRT monitors are. Use an antistatic cloth to remove dust and cat hair from the screen. To remove the sneeze globs, gently rub the screen with a soft towel.

Fancy LCD displays

Eventually, your computer will be connected to a flat-panel LCD monitor, similar to the screens used on PC laptops. Not only are these monitors lightweight, thin, and beautiful to look at, but they'll also induce envy into anyone who sees them. The bad news? They're more expensive than their CRT counterparts.

✔ If you want to go LCD monitor shopping, forget the graphics! The best judge of an LCD screen is text. Fire up a word processor in the store and see how the text looks. Some LCD monitors display glorious graphics but tepid text.

✔ The best LCD monitors to get are those that come with their own digital graphics adapter. They typically plug into the AGP (Accelerated Graphics Port) slot on your PC's motherboard, so make sure your PC has an AGP slot before buying one.

✔ Quite a few LCD monitors also plug into standard VGA ports. No problem there.

✔ A 15-inch LCD monitor has approximately the same viewing area as a standard 17-inch monitor, which is due to the LCD monitors being wider than most CRT monitors.

✔ LCD monitors are available in just about every size, from 14 inches diagonally up to 21 inches. Those 21-inch monsters are beautiful but very expensive.

✔ Frequency, or the scan rate, is very important to an LCD monitor. Some monitors are designed to display only one resolution very well. If you have such an LCD monitor, then set it to that proper resolution. For example, some 15-inch LCD monitors work best at a resolution of 1024 x 768 pixels. Anything else looks yucky, or there may be "rivers" of jiggling pixels running down the screen.

✔ Be sure to check the viewing angle on an LCD monitor, which is the number of degrees to the left or right of the monitor at which the image fades. Monitors with a 160-degree or wider viewing angle are best.

All About Graphics Adapters

The secretive, internal part of a PC's video system is the graphics adapter. It's an expansion card that plugs into your PC's motherboard and gives your computer the ability to display lovely text and graphics on the monitor.

Graphics adapters come in various price ranges and have features for artists, game players, computer designers, and regular Joes like you and me and guys named Joe. Here's the quick roundup:

✔ The measure of a graphics adapter is how much memory (video RAM) it has. Most adapters come with around 8MB or 16MB of memory. The more expensive, fancier models can have up to 64MB. Wow.

✔ The more memory the graphics adapter has, the higher the resolutions it can support and the more colors it can display at those higher resolutions.

✔ Many graphics adapters are advertised as supporting 3-D graphics. That's okay, but they work only if your software supports the particular 3-D graphics offered by that graphics adapter. (If so, the side of the software box should say so.)

✔ If your PC has a DVD drive, you need a graphics adapter capable of producing the DVD image on the monitor. The graphics adapters typically have an S-Video Out port on them, which lets you connect a TV to the computer for watching things on a larger screen.

✔ Some high-resolution graphics systems are applicable only to certain kinds of software. Computer graphics, CAD, and animation and design are all areas where paying top dollar for your display is worth it. If you're using only basic applications, such as a word processor, you don't need a top-dollar graphics adapter.

Tweaking the Display in Windows

The knobs on your monitor control the monitor. To control the graphics adapter — which really does all the work — you need to use Windows. Specifically, you use the Display icon in the Control Panel to tweak various aspects of your monitor's display.

The following sections discuss various strange and wondrous things you can do in the Display Properties dialog box, summoned by the Display icon in the Control Panel. But first, here's how you display the Display Properties dialog box:

1. **Right-click the desktop.**

   This summons the desktop's shortcut menu, the fastest way to get to the Display Properties dialog box in any version of Windows.

2. **Choose Properties.**

   This action conjures up the Display Properties dialog box, similar to what's shown in Figure 11-4.

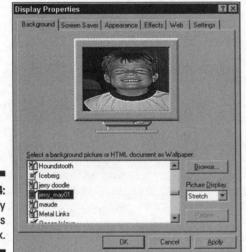

Figure 11-4: The Display Properties dialog box.

3. **Mess with the Display Properties dialog box.**

   You can change the desktop's background, add a screen saver, and change the system colors or screen resolution. The sections that follow outline how to perform these miracles.

4. **Close the Display Properties dialog box.**

   When you're done, you can click the OK button to keep your changes, or click Cancel to go back to the way things were.

You can also summon the Display Properties dialog box from the Control Panel, but in half a dozen years of using Windows, I've rarely done that.

Some Display Properties dialog boxes may have custom tabs for your display adapter.

Oh, yes: As you would expect, the Display Properties dialog box in Windows XP does things a wee bit different. Exceptions are noted in the sections that follow.

Changing the background (wallpaper)

The background, or *wallpaper,* is what you see when you look at the desktop. You can see a pattern or a pretty picture or just about anything other than the dingy gray that Windows really wants to display.

Summon the Display Properties dialog box, as described in the preceding section. Make sure the Background tab is forward, as shown in Figure 11-4.

You can put an image up on the desktop in two ways. The first is with a graphical image or *wallpaper*, and the second is with a pattern.

The scrolling list shows a bunch of graphics files you can apply to the desktop. Or you can use the Browse button to seek out and find another image anywhere on your PC's hard drive.

If the image is large enough, it can cover the entire screen. If it's small, you may want to tile it on the screen, in which case you'd select Tile or Stretch from the drop-down list.

To use a pattern you must choose "(None)" from the Wallpaper list, then click the Pattern button. A bunch of them are displayed, each of them equally boring. Or you can create your own, which is fun so I need not go into any detail about it here. Click OK when you're done messing with the patterns.

To apply your new wallpaper image or pattern, click OK to close the Display Properties dialog box.

- ✔ In Windows XP, click the Desktop tab to set the wallpaper. Windows XP doesn't have a desktop pattern option.

- ✔ Anytime you select a new pattern or wallpaper, it appears in the mini-monitor preview window. It's rather small, so the effect isn't stunning. If you want to see a true preview, click the Apply button.

- ✔ If you created your own graphics file, you can use it as the wallpaper. First, the graphics must be a bitmapped image or BMP file. You can also use GIF files, but you have to use the Browse button to locate and select them. (See Chapter 17 for information on scanning in images to be used as wallpaper.)

Adjusting the resolution and colors

The Settings tab in the Display Properties dialog box (Figure 11-5) is where you tweak your monitor's color and resolution. You can have only so much of both, and this part of the dialog box lets you see just how much you can get away with.

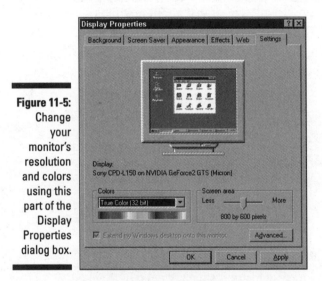

Figure 11-5:
Change your monitor's resolution and colors using this part of the Display Properties dialog box.

I'm not going to go through all the details here. Basically, you select your colors first, from 16 colors on up to 16 bit or 32 bit or whatever huge value Windows gives you.

Next, select a resolution. You notice that the mini-monitor preview window changes to reflect your choice. And if you select a higher resolution, don't be surprised if the number of colors decreases. These two things are linked, in case you haven't guessed.

To preview changes, click the Apply button. Your monitor may blink or flicker, and Windows asks if everything is okay. Click the OK button if it is.

✔ Higher resolutions work best on larger monitors. But remember that the maximum resolution and color settings you get depend on the graphics adapter and not the monitor size.

✔ Some computer games change the monitor's resolution to allow the games to be played. This is okay, and the resolution should return to normal after playing the game.

✔ Some kids' games demand that resolution be set to exactly 256 colors. It will say so when you install the program.

✔ If you have trouble seeing tiny images on the screen, consider the 800 x 600 or even the 640 x 480 resolution. Also, click the Effects tab in the Display Properties dialog box and put a check mark in the Use Large Icons check box.

✔ If you cannot reset the resolution higher than 640 x 480 then either the computer is in "Safe Mode" (and will say so in every corner of the screen), or you need to upgrade your video drivers. Refer to Chapter 27 for information on Safe Mode. The last section in this chapter has information on updating your PC's video drivers.

Adding a screen saver

Eons ago, PC monitors were susceptible to the dreaded *phosphor burn-in*. After time, the same image became *etched* on your screen. Visions of 1-2-3 or WordPerfect would haunt DOS users, even with the monitor turned off!

One of the preventative measures against phosphor burn-in was to run a screen-saver program. That program would blank the monitor. So after several minutes of inactivity — no typing or moving the mouse — the screen went blank. Touching the mouse or pressing any key resumed computer operation, but the screen saver saved the monitor from phosphor burn-in.

Beware the Web wallpaper!

Q: I chose a wallpaper pattern I liked, but now I cannot see any of my desktop icons! They're all there, because if I'm lucky I can click them. But I can't otherwise see them. What did I do?

A: You chose a Web-based Wallpaper, which sometimes hides things on the desktop. For example, some images listed in the Display Properties/Background dialog box can only be displayed if you activate the "Web view" for the desktop. (This is one of the many Internet-based "features" offered by Windows.) So you get a pretty picture, but because it's a Web view, some things on the screen may not look right.

To disable Web view, click the Web tab in the Display Properties dialog box. Remove the check mark by "Show Web content on my Active Desktop." That fixes it.

By the way, if you *really* like the Web wallpaper image, you can use any graphics program to convert it from a JPEG or GIF file into the native BMP format used by Windows. That way you can see the graphic image on the desktop without having to mess with Web view.

Easing monitor sickness

Q: I wrote to you awhile back about how to deal with motion sickness while on the computer. You wrote back with the good idea of an antiglare screen, which does help, but I had already purchased one, and I was still getting sick.

I wanted to share with you a suggestion that my sister-in-law gave me. She needed to find some motion sickness bracelets for her car travel. Well, I thought, if they work for cars why not computers? They definitely help! They are

called Travel-Eze wristbands, and I bought them at Walgreens. I doubt that they are strong enough for a person like me to play games on the computer, but they really seem to be help- ing me with just normal stuff.

A: Your suggestion is passed on, and thank you! Also, the reader points out that you can tap on certain pressure points on the wrist and behind the ear to alleviate some forms of motion sickness.

Fortunately, today's monitors are less likely to suffer from phosphor burn-in. Still, the screen saver remains, mostly as a toy. (Though in Windows 98/Me, using a screen saver is the best way to password-protect your PC. More on that in a moment.)

To set a screen saver, click the Screen Saver tab in the Display Properties dialog box. Figure 11-6 shows what it may look like.

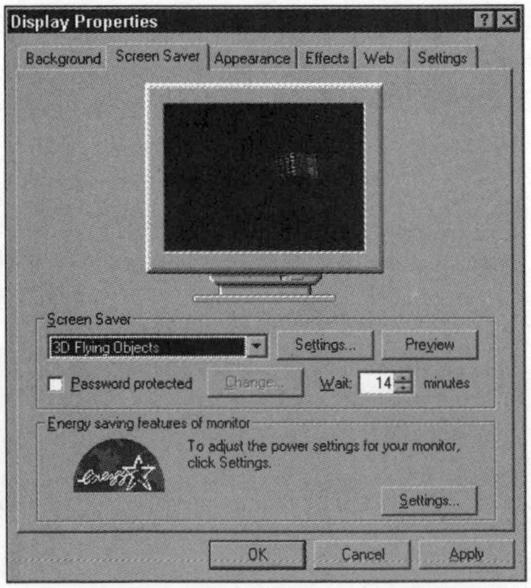

Figure 11-6: Select a screen saver here.

You select a screen saver from the Screen Saver drop-down list. The preview window (screen) in the dialog box shows you what you're getting yourself into.

Click the Settings button to make adjustments for your chosen screen saver.

In the Wait box, enter the number of idle minutes after which you want the screen saver to kick in.

Click the Preview button to see what the screen saver does in full-size mode. (Move the mouse a tad to turn the screen saver off.)

✔ A safe key to press for switching off the screen saver is Ctrl. Unlike other keys on your keyboard, this key doesn't mess with any application that appears after the screen saver vanishes.

✔ No, pressing Ctrl doesn't switch off the screen saver; it merely hides it so you can see the desktop again.

✔ A cool way to switch off the screen saver is to pound your desk with your fist. That jostles the mouse and deactivates the screen saver.

✔ The Password Protected check box allows you to put a password on your screen saver (set with the Change button). This is a great way to protect your PC when you're away; only by knowing the password (or resetting the PC) can you stop the screen saver and use the computer.

✔ If you forget the password, you have to reset the computer to regain control. There's no other way around it.

Downloading screen savers from the Internet

Q: I just downloaded a screen saver from the Internet. How do I get it to work in Windows? It doesn't show up in the Screen Saver dialog box?

A: Two things. First, beware of downloading screen saver (as well as desktop theme) files from the Internet. Although some of them are legitimate screen savers, some of them are invasive ads that are impossible to uninstall or remove. If you download such a screen saver, then you're pretty much stuck with it. So be careful!

Now if you still want to download a screen saver, you need to save the file into the Windows\System folder for Windows 98/Me, or the WINNT\System32 folder for Windows 2000. After you do that, you can summon the Display Properties dialog box and see the custom screen saver in the list.

Dueling Monitors

As an amazing trivial fact, your PC can handle two or more monitors. Windows displays information on both monitors, giving you lots of roomy desktop real estate. To enable this feat you need to buy a second monitor *plus* a second graphics adapter for your PC. (Or you can use one of the dual-display graphic adapters available.)

Briefly, the process works like this. These are simplified steps. Unless you really know what you're doing, I recommend having your dealer or an experienced user set all this up.

1. **Turn off your computer and remove your existing graphics adapter.**

2. **Install the second adapter.**

   This is necessary to properly load the drivers for that adapter. Note that only one of the adapters can use the AGP port; the second adapter must be a PCI adapter.

3. **Attach the second monitor to the second adapter and turn on the computer.**

4. **Install the software and drivers for that adapter.**

   Make sure it's operating properly.

5. **Turn off the computer.**

6. **Reinstall the first adapter and its monitor.**

7. **Turn on the computer.**

From this point on, the computer should start up and load the drivers for both adapters. One will be the primary adapter/monitor. That will display Windows, the desktop, taskbar and all that. The second monitor will display a message that tells you how to finish the job. Heed those instructions. If not, then something is messed up and you'll have to phone the graphics adapter manufacturer's tech support line for help.

- ✔ Only the "Professional" version of Windows XP supports multiple monitors.

- ✔ The two monitors show up in the Settings tab in the Display Properties dialog box. You can drag each monitor's icon around to better position its images.

- ✔ Each monitor can have its own resolution and settings. Just select the monitor from the Display drop-down list and select the necessary settings.

- ✔ The desktop image appears on both monitors.

- ✔ You can drag windows from one monitor to the other. It's really kind of neat to see.

✔ Games run only on your main monitor (the one that's active when the PC first starts). DOS programs also run on the main monitor only. In the future, some games may take advantage of multiple monitors, but I wouldn't count on it. (Two monitors is just too weird.)

✔ Maximizing a window enlarges it to fill the entire screen of one monitor only. You can, however, stretch a window across several monitors.

Basic Monitor Troubleshooting

Most video troubleshooting has to deal with the graphics adapter. Monitors rarely screw up, and if so chances are they should be replaced. But display adapters go bonkers more often and truly drive you nuts. For example, you start the computer and suddenly the resolution is all tweaky or things are so *huge* that you can't use the mouse to click any button. It's times like those that you seriously want to douse the computer with lighter fluid and set the whole thing ablaze.

Fixing the big things

Sometimes the screen displays an image that's just too big to be useful. This usually happens when you mess around in the Appearance tab of the Display Properties dialog box. Oops!

The solution is to start the computer in Safe Mode. In that mode, the settings return to normal, so you can return to the Display Properties dialog box and change things back. Refer to Chapter 27 for information on starting the computer in Safe Mode.

What's a screen dump?

No, a screen dump is not a pile of old monitors somewhere in the desert.

A *screen dump* is the process of taking the information on your computer screen and sending it off to the printer or to a file. Under DOS, the magic Print Screen key on the keyboard initiated this procedure. In Windows, the Print Screen key does kind of the same thing, but nothing is printed.

In Windows, when you press the Print Screen key, you take a snapshot of the desktop. All that graphical information is saved as a graphic image in the Clipboard. You can then paste the image into any program that can swallow graphical images. So even though nothing prints, you still get a dump of what was on the screen.

Reinstalling the graphics adapter driver

The most common monitor error I get in my electronic mailbox concerns people whose graphics adapters suddenly turn stupid. For some reason, the display is set to 640 x 480 mode with only 16 colors. And, try as they might, they just cannot reset to anything higher. This can be mondo frustrating.

The solution is to reinstall your PC's graphics adapter driver. That's the software that controls the graphics adapter. It's most likely already on the computer, so you need follow only a few steps to get the driver back into place:

1. **Open the Display Properties dialog box as covered earlier in this chapter.**

2. **Click the Settings tab.**

3. **Click the Advanced button.**

   This action displays your graphics adapter's dialog box.

4. **Click the Adapter tab.**

5a. **In Windows 98/Me, click the Change button.**

5b. **In Windows 2000/XP, click the Properties button to display yet another dialog box. In that dialog box, click the Driver tab and then click the Update Driver button.**

   No matter how you get there, eventually a wizard appears that walks you through the steps required to set up a new driver for your graphics adapter.

   Generally speaking, the options preselected in the wizard are your best choices. Chances are that you'll find the driver software on the computer, in which case you merely need to reinstall it.

In some cases you may need to reset the computer. Do so if asked.

If the drive cannot be found, you might consider searching for a new driver on the Internet. Refer to the driver's name as displayed in Step 3's dialog box (above). Search the Internet for that name, and you might be able to find newer, better drivers on the manufacturer's Web site.

Chapter 12

Eeek! (The Mouse Chapter)

● ●

● ●

The Macintosh may have been the first personal computer to come with a mouse, but today it's hard to find any PC that's sold without its own mouse. Some mice are fun, like the wacky models Logitech sells. Other mice, like the IBM computer mouse (which has the serious IBM letters etched into its case), are meant strictly for business. Regardless, a mouse is a necessary thing to have, especially when you're using a graphically drunk operating system like Windows.

> ✔ Doug Englebart invented the computer mouse at the Stanford Research Institute in the 1960s. (Apple computer didn't "invent" it for the Macintosh.) Doug received only $10,000 for his invention, but in 1997, he won the $500,000 Lemelson-MIT Prize for American Innovation.
>
> ✔ The plural of computer mouse is *mice.* One computer has a mouse. Two computers have mice.

Say "Hello" to the Mouse

A computer mouse is a little plastic rodent running around on your desk. It looks like a bar of soap with a large, rolling ball embedded in its belly. On the top, you find at least two push buttons. A tail, or cord, runs from the mouse into the back of your PC. Figure 12-1 shows a typical mouse.

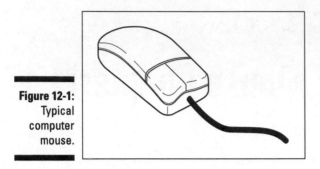

Figure 12-1:
Typical
computer
mouse.

You need a mouse, especially in an operating system like Windows, to control graphics and graphical whatnots on the screen. The mouse makes an ideal companion to the keyboard, helping you get work done in a graphical madhouse like Windows.

✔ Your PC may have come with a specific mouse, but you can always buy a better replacement! Refer to the section "Types of Mice," later in this chapter, for some of the varieties.

✔ Designate a special mouse area on your desk and keep it clear of desk debris so that you have room to move the mouse around. An area about the size of this book is typically all you need to roll the mouse around.

✔ A mouse works best when moved across a *mouse pad*, which is a small piece of plastic or foam rubber that sits on your desk. The mouse pad provides more traction than your slippery desktop. Also, it reminds you to keep that area of your desk clean.

✔ The best mouse pads have rough surfaces, which the mouse can really grip. Poorly designed mouse pads are slick and should be avoided. Also, having an image on your mouse pad is a status symbol. Kinkos and other places even let you create your own mouse pad image using any photograph.

Types of Mice

There are many species of computer mice. Beyond the common bar-of-soap model are upside-down mice, mice with too many buttons, radio mice, pen mice, and on and on. The sections that follow describe various types of computer mice you can buy.

✔ I even saw a mouse with 52 buttons on it, allowing you to use it as a keyboard. (I wonder why the thing never caught on?)

✔ Another type of mouse is the USB mouse. Though it's not different-looking, it does connect to the PC via the USB port. See Chapter 8 for more information on the USB port.

The wheel mouse

The wheel mouse has an extra button between the two standard buttons. That button is a wheel, which you can spin up or down to scroll a document in those few Windows programs that obey the wheel mouse. Or you can press and hold the wheel button to *pan* the document up or down or left or right.

- Most of the new mice sold today have little wheels in them. In the future, I predict that all computer mice will have wheels.

- The Microsoft version of the wheel mouse is called the IntelliMouse.

- Not every application obeys the wheel button's movements. So if the wheel button doesn't scroll a document, for example, don't blame the mouse.

The optical mouse

The latest in computer mouse technology is the optical mouse, which has no ball! No, the optical mouse uses an infrared sensor to track its movements over any surface. This eliminates the need for a mouse pad and allows you to slide the mouse directly on your desktop.

- The fanciest of all the optical mice is the Microsoft IntelliMouse Explorer. It's a standard IntelliMouse (with the wheel button), plus it's optical. And it looks like a tiny spaceship that's landed near your keyboard. Very cool.

- A special version of the IntelliMouse Explorer comes with two or three extra buttons, which help you navigate through the Internet. There is a "forward" button and a "back" button as well as another tiny button I just noticed and have no idea what it does.

- Though the optical mouse doesn't need a mouse pad, you must slide it over a surface that isn't too shiny or uniform in color. If you notice that the mouse isn't responding properly, then you'll need to use a mouse pad of sorts (basically anything flat that has printed material on it).

The upside-down mouse (the trackball)

A trackball mouse looks like a regular mouse turned upside down, as shown in Figure 12-2. Instead of rolling the mouse around, you use your thumb or index finger to roll the ball itself. The whole contraption stays stationary, so it doesn't need nearly as much room, and the cord never gets tangled.

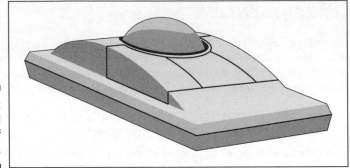

Figure 12-2:
A trackball
type of
mouse.

Trackballs aren't for everyone. The only crowd that really loves them is the artist types, who prefer the precise movements the trackball gives you. Are you wearing all black? Have on a beret? If so, you'll probably love a trackball mouse.

Connecting the Mouse

The computer's mouse plugs into the mouse connector on the back of the console. Simple.

Serial mice plug into the computer's serial port. If you have a serial mouse, plug it into COM1, because COM2 is often used as the modem port and plugging the mouse into COM2 can cause problems.

If your PC uses a USB mouse, plug it into the USB port. There is usually a spare USB port on the keyboard, if your PC is so equipped.

- ✔ It's a good idea to turn your computer off before you connect or disconnect the mouse.
- ✔ You don't need to turn the computer off before connecting a USB mouse; USB is designed that way.
- ✔ USB and other PC ports are covered in Chapter 8.
- ✔ The mouse may come with its own software, which you install by using the Windows handy install program thingy. See Chapter 19.
- ✔ The tail points *away* from you when you use the mouse. (Oh, I could tell a story here about a former boss, but I won't.)

Using Your Computer Mouse

The computer's mouse controls a pointer or mouse cursor on the screen. When you move the mouse around by rolling it on your desk, the pointer on the screen moves in a similar manner. Roll the mouse left, and the pointer moves left; roll it in circles, and the pointer mimics that action; drop the mouse off the table, and your computer yells out, "Ouch!" (Just kidding.)

You don't need to squeeze the mouse; a gentle grip is all that's necessary.

- Most people hold the mouse in their palm with their thumb against the left edge and their ring finger against the right edge. The index finger and middle finger can then hover over the buttons along the top. (If this were medieval times, the mouse would be a fist weapon, not a finger weapon.)

- The first time you use a mouse, you want to move it in wild circles on your desk so that you can watch the pointer spiral on the screen. This urge takes a long time to wear off (if it ever does).

- When the mouse cord becomes tangled, raise the mouse in your hand and whip it about violently.

 - The best way to learn how to use a computer mouse is to play a computer card game, such as Solitaire or FreeCell (both of which come with Windows). You'll have the mouse mastered in only a few, frustrating hours.

Point the mouse

When you're told to *point the mouse,* it means you move the mouse on the desktop, which moves the mouse pointer on the screen to point at something interesting (or not).

Try not to pick the mouse up and point it at something like a TV remote control. It just doesn't work that way.

Click the mouse

A click is a press of the mouse button.

Often you read *click the mouse on the OK button.* This instruction means a graphic or something-or-other is on the screen with the word OK on it. Using the mouse, you move the pointer over the word OK. Then, with your index finger, click the mouse button. This action is referred to as *clicking the mouse on something* (though you could roll the mouse around on your forehead and click it there if you like — just make sure no one's looking).

✔ The button to click is the *left* mouse button, the one under your index finger. That's the main mouse button.

✔ If you need to click the right button, the instructions will tell you to *right-click* or to *click the right mouse button.* Same for the wheel button, should your mouse have one of those.

✔ When you push the button on your mouse, it makes a clicking noise. So most programs tell you to *click* your mouse button when they really mean for you to *press* the mouse button.

✔ You also click the mouse to *select* something. So if the instructions say *Select the Drive C icon,* they mean to click the mouse on the Drive C icon.

✔ When clicking the button, push it down once and release it. Don't hold it down continuously. (Actually, it makes two clicks — one when pushed and another when released. Is your hearing that good?)

✔ Sometimes you may be asked to press a key combination along with clicking the mouse. A popular combo is Ctrl+click, which means to press and hold down the Ctrl (control) key on your keyboard before you click the mouse button.

Double-clicking the mouse

A double-click is two rapid clicks in a row. You do this in Windows to open something.

✔ The time between clicks varies, but it doesn't have to be that quick.

✔ Try not to move the mouse around between the clicks; both clicks have to be on the same spot.

✔ Oh, there are also triple, quadruple, and quintuple clicks as well. It's all the same idea; click the mouse more than once in the same spot. (I've never needed a sextuple click.)

✔ If you double-click your mouse and nothing happens, you may not be clicking fast enough. See the section "Double-clicking doesn't work!" later in this chapter.

Dragging the mouse

You drag with the mouse to select a group of items on the screen or to pick up and move something.

To drag with the mouse, follow these steps:

1. Point the mouse cursor at the thing you want to drag.

2. **Press and hold the mouse's button.**

   That's the left button. Press and hold the button down — don't click it! This action has the effect of picking up whatever the mouse is pointing at on the screen.

   If it's not picking up something, a drag also selects objects by drawing a rubber-band-like rectangle around them.

3. **Move the mouse to a new location.**

   The drag operation is really a *move;* you start at one point on the screen and move (drag) the whatever to another location.

4. **Release the mouse button.**

   Lift your finger off the left mouse button. You're done dragging.

When you release the mouse button, you let go of whatever it was you were dragging.

- You can also drag to select a group of items. In this case, dragging draws a rectangle around the items you want to select.

- Dragging is used in many drawing and painting programs to create an image on the screen. In this sense, dragging is like pressing a pen tip or paintbrush to paper.

- You can also drag using the right mouse button instead of the left. This action is usually called a right-drag.

- Sometimes you may be asked to press and hold a key while dragging, referred to as a Ctrl+drag (Control+drag) or Shift+drag or some other key combination. If so, press that key — Ctrl, Shift, Alt, or whatever — *before* you first click the mouse to drag something.

Tweaking the Mouse in Windows

Lurking in the Control Panel is the Mouse icon, which opens up the Mouse Properties dialog box, which is where you can tweak your mouse. The following sections describe a few handy things you can do there. Here are the general steps you take to open the Mouse icon up for business:

1. **Open the Control Panel.**

   From the Start menu, choose Settings⇨Control Panel. The Control Panel's main window appears.

2. **Open the Mouse icon.**

Mouse

Funny how that mouse icon looks like the type of mouse Microsoft is currently selling. Oh, whatever. Double-click the Mouse icon. This action brings forth the Mouse Properties dialog box, looking similar to Figure 12-3. (Not all Mouse Properties dialog boxes look alike; custom mice have more tabs and different options.)

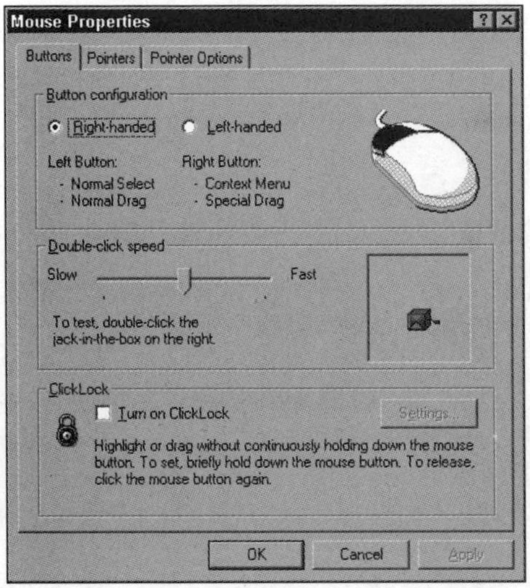

Figure 12-3:
The Mouse
Properties
dialog box.

3. **Goof around in the Mouse Properties dialog box.**

   Several subtle things are permissible in the Mouse Properties dialog box. A few of the more popular ones are discussed in the sections that follow.

4. **Close the dialog box.**

   When you're done messing around, you have two choices: Click the OK button to keep your changes, or click Cancel to return to the way things were before.

Hunting down the Mouse Properties dialog box in Windows XP works like this:

1. **Choose the Control Panel from the Start menu.**

2. **Choose Printers and Other Hardware.**

3. **Choose the Mouse.**

   And there it is.

Remember that you need to click only once on items to select *and* open them in Windows XP.

"Double-clicking doesn't work!"

If you can't seem to double-click, one of two things is happening: Either you're moving the mouse pointer a little bit between clicks, or the double-click *rate* is set too fast for human fingers to manage.

1. **Bring forth the Mouse Properties dialog box, as discussed in the preceding section.**

2. **Click the Buttons (or Activities) tab.**

   What you're looking for is the Double-Click Speed area, which appears in the middle of Figure 12-3.

3. **Adjust the slider Slow or Fast to change the double-click speed.**

4. **Test the new setting.**

   To test this setting, first click the Apply button. This action resets Windows to your new mouse specifications. Then double-click the graphic in the test area. If the graphic changes, then you have a proper double-click speed set.

5. **Click OK to close the Mouse Properties dialog box.**

Messing with the mouse pointer

Windows tries to communicate certain things to you using the mouse pointer. You can see what it's trying to tell you by visiting the Pointers tab in the Mouse Properties dialog box. Figure 12-4 offers a peek.

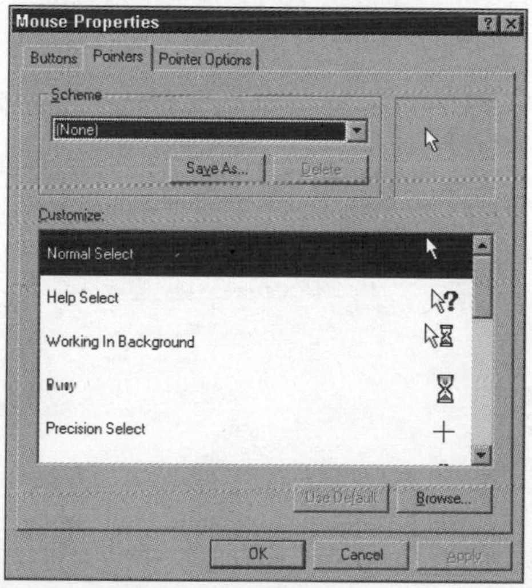

Figure 12-4:
Choose another mouse pointer.

The scrolling list shows the different pointers that appear when Windows is busy, selecting text, resizing something, and so on. The nifty part is that you can change the way those pointers look.

To change an individual pointer, double-click that pointer in the scrolling list. A Browse dialog box appears, from which you can choose any of a number of pointers — even an animated cursor that dances or throbs or whatever.

You can change all the pointers en masse by choosing a Scheme from the drop-down list.

You can download cursor files or get disks full of them. If so, save these cursor files in the Cursors folder in the Windows main folder. (The pathname is C:\WINDOWS\CURSORS; in Windows 2000 it's C:\WINNT\CURSORS.) That way they show up in the list when you select a new pointer in the Browse dialog box.

"I'm a southpaw, and the buttons are backward!"

Hey, Lefty, if you just can't stand the idea of using a mouse in the right-hand/left-brain dominated world, you can switch things over — even putting the mouse on the nontraditional left-hand side of your PC keyboard. (Oh, brother. . . .)

Summon the Mouse Properties dialog box using the instructions offered in "Tweaking the Mouse in Windows," earlier in this chapter. In the Buttons (or Basics) panel, click the proper button to select a left-handed mouse. This action mentally switches the buttons in the Windows head: The right button takes on left-button tasks and vice versa.

✔ This book and all manuals and computer books assume that the left mouse button is the main button. Right-clicks are clicks of the right mouse button. If you tell Windows to use the left-handed mouse, these buttons are reversed. Keep in mind that your documentation will not reflect that.

✔ There is no setting for ambidextrous people, wise guy!

Mouse Woes

Mice can be reliable and trustworthy, but every so often, they annoy you by not working properly. The following sections provide some mouse mainte- nance and troubleshooting information for those desperate times when it's needed.

Cleaning your mouse

Your desk constantly collects a layer of dust and hair, especially if you have a cat around or a picture of a cat on your mouse pad. If your mouse isn't behav- ing the way it used to, you may need to clean it. This is easy to do yourself; there's no need for the repair shop or a guy in a van.

To clean a traditional, ball-in-the-belly mouse, turn it over and you'll see a little round plate holding the ball in place. Push or twist the plate to open. The plate comes off, and the ball falls out, rolling off the desk, and under your chair.

Pull out any hair or debris from the mouse-ball hole and brush any stray offal off the ball itself. Check the rollers inside the ball hole to see if they have any scum on them. If so, carefully remove the scum using a pin and a pair of tweezers. Put the ball back inside, reattach the plate, and you're on your way.

- Optical mice don't have balls, so there's really nothing in them to clean. However, you will occasionally have to pull hair from the optical sensor's hole. Use a pair of tweezers for this, pulling any cat or human hair out of the hole. (You'll know when this needs to be done because the optical mouse will behave erratically.)

- Try to keep the mouse pad clean as well: Brush it off occasionally to clear away the potato chips, drool, and other detritus that accumulates there.

The mouse is a slug

Slow mice happen over time. Why? Who knows. If you've cleaned and cleaned your mouse and it's still playing dead or cross-eyed, then toss that sucker out! I'm serious: Buy another mouse.

Computer mice typically work well for two to three years. After that, for some reason, they get sluggish and jerky. Rather than pound your mouse into your desktop, just break down and buy a new one. You'll be amazed at how much better it works and how much more calmly you use the PC.

The vanishing or stuck mouse

After a terrifically productive session of managing your files, you may suddenly notice that your mouse is gone.

No! Wait, there it is!

But then it's gone again, vanishing in and out like a Cheshire cat. I have no idea why this is so.

Or the mouse pointer may just sit there dead on the screen. You move the mouse. Nothing. You motivate the mouse with your handy repertoire of nasty epitaphs. Nothing. You slam the mouse into your desktop. Nothing. Nothing. Nothing.

The solution: Restart Windows. See Chapter 2.

Chapter 13

The Keyboard Chapter

Y ou probably have keys, a whole ring full of them. I used to think the more important you were, the more keys you had. That still may be true.

Pianos have 88 keys, 55 white and 33 black. They can take years to master.

Your computer has a keyboard with over 100 keys on it. Often you're expected to master it in less than a week. Egads! Then what are you wasting time for? Hurry up and read this, the keyboard chapter!

Know Thy Keyboard

Your keyboard is the direct line of communication between you and the computer. The computer has no ears. You can try yelling. You can wave your arms. But the computer hears nothing unless you type something on the keyboard.

Your typical PC keyboard

The typical PC keyboard is shown in Figure 13-1. The nerds call it the *enhanced 104-key keyboard*. Yes, it has 104 keys on it. You can count them yourself, if you have the time.

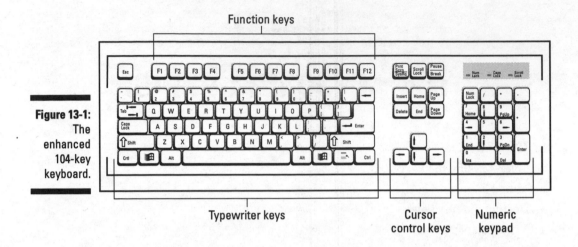

Figure 13-1:
The enhanced 104-key keyboard.

- ✔ Older keyboards lacked the three special "Windows" keys that appear on newer keyboards.

- ✔ Some keyboards have special Internet keys on them. These appear as a row of buttons above the function keys. These Internet keys are non-standard and perform specific operations that the typical PC keyboard doesn't handle. See the section "Special keys on special keyboards" for more information.

Basic keyboard layout

Four main areas are mapped out on your PC's keyboard, as shown in Figure 13-1:

Function keys: These keys are positioned on the top row of the keyboard. They are labeled F1, F2, F3, and on up to F11 and F12.

Typewriter keys: These keys are the same type of keys you'd find on an old typewriter: letters, numbers, and punctuation symbols.

Cursor-control keys: Often called arrow keys, these four keys move the text cursor in the direction of their arrows. Above them are more cursor control keys — the six pack of Insert, Delete, Home, End, PgUp, and PgDn.

Numeric keypad: Popular among bank tellers with zippy fingers, the numeric keypad contains the calculator-like keys.

- The numeric keypad has a split personality. Sometimes it's used to generate numbers, other times it duplicates the cursor keys. See the section "Keys to change the keyboard's mood," later in this chapter, for more information on this duplicity.

- The cursor-control keys are used to move the text cursor around, which typically looks like a blinking toothpick when you type or edit text in Windows. The mouse pointer is often called the cursor, though the cursor keys don't move it around.

- The PgUp and PgDn keys stand for Page Up and Page Down. The labels on the key caps may be fully spelled out or abbreviated.

- Insert and Delete are editing keys, often used with the cursor keys.

- The Print Screen key may also be labeled PrtScr or Print Scrn.

So where is the Any key?

Though the message isn't as common as it was in the olden days, you may someday see "Press any key to continue" displayed on the screen. So where is the elusive *Any* key?

Any key refers to, literally, any key on your keyboard. But why beat around the bush: When a message says to press the Any key, press the spacebar.

- If you can't find the spacebar, or you think it's the place where you order drinks on the Starship Enterprise, press the Enter key.

- So why does the message say, "Press any key" instead of saying "Press the spacebar to continue"? I guess it's because the idiot programmers want to make things *easy* for you by giving you the whole keyboard to choose from. And if that's really the case, why not just break down and say, "Slap your keyboard a few times with your open palms to continue"?

Know your ones and zeros

On a typewriter, the lowercase letter *L* and the number 1 are often the same. In fact, I remember my old Royal upright lacked a 1 key altogether. Unfortunately, on a computer there is a big difference between a one and a little *L*.

If you're typing **1,001**, for example, don't type l,00l by mistake — especially when working with a spreadsheet. The computer will gag.

The same holds true for the uppercase letter *O* and the number 0. They're different. Use a zero for numbers and a big *O* for big O things.

Sometimes zero is displayed with a slash through it, like this: Ø. That's one way to tell the difference between O and 0, but it's not used that often.

Where is the Help key?

Whenever you need help in Windows, whack the F1 key. F1 equals help — no way to commit that to memory. However, I've included a little fake key cap cover on this book's Cheat Sheet. Clip it out and paste it over the F1 key on your keyboard.

What are those weird Windows keys?

Most PC keyboards today sport three new keys: the Windows key, the Shortcut Menu key, and yet another Windows key. They sit between the Alt and Ctrl keys on either side of the spacebar (refer to Figure 13-1).

 The Windows key serves the same purpose as pressing Ctrl+Esc: It pops up the Start menu thing. You can also use it for a few quick shortcuts, as shown in Table 13-1.

Table 13-1	WinKey Shortcuts
Key Combo	*Function*
WinKey+D	Displays the desktop (minimizes all Windows)
WinKey+E	Starts Windows Explorer
WinKey+F	Displays the Find Files/Search Results dialog box
WinKey+R	Displays the Run dialog box

Shortcut to the old graveyard

The Shortcut Menu key displays the shortcut menu for whatever item is currently selected on the screen. This is the same as right-clicking the mouse when something is selected.

Keys to change the keyboard's mood

Several keys affect the way the keyboard behaves. The first three of these keys are the Lock sisters:

Caps Lock: This key works like holding down the Shift key, but it produces only capital letters; it does not shift the other keys as a typewriter's Shift Lock key would do. Press Caps Lock again, and the letters return to their normal lowercase state.

Num Lock: Pressing this key makes the numeric keypad on the right side of the keyboard produce numbers. Press this key again, and you can use the numeric keypad for moving the text cursor around on the screen.

Scroll Lock: This key has no purpose in life. Some spreadsheets use it to reverse the function of the cursor keys (which move the spreadsheet instead of moving the cell highlight). Scroll Lock does little else important or famous.

Other keys that affect the way the keyboard behaves are the modifier keys. These keys work in combination with other keys to do various interesting and unbelievable things:

Shift: Hold down the Shift key to make capital letters. By pressing the Shift key, you also can create the %@#^ characters that come in handy for cursing in comic strips. When you release the Shift key, everything returns to normal, just like a typewriter.

Ctrl: The Control key, abbreviated as Ctrl, is also used like the Shift key; you press it in combination with another key. In most Windows programs, the Ctrl key is used with various letter keys to carry out specific commands. For example, if you hold down the Ctrl key and press S (Ctrl+S), you save something. Likewise, in most programs, you press Ctrl+P to print, and so on for each clever letter of the alphabet.

Alt: Like the Shift and Ctrl keys, the Alt key is used in combination with other keys to carry out commands. For example, holding down the Alt key and pressing the F4 key (Alt+F4) closes a window on the desktop. You press and hold the Alt key, tap the F4 key, and then release both keys.

Here are more thoughts on these, the moody keys on your keyboard:

- ✔ The Caps Lock, Num Lock, and Scroll Lock keys have lights. When the light is on, the key's feature is turned on.

- ✔ On most computers the Num Lock is already on when the computer starts. Annoying, huh?

- ✔ If you type **This Text Looks Like A Ransom Note** and it looks like tHIS tEXT lOOKS lIKE a rANSOM nOTE, the Caps Lock key is inadvertently turned on. Press it once to return everything to normal.

- ✔ If you press the Shift key while Caps Lock is on, the letter keys return to normal. (Shift kind of cancels out Caps Lock.)

- ✔ Even though you may see Ctrl+S or Alt+S with a capital *S,* this doesn't mean you must type Ctrl+Shift+S or Alt+Shift+S. The *S* is simply written in uppercase because Ctrl+s looks like a typesetting error.

- ✔ Don't be surprised if these shift keys are used in combination with each other. I've seen Shift+Ctrl+C and Ctrl+Alt. You use Ctrl+Esc to pop up the Start menu. Just remember to press and hold the Shift keys first, and then tap the letter key. Release all the keys together.

- ✔ Some manuals use the term ^Y rather than Ctrl+Y. This term means the same thing: Hold down the Ctrl key, press Y, and release the Ctrl key.

- ✔ With some programs, you do press the Alt or Ctrl keys by themselves. For example, you can press the Alt key to activate the menu bar in a Windows program. In Windows 2000/XP, pressing the Alt key by itself displays the underlined hot keys on the menu bar or in a dialog box.

The all-powerful Enter key

Nearly all PC computer keyboards have two keys labeled Enter. Both keys work identically, with the second Enter key placed by the numeric keypad to facilitate rapid entry of incorrect numerical values.

So what is the Return key? Many early computers sported a Return key. Essentially, it's the same thing as the Enter key. I bring this up because I just saw a manual the other day that said to *press Return*.

There is no Return key!

Press the Enter key when some dopey manual suggests that you press Return.

- ✔ Pressing the Enter key is the same as clicking OK in a dialog box.

- ✔ In your word processor, only press Enter at the end of a paragraph.

- ✔ In a Web browser, you press the Enter key after typing a Web page address to view that page (well, eventually).

- ✔ Don't press Enter after filling in a text box inside a dialog box. Use the Tab key to move from text box to text box. This rule also applies when using some database programs; use the Tab key to skip merrily between the fields. La, la, la.

- ✔ The difference between Enter and Return is only semantic. Enter has its roots in the electronic calculator industry. You pressed Enter to enter numbers or a formula. Return, on the other hand, comes from the electronic typewriter. Pressing Return on a typewriter caused the carriage to return to the left margin. It also advanced the paper one line.

The Tab key

The Tab key is used two different ways on your computer.

In a word processor, you use the Tab key to indent paragraphs — just like the old typewriter's Tab key.

In a dialog box, you use the Tab key to move between the gizmos in the dialog box. Use Tab instead of Enter, for example, to hop between the First Name and Last Name fields. This also holds true for filling in a form on the Internet: Use the Tab key, not Enter, to fill in the blanks.

- The Tab key often has two arrows on it — one pointing left and the other right. These arrows may be in addition to the word *Tab,* or they may be on there by themselves to confuse you.

- Actually, the arrows move both ways because Shift+Tab is a valid key combination. For example, pressing Shift+Tab in a dialog box moves you "backwards" through the options.

- The computer treats a tab as a single, separate character. When you backspace over a tab in a word processing program, the tab disappears completely in one chunk — not space by space.

Slashing about

Two slash keys are on your keyboard, and you can easily be confused.

The forward slash (/) leans forward (duh!), like it's falling to the right. You use this slash primarily to denote division, such as 52/13 (52 divided by 13).

The backslash (\) leans to the left. You use this character in *pathnames,* which are complex and discussed only near the end of Chapter 5, where no one can find them.

Escape from Windows!

The one key that says "Hey! Stop it!" to Windows is the Escape key, labeled Esc on your keyboard.

Pressing the Esc key is the same as clicking Cancel or "No Way" in a dialog box. And it closes most windows, but not all, just to keep you guessing.

- Esc can be a good pinch hitter to try first when something goes awry.

- To close any window or quit any program, use the mysterious Alt+F4 key combination.

At a nerd cocktail party.

> **LANCE:** Say, Shelia, I'll bet you didn't know that the ASCII code for the Escape key is 27.
>
> **SHELIA:** Not only that, Lance, but it's 1B in hexadecimal.
>
> **BOTH:** Ha-ha-ha-ha-ha!

Don't bother with these keys

Some keys on the keyboard meant something to some old program, now long forgotten. I'm wishing this on the Windows and Shortcut Menu keys myself. But until they become useless, the following keys no longer hold any meaning for Windows:

Pause. Honestly, the Pause key doesn't work in Windows. In DOS, it would pause output. So if you were displaying a long file on the screen, you could press the Pause key, and everything would stop. In Windows, the Pause key does nothing. And Windows is so slow anyway, who would want to pause it?

SysRq. The System Request (Ah! That's what it means!) key was supposed to be used for the next version of DOS. But a next version of DOS never came about, nor was a use ever found for the SysRq key. Though it lingers on the keyboard's face like an ugly mole.

Break. By itself, the Break key does nothing. When used in combination with the Ctrl key (Ctrl+Break), the Break key could be used to stop old DOS programs. In Windows, though, Break does nothing.

Other strange and useless key thoughts:

- ✔ The Pause key may also be labeled Hold on some keyboards.

- ✔ The Pause key does work in some games. It pauses play so you can talk on the phone without letting your boss know that you're playing Lesbian Retirement Home Commandos.

- ✔ If you ever do use the DOS window and need to stop a program, then you can use either Ctrl+Break or Ctrl+C — assuming you can remember either one.

- ✔ Why is the key called Break? Why not call it the Brake key? Wouldn't that make sense? Who wants a computer to break, anyway? Golly.

TIP

"Must I learn to type to use a computer?"

No one needs to learn to type to use a computer. Plenty of computer users hunt and peck. In fact, most programmers don't know how to type; they sit all hunched over the keyboard and punch in enigmatic computer languages using greasy, garlic-and-herb potato chip-smeared fingers. But that's not being very productive.

As a bonus to owning a computer, you can have it teach you how to type. The Mavis Beacon

Teaches Typing software package does just that. Other packages are available, but I personally love the name "Mavis Beacon."

Trivia: A computer software developer once halted all development and had his programmers sit down and learn how to touch type. It took two whole weeks, but afterward, they all got their work done a lot faster and had more time available to break away and play games.

Special keys on special keyboards

If 104 keys on the keyboard just aren't enough, you can venture out and buy special keyboards that sport *even more* keys. Or perhaps your computer came with such a keyboard. Typically they have a row of buttons along the top, right above the function keys. These buttons carry out specific tasks, such as connecting to the Internet or adjusting the computer's sound volume.

The buttons on these keyboards are nonstandard. That means that they don't come with the typical PC keyboard and must be supported by using some special program run on the computer. It's that program that controls the keys and their behavior. So if the keys don't work, then it's a problem with the special program and not anything that Windows or your computer is doing wrong.

Clever Windows Key Combinations

Windows isn't totally limited to using the Mouse for getting things done. There are plenty of key combinations that empower your fingers with electrifying commands designed to jolt Windows into obedience. Yea, Windows shudders at any of the commands listed in Table 13-2.

Table 13-2	Windows Key Combinations
Key Combo	*Command*
Alt+Tab	Switch to the next window/program
Alt+Shift+Tab	Switch back to the previous window/program
Alt+Esc	Cycle through running programs
Ctrl+Esc	Display the Start menu
Alt+F4	Close the current window
Shift+[*cursor key*]	Select text in the direction of the cursor key
Alt+↓	Display a drop-down list
F10	Activate the menu bar
Alt+Enter	Display a window's Control menu.

Don't memorize this list! Instead, put a bookmark on this page and refer to it any time you want to make the mouse seethe with jealousy.

The Keyboard Follies

Keyboards aren't without their sticking points — and I don't mean what happens when you spill a cola in there. The following sections mull over some of the more trying times you may have with your PC keyboard.

"My keyboard beeps at me!"

Common problem. Many potential causes and cures.

Reason 1: You can't type anything! Whatever program you're using doesn't want you to type or expects you to be pressing some other key. Remember that in Windows you can only use one window at a time — even if you're looking at another window.

Reason 2: You're typing too fast. The PC's keyboard can only swallow so many keys at once. When its li'l stomach is full, it starts beeping at you until it can digest.

Reason 3: You have a keyboard beep feature turned on. Have your guru run your PC's Setup program to eliminate the beep. Or have him or her discover which program produces the beep and eliminate that.

Reason 4: The computer is dead! Refer to Chapter 2 for information on Restarting Windows.

"Oops! 1 just spilled java into the keyboard!"

Sooner or later, you'll spill something gross into the keyboard. The grossest liquids are thick or sugary: soft drinks, fruit juice, cheap sherry, or St. Bernard drool (not sugary, but thick). These things can seriously damage the keyboard. Here's what to do:

1. **Pick up the glass or push the St. Bernard out of the way.**
2. **Save your work (if the keyboard is still functional), turn off the computer, and unplug the keyboard.**
3. **Turn the keyboard upside down and give it a few good shakes (away from your coworkers' keyboards, if possible).**
4. **Use a sponge to sop up as much stuff as possible and then just let the keyboard dry out.**

   It usually takes about 24 hours.

Surprisingly enough, the keyboard will probably still work, especially if the beverage didn't contain much sugar. Unfortunately, it may not work. The keyboard contains special circuitry, and if that circuitry is damaged, you may need to buy yourself another keyboard. (At least that's cheaper than buying a whole new PC.)

Some companies sell plastic keyboard covers. These covers are custom fitted to the keyboard and work well. Smokers, especially, should consider purchasing one.

"Ouch! My wrists hurt!"

Repetitive anything can be bad: smoking, eating, drinking, running for Congress, and typing on your computer keyboard. This can be a serious problem, especially if you rely on your computer for your job.

Many typists suffer from something called Carpal Tunnel Syndrome, also called Repetitive Stress Injury (RSI).

RSI is a soreness caused when muscles rub against each other in a small wrist passage called the carpal tunnel (the names Lincoln Tunnel and Holland Tunnel are already copyrighted by the State of New York). The carpal tunnel collapses, changes from a horseshoe shape into something narrower that causes the muscles (tendons, actually) to rub.

Various solutions are available for this problem. Some sufferers wear expensive, reinforced gloves that, if they don't actually help alleviate the pain, at least draw sympathetic stares from onlookers. And crunching your wrist by squeezing your palm below the thumb and little finger can help. But the best thing to do is to avoid the problem in the first place.

Here are several things you can do to avoid RSI:

Get an ergonomic keyboard. Even if your wrists are as limber as rubber tree plants, you may want to consider an *ergonomic* keyboard. That type of keyboard is specially designed at an angle to relieve the stress of typing for long — or short — periods of time.

Use a wrist pad. Wrist pads elevate your wrists so that you type in a proper position, with your palms *above* the keyboard, not wresting below the spacebar. Remember Sister Mary Lazarus and how she whacked your slouching wrists? She was right!

Adjust your chair. Sit at the computer with your elbows level with your wrists.

Adjust your monitor. Your head should not tilt down or up when you view the computer screen. It should be straight ahead, which doesn't help your wrists as much as it helps your neck.

- ✔ Ergonomic keyboards cost a little more than standard keyboards, but they are well worth the investment if you type for long hours, or at least want to look like you type for long hours.

- ✔ Some mouse pads have built-in wrist elevators. These are great for folks who use mouse-intensive applications.

- ✔ Many keyboards come with adjustable legs underneath for positioning the keys to a comfortable angle.

TECHNICAL STUFF

For those forced to do math on the computer

Clustered around the numeric keypad, like campers roasting marshmallows around a fire, are various keys to help you work with numbers. Especially if you're dabbling with a spreadsheet or other number-crunching software, you'll find these keys come in handy. Take a look at your keyboard's numeric keypad right now just to reassure yourself.

What? You were expecting a ×_or + key? Forget it! This is a computer. It uses special oddball symbols for mathematical operations:

- ✔ + is for addition.
- ✔ - is for subtraction.
- ✔ * is for multiplication.
- ✔ / is for division.

The only strange symbol here is the asterisk for multiplication. Don't use the little X! It's not the same thing. The / (slash) is okay for division, but don't waste your time hunting for the ÷ symbol. It's not there.

Chapter 14

Adventures in Printerland

• •

• •

*I*f your computer were a theme park, then it would have to be divided into various "lands" (or "*lands" to use computer lingo). There would be Internetland, Hardwareland, LANland, I/Oland, Peripheraland, and so on. But would anyone really care about Printerland? Would it be too obscure? Not as useful as the attractions in Monitorland or the thrill rides in Keyboardland, Printerland would be noisy. And the guests would complain how the log ride used real ink that stained. Ugh.

Fortunately, the printer is not some obscure theme in an amusement part. There is no log ride, nor the kiddies' favorite Page Eject Drop of Doom. The printer lacks flash and rarely gets attention, but that just might be because it does its job without causing you much stress. Ahhhh . . . That's nice. No stress. Definitely not amusement park material.

Hello! I'm Mindy, and I'll Be Your Printer

Printers are devices that produce an image on paper. The image can be text or graphics, in color or in black ink. Using the printer is often the last step in creating something on the PC. It's the end result of your labors. Therefore, the image produced must be as good as possible.

Two major types of printers are popular today: *inkjet* and *laser.* The following sections discuss the merits of each and how they work.

- ✔ Printers are judged by the quality of image they produce.

- ✔ Printers are also judged by their price. Generally speaking, you can pay anywhere from just over $100 to thousands of dollars for a printer.

- ✔ Printers were once judged by their speed, but printer speed just isn't a big issue anymore.

- ✔ The printer produces *hard copy,* which is anything you do on your computer screen that eventually winds up on paper.

The Ever-Popular Inkjet Printer

Inkjet printers are the most popular type of computer printer sold today. They produce high-quality text or graphics on just about any type of paper. Some specialized inkjets are photo printers, capable of photographic quality output.

Figure 14-1 illustrates a typical inkjet printer, which looks a lot like my inkjet printer. I've flagged important things in the illustration.

Inkjet printers work by literally lobbing tiny balls of ink on paper. The teensy tiny ink balls stick to the paper, so this type of printer needs no ribbon or toner cartridge; the ink is jetted out directly, which is how the printer gets its name.

Inkjet printers come with both color and black inks. The ink is stored in tiny cartridges, typically one cartridge contains black ink and another contains three ink colors. Photo printers have one black ink cartridge and a color ink cartridge that contains four ink colors.

These printers are inexpensive, which is probably why they're so popular. The price range is from under $100 (which is still a good printer) to several hundred dollars, depending on what extra features you need. This price range is what makes the inkjet printer one of the best suited for any PC.

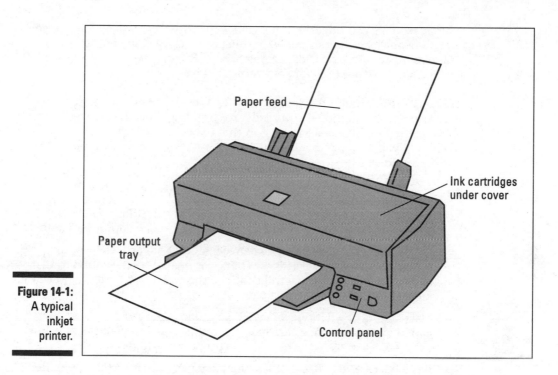

Paper feed

Ink cartridges under cover

Paper output tray

Figure 14-1:
A typical
inkjet
printer.

Control panel

✔ Inkjet printers are by no means messy. The ink is dry on the paper by the time the paper comes flopping out of the printer.

✔ Low-end inkjet printers cost less because they're dumb; they contain no internal electronics to help create the image. Instead, the computer is required to do the thinking, which slows things down a tad. When you pay more for an inkjet printer, the smarts are usually included with the printer (and the price).

✔ High-priced inkjet printers usually offer a higher quality output, faster speed, more printing options, the ability to print on larger sheets of paper, and other nifty options.

Going broke buying ink cartridges

Gillette made his fortune by giving away the razor and selling the blades. It was a brilliant idea, one that entrepreneurs have tried to emulate for over 100 years, with mixed results. Inkjet printers are one of the more successful emulations of Gillette's idea (though attempts to shave with an inkjet printer have proven futile). The inkjet printers themselves are cheap. Where you pay through the nose is for the ink cartridges.

Inkjets need ink cartridges to print. And when those cartridges run dry you must buy new ones. For example, printing a very large blue poster utterly drained the color ink cartridge on my printer. Replacement cost: $25. And that's cheap! I've paid $50 for some ink cartridges.

There's no way around this insanity, either. Where you could once abuse a typewriter ribbon until it was threadbare, your inkjet printer refuses to print if one of its ink cartridges is empty. Even if the color cartridge still has plenty of red and yellow ink, if the blue ink is low or missing, you must replace the entire cartridge.

✔ If possible, try to buy inkjet cartridges in bulk.

✔ Several online and mail-order dealers offer cheap prices on ink cartridges, better than you'll find locally or in an office supply superstore.

✔ Please do not respond to the spam e-mail that advertises low prices on replacement ink jet cartridges. The fewer people who respond to that spam, the less likely they will continue to send it out. (See Chapter 24 for more information on e-mail spam.)

✔ Make a note of what type of inkjet cartridges your printer uses. Keep the catalog number somewhere handy, such as taped to your inkjet printer's case, so you can always reorder the proper cartridge.

✔ If the ink cartridge has nozzles, then you can refill it on your own. Refill kits are sold everywhere, and they're cheaper than continually buying new cartridges. However, they work best if the cartridge has nozzles. If the cartridge is just a storage bin, then you're better off buying new ones.

✔ Always follow the instructions for changing cartridges carefully. Old cartridges can leak and get messy ink all over. I suggest having a paper towel handy and putting the used cartridge in a baggie while you walk to the trashcan.

✔ You don't always have to print in color with an inkjet printer! You can also just print in black ink, which saves the (often spendy) color cartridge from running low. The Print dialog box (covered later in this chapter) often has an option that lets you choose whether you want to print with color or black ink.

Buying special paper

Don't let the expensive paper ads fool you; your inkjet printer can print on just about any type of paper. Even so, the pricey paper *does* produce a better image.

My favorite type of inkjet paper is called *laser paper*. It has a polished look to it and a subtle waxy feel. Colors look better on this paper, and black-ink text documents have a much nicer feel than printing on regular photocopier paper.

The best (and most outrageously expensive) paper to buy is special photographic paper. Using this paper with your printer's high-quality mode prints color images that look just like photographs. But at $1 per sheet, this is the kind of paper that's best used for special occasions.

Another fun paper: iron-on transfer paper. With this paper, you can print an image (reversed) and then use an iron to *weld* that image to a T-shirt. This is popular for those "These are my grandkids" types of T-shirts you see fat guys wearing at the fair.

Laser Printers from Beyond Infinity

If inkjet printers are for fun, laser printers are for work. Used primarily in the office place, laser printers are great for producing both text and graphics, typically in black and white though color laser printers are available — and outrageously expensive.

Figure 14-2 illustrates a typical laser printer, which usually resembles a squat copy machine. Paper is fed into the printer via a tray. The paper scrolls through the printer, and the final result snakes out the top.

Laser printers work like photocopiers. The difference is that the computer creates the image and etches it using a laser beam instead of using a mirror and the magic moving bar of light.

Generally speaking, you'll pay more for a laser printer than you will for an inkjet. But for that money you get a faster printer, one that prints a higher quality image, and one that's less expensive to maintain; while toner drums are costly ($90 and up), they don't need replacement as often as ink cartridges.

✔ Laser printers make their images using heat. The laser beam etches an image on a *drum*. That drum is then dusted with something called *toner*. The toner sticks to the drum where the laser beam etched the image. The drum then rolls over the paper where a heated roller literally welds the image to the paper. The process is so ingenious you'd think aliens thought of it first, but they didn't.

✔ Be careful when changing toner cartridges! They're not as potentially messy as ink cartridges (which can leak), but if dropped or damaged, the toner cartridges can leak dusty toner. The toner gets everywhere, and it's not the most healthy substance.

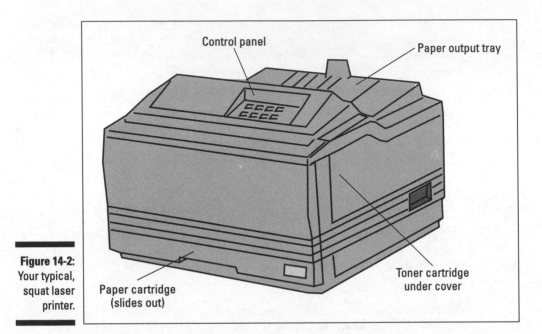

Control panel

Paper output tray

Figure 14-2:
Your typical,
squat laser
printer.

Paper cartridge
(slides out)

Toner cartridge
under cover

Examining Your Printer's Control Panel

Every printer has a control panel. The fancy models have LCD screens that display lots of text: `Printer jammed; I'm out of paper; That's plagiarism;` and so on. Other printers, less fancy, may just have an on-off button and a page eject button. Whatever; look at your printer's panel now.

You should locate two things on the panel:

✓ The on-line or select button

✓ The form feed button

The purpose of the on-line or select button is to tell your printer whether or not to ignore the computer. When the printer is off-line or deselected, the computer can't print. You would take the printer off-line if, for example, you had to un-jam it or if you wanted to eject a page of paper.

The form feed button is often necessary to eject a page of paper from the printer. Right now I can't think of any specific instances when you'd need to do that, but I know I've had to write about it enough that it's not a blue-moon type of activity.

✔ The computer can print only when the printer is on-line or selected.

✔ My inkjet printer has only two buttons, on-line and form feed. You can carry out other printer functions by using a special dialog box in Windows.

✔ Some laser printers may have an on-line button but no form feed button. In that case, you need to refer to your printer's manual for information on doing a form feed, which involves choosing a menu item or pressing a combination of keys somehow.

✔ Speaking of manuals, it's a good idea to keep your printer's manual handy. You may never read it, but if your printer suddenly pops up and displays Error 34, you can look up what Error 34 is in the manual and read how to fix it. (This is the voice of experience talking here.)

Setting Up Your Beloved Printer

Printers are one of the easiest devices to set up and configure.

1. **Turn everything off: computer, printer, everything.**

2. **Plug the printer into the PC's console.**

   Start with the printer cable. Oops! The printer didn't come with a cable? Ugh. You need to buy a cable.

   Plug one end of the cable into the printer, the other goes into the computer's *printer port*. If you have a USB printer, then plug the USB cable into your console's USB port.

   The cable has different ends, so you can't screw anything up.

3. **Plug the printer into the proper power socket.**

   Do not plug the printer into a UPS. And you should plug laser printers directly into the wall, not into a power strip or UPS. See Chapter 2 for more information.

There. You're done with hardware installation.

✔ Placing your printer somewhere within arm's reach of your PC helps.

✔ If your PC has more than one printer port, plug your printer into LPT1, the first printer port.

✔ Some USB printers demand to be directly connected to the computer, not plugged into a USB hub.

- A single computer is capable of handling two printers. You need a second printer port on your PC, but you must have a terribly big ego to be that possessive.

- If you have some type of device (CD-R/RW, DVD, scanner, or whatever) connected to your PC's printer port, then you need to plug the printer into that device and not into the console directly. The device will have two connectors on its rump. One is labeled for the cable that goes to the console; the other is labeled for the printer.

Loading it with paper

Stick a ream of paper into your printer. Yes, your printer needs paper. The days of printing on thin air and magic tablets are still in the future.

For inkjet printers, load the paper in the tray, either near the printer's bottom or sticking out the top.

Laser printers require you to fill a cartridge with paper, similar to the way a copy machine works. Slide the cartridge all the way into the printer after it's loaded up.

- Always make sure that you have enough printer paper.

- You can buy standard photocopier paper for your printer.

- Some printers are capable of handling larger-sized paper, such as legal or tabloid sizes. If so, make sure you load the paper properly and tell Windows or your application that you're using a different-sized sheet of paper.

- Check your printer to see how the paper goes in, either face down or face up. And note which side is the top. This info helps you when loading things such as checks for use with personal finance software. (See the section "Important Printer Points to Ponder" at the end of this chapter.)

- Avoid using erasable bond and other fancy dusted papers in your laser printer. These papers have talcum powder coatings that come off in your laser printer and gum up the works.

Loading it with ink (or the ink substance)

Before you can print, you need to infuse your printer with the inky substance.

Inkjet printers use little ink cartridges. Carefully unwrap the foil around the new cartridge. Remove any tape or covering, per the package's instructions. And insert the ink cartridge into the printer, again following the instructions for your specific ink printer.

Laser printers require drop-in toner cartridges. They're easy to install and come with their own handy instructions. Just don't breathe in the toner or you'll die. Some manufacturers sell their cartridges with return envelopes so you can send the old cartridge back to the factory for recycling or proper disposal.

✔ I suggest buying rubber gloves (or those cheap plastic gloves that make you look like Batman) and using them when changing a ribbon or toner cartridge.

✔ Another option for an old toner cartridge is recharging. You can take it to a special place that will clean the old cartridge and refill it with toner. This process actually works and is often cheaper than buying a whole new cartridge.

Telling Windows about Your Printer (Software Installation)

Most likely, you set up Windows to work with your printer when you first brought your PC home. One of the first setup questions Windows asks is, "Which printer are you using?" and you, or someone else, followed the steps and chose the proper printer. No sweat.

If you just bought a new printer, however, you need to set up that one manually. Connect your printer to the PC if you haven't already (see "Setting Up Your Beloved Printer," earlier in this chapter). Make sure that your printer is on, loaded with paper, and ready to print. Then tell Windows all about your printer by heeding these steps:

1. **Open the Printers folder.**

   This is done by choosing Settings⇨Printers from the Start menu. The Printers folder window lists all the printers you may already have connected to your PC, network printers, plus the holy Add Printer icon.

   In Windows XP, choose the Control Panel from the Start menu and then click the Printers and Other Hardware link. Click the Add a Print task and skip to Step 3.

2. **Open the Add Printer icon.**

Add Printer

   Double-click the Add Printer icon to open it.

   Look, Ma! It's the Add Printer Wizard!

3. **Click the Next button.**

The steps that follow vary, depending on your version of Windows. Here's my advice:

- Only select the network printer option if you're on a network. In that case, it's probably best to ask your network guru for help on this (though it's rather easy if you're used to using the network in Windows).

- Windows may be able to automatically detect your printer, especially if you're using a USB printer. Otherwise, you need to know the printer's manufacturer and model number. You pick both of those items from a dialog box the Wizard presents.

- You also need to know how the printer connects to the computer. As stated earlier in this chapter, that's most often through the printer port LPT1.

- Windows may ask for its distribution CD to load the printer driver files. If you don't have the CD, then try using the location `C:\Windows\Options\CABS`. Windows may be able to find the files there.

- If your printer came with its own CD, you may need to install programs from that CD to begin or finish the printer installation. Refer to the documentation that came with the CD.

4. **The final installation step is to print a test page on your printer.**

Personally, I'm shocked that the test page isn't a catalog and order form for Microsoft products. But it ensures that your printer is connected properly and everything is up to snuff. It's very gratifying to see that page print.

Basic Printer Operation

Here are the steps required to turn on your printer:

1. **Flip the switch.**

- Always make sure that your printer is on before you start printing. Like, duh.

- Your laser printer doesn't need to be on all the time. Laser printers draw lots of power when they're on, even more when they're printing. Unless you have one of those power-saving laser printers, only turn on your laser printer when you need to print.

- You can leave inkjet printers on all the time because they don't use much power.

Printing something, anything

Under Windows, printing is a snap. All applications support the same print command: Choose File⇨Print from the menu, click OK in the Print dialog box, and — zit-zit-zit — you soon have hard copy.

- ✔ The common keyboard shortcut for the print command is Ctrl+P.
- ✔ Many applications sport a Print toolbar icon. If so, you can click that button to quickly print your document.
- ✔ The Print toolbar icon does not summon the Print dialog box. It just prints the entire document. To summon the Print dialog box, you must use Ctrl+P or choose File⇨Print from the menu.
- ✔ It's usually a good idea to preview your printing before you condemn even more of our North American forests to death. Many Windows programs have a File⇨Print Preview command that lets you pore over the page before it's splattered all over a tree slice. Save an owl (or something like that).

I want to print sideways

Printing on a sheet of paper long-ways is called printing in the *landscape* mode. Almost all Windows programs have this option.

From the Print dialog box, click the Properties button. Click the Paper tab in your printer's Properties dialog box, as shown in Figure 14-3. Click the Landscape option. Click OK to close the dialog box, and then click OK in the Print dialog box to print in the landscape mode.

- ✔ In Windows XP, click the Preferences button in the Print dialog box. Then use the Layout tab to set the paper's orientation.
- ✔ Some programs may not use the Paper tab in the printer's Properties dialog box. For example, in Microsoft Word, it's the File⇨Page Setup command, Paper Size panel. Whatever.

Once is not enough

Q: In your book you say that you should recharge a used laser toner cartridge only once. This isn't so. Today's modern toner recharging methods allow you to reuse one cartridge several times.

A: I stand corrected. At $120 for a new cartridge, recharging is a handy and inexpensive option.

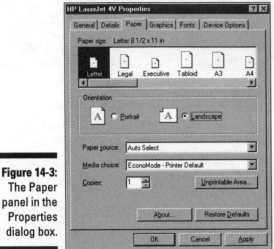

Figure 14-3:
The Paper
panel in the
Properties
dialog box.

Printing the screen

Even though the keyboard has a button named Print Screen, it won't send a copy of the screen to the printer. At least not directly. If you really need a printed copy of the Windows desktop or some window on the screen, follow these steps:

1. **Arrange the screen so that it looks the way you want it printed.**

2a. **If you want a snapshot of the whole screen, press the Print Screen key.**

2b. **If you want a snapshot of only the top window on the screen, press Alt+Print Screen.**

3. **Open the Paint program.**

   From the Start menu, choose Programs➪Accessories➪Paint.

   The Paint program appears on the screen.

4. **Choose Edit➪Paste.**

   This action pastes the image into the Paint program.

   If a warning dialog box tells you the image is too big, click the Yes button.

5. **Print the image.**

   Choose File➪Print to summon the Print dialog box.

6. **Click OK to start printing.**

If the image is very large, you might want to take advantage of the File⇨ Print Preview command. It shows you how the final image will look, as well as how many pages it will print on (if it's incredibly huge).

Feeding an envelope

To stick an envelope into your printer, just shove it into the special slot. Oftentimes you must open a hatch on the front of the computer to reveal the slot. A special illustration on the hatch tells you which way to place the envelope: face up or down, and top right or top left. Then you tell your software to print the envelope and — *thwoop!* — there it goes and comes back again, complete with a nifty address.

✔ Obviously, feeding an envelope to a printer is different for each type of printer.

✔ Pay attention to how the envelope feeds in. Does it go in long-ways or wide-ways, up or down, top or bottom?

✔ Also obviously: Each program has a different command for printing envelopes. Typically, you have to tell the program how the envelope goes into your printer so that it knows in which direction to print the address.

✔ Some printers require you to press the On-line or Select button to print the envelope. For example, on my printer I set up everything and stick the envelope in the hatch, and then I print with my software. After a few seconds, the printer's display says, "Me feed!" which I properly interpret to mean, "Press my On-line button, doofus!" which I do, and then the thing prints.

Important Printer Points to Ponder

Printers don't come with cables! You must buy the cable in addition to the printer.

The printer cable can be no more than 20-feet long. That length is ridiculous, of course, because the best place for your printer is within arm's reach. (USB cables can be no longer than about 12 feet.)

Printers don't come with paper. Always buy the proper paper for your printer. And stock up on it, too; go to one of those discount paper warehouse places and buy a few boxes.

Never let your printer toner get low or ink cartridges go dry. You may think squeezing every last drop of ink saves you money, but it's not good for the printer.

Laser printers sometimes show a *toner low* light or warning message. When you first see it, you can take the toner out of the printer and rock it from side to side. Doing so redistributes the toner and gets more mileage from it. But you can do it only once! Replace the old toner as soon as you see the *toner low* light again.

Inkjet printers generally warn you that the ink cartridge is low, either on their panel or on your computer's screen. Change the ink cartridge at once! Some printers are really stubborn about this.

Most printers have little pictures on them that tell you how the paper goes into the printer. Here is how those symbols translate into English:

- ✔ The paper goes in face down, top side up.
- ✔ The paper goes in face down, top side down.
- ✔ The paper goes in face up, top side up.
- ✔ The paper goes in face up, top side down.

If one side of the paper has an arrow, it usually indicates whether the top side is up or down. Then again, this could all be wrong, and what they're telling us is that we need to start using stone tablets all over again.

Chapter 15

The Very Model of a Modern Modem

Computer communications have come a long way. Modems were once options and considered a pricey peripheral. Not any more! Recently I ordered a PC without a modem, and the dealer thought I was nuts. O, how times have changed!

This is your modem chapter. It's a hardware chapter, because the software side of using a modem is all Internet, Internet, Internet, which I cover in Part V of this book. This chapter explains modem mania without getting lost in the jumbled jungle of jargon that confounds computer communications.

What Does a Modem Do?

Poetically, a modem takes the rude ones and zeros of computer language and translates them into tones, literally singing binary information over the phone lines to other modems. The other modems then take the song and translate it back into ones and zeros for the other computers.

Scientifically, the modem takes digital information from your computer and translates it into analog signals (sounds) that can be sent over common phone lines. Converting the digital information into analog is called *modulation*. Converting back the other way is *demodulation*. So a modem is a MOdulator-DEModulator.

- ✔ You (the human) don't actually use the modem directly. Instead, communications software is responsible for sending and receiving information using the modem.

- ✔ The communications software dials the modem, connects with another modem, and then gets the two computers to talk.

- ✔ Most modems plug into serial ports. This is true even if you have an internal modem. Refer to Chapter 9 for the lowdown on ports.

- ✔ Some high-speed modems pretend that they are plugged into your computer's networking hardware. This sounds complex, but it's a faster way to communicate with the computer.

- ✔ There are more modem jokes in the computer world than anything else, typically with the punch line, "How many *modem* do you want?"

Modem Features

A bazillion different types of modems are available — internal and external models, models with different speeds and features, different brand names, and prices from super cheap to down-payment-on-a-house expensive. It's modem madness!

Does it live inside or outside the computer?

Modems come in two main breeds:

Internal: This type of modem fits inside your computer console. It's the most common breed, because most computers are sold with internal modems preinstalled.

External: This type of modem lives in its own box that sits outside your computer console. It exists primarily as an upgrade for earlier, noninternal modem bearing computers.

Both types work in exactly the same way; the external modem just has a little plastic box housing the mechanism, plus an extra power cord and cable connecting it to a serial port.

✔ Internal modems are cheaper. They plug into an expansion slot inside your computer. The back of the card is visible at the back of your computer; that's where its phone lines plug in and hang out.

✔ External modems cost more because you have to pay for their plastic box. You also have to buy a serial cable to connect it to your PC's serial port.

Normally I would list the plusses and minuses of each modem type here, but because internal modems are pretty much The Standard, there's no need to blather on about any differences. For posterity, know that I love external modems more than internal. Heck, I still have all my external modems and they all still work. So there!

I feel the need for speed

Just as some computers are faster than others, some modems are faster than others. But all modems are relatively compatible: The fastest modems can still talk to the slower ones.

Most modems sold today run along at a 56K clip, where K is kilobits per second or how many bits a modem can squirt through the phone line in one second. Slower modems are out there, and just because the modem is capable of 56K doesn't mean you'll always connect at that speed. For example, most AOL connections run at 28K maximum.

✔ To go faster than 56K, you need a type of modem that doesn't use standard phone lines, such as a DSL, cable modem, or some other expensive and terrifying technology. See the section "The merry land of modems," later in this chapter, for the full details.

✔ Modem speed is measured in kilobits per second. Most people use the term "K" as the speed rating, or often Kbps. In the olden days "bps" was the rating, but because modern modems run at 1000's of bps, the K was adopted instead.

✔ That's not the same K as used to measure memory or disk size. A 100KB file is 100 kilobytes or approximately 100,000 bytes in size.

✔ You're probably reading this sentence at what would be equivalent to 300 bps (.3K). But at that slow speed, downloading a Web page would take several minutes.

✔ Windows tells you the modem's connection speed whenever a connection is made. You'll note that the speed is always less than the modem is physically capable of. That lower speed is due to the phone line conditions and general shape of the connection. Sometimes it will be good and fast, other times it will be slower. There is generally nothing you can do to improve the speed (despite all the ads on the Internet to the contrary).

✔ Some people use the word *baud* to describe modem speed. That's inaccurate. The correct term is bps. Correct them enthusiastically if you want to sound like a true computer geek.

"What is this fax-modem thing?"

Modem developers noticed the similarity between modem technology and fax machine technology several years back. They could easily combine the two, and the result was called a *fax modem*.

With the proper software, a fax modem can communicate not only with other PCs and modems, but also with fax machines. It was a glorious day for the computing masses back then.

Today, nearly all modems have the ability to send or receive a fax. It's like having automatic transmission in your car; it's just not a big enough deal to brag about any more.

To use your modem like a fax machine, you need special fax software. Some versions of Windows come with a program called Microsoft Fax to do the job. Fortunately, your modem probably came with special fax software that's (I'll bet a billion dollars) much, much easier to understand and use than anything Microsoft could dream up.

The merry land of modems

Long ago there were only two kinds of modem: smart and dumb. I'm not making that up!

Modems were called *smart* if they could dial the phone and answer and if software could control them.

Dumb modems (and this term truly opens up a can of worms) were simple devices usually controlled by two or more switches. You would manually dial a phone number, and then turn on the modem or put the telephone handset into a cradle. Dumb. Dumb. Dumb.

Today, all modems are smart. But within the smart-modem world different types of modems are available. Some are designed to operate a certain way, and others require a special service to utilize their extra speed. Here's the short list, and a summary appears in Table 15-1:

Typical, standard modem. Standard, off-the-shelf modems can connect to your existing phone system. The price varies with the speed; the current top speed of 56K costs you anywhere from $50 to $150, depending on the modem's make and model.

WinModem. This type of modem contains no real smarts. Instead, the computer does the processing. This may sound like a lot of overhead, but the advantage is that you can upgrade the modem's smarts using software. Buying a new modem is a thing of the past; just upgrade the soft-modem software, and you have a brand new modem. Or so they say.

ISDN modem. The next step up from the traditional modem is the ISDN model. It requires that you have ISDN service, which your phone company can install (and gladly charge you for), and it's available almost everywhere. Beyond that you need an ISDN modem, which more than doubles the speed of your Internet connection.

DSL modem. This type of modem gives you fast access by taking advantage of unused frequencies in the phone line, like those pauses when your teenager is saying, "I dunno, what do you want to do?" Aside from limited availability, the only drawback is that you must be within a few miles of the phone company's main office to get DSL service. Oh, and it's expensive, too. And if it breaks, it takes the phone company a long, long time to fix it. (Actually, the phone company and your ISP bicker about who's job it is to fix things.)

Satellite modem. Combined with an outdoor antenna and a subscription to the satellite service, this is one of the fastest modem options available. In some configurations, the modem provides both sending and receiving abilities. In other configurations, the satellite only sends information from the Internet; you still need a standard phone-line modem to send information to the Internet.

Make 'em all jealous with a T1 line!

The fastest of the fastest ways to connect your computer to the Internet is the T1 line. This is a dedicated digital phone line that the phone company connects directly to your home or office.

T1 comes in speeds from 56K on up to about 1,500K, but it comes at a price. Not only do you need to pay for the T1 line (both to the phone company and your Internet Service Provider),

but you'll also need a special piece of hardware called a router and a dedicated computer or "server" to handle the whole job. This is a lot of work and expense, but if you want to drive the Cadillac of Internet connections, it's the way to go.

Faster than the T1 is the T3, though this type of connection is used primarily by big businesses or Internet Service Providers themselves.

Cable modem. This type of modem is the fastest you can buy, often faster than the computer can keep up with! Two ugly downsides: You need to live in an area serviced by a cable company that offers cable-modem access, and when more of your neighbors begin using their cable modems, the overall speed decreases. But at 2:00 a.m., your cable modem *smokes!*

- The plain old telephone system modem is also known as a POTS modem. POTS is Plain Old Telephone System.

- ISDN stands for Integrated Services Digital Network.

- Another advantage of ISDN is that you can often receive faxes and use a standard telephone on the same line as your modem connection.

- DSL stands for Digital Subscriber Line. There are variations, such as ADSL and other *something*-DSL options. Your phone company knows more about this than I do.

- ISDN, xDSL, satellite, and cable services charge you additional fees for connecting. So in addition to paying more for a fancy modem plus paying for Internet access, you must pay for the connection.

Table 15-1	Comparison of Modems, Price, and Speed	
Modem Type	*Average Price*	*Speed (in bps)*
Standard	$80	56K
Soft modem	$140	56K
ISDN modem	$300	128K up to 512K
Satellite modem	$300	512K
DSL modem	$400	8,000K
Cable modem	$180	30,000K

Connecting Your Modem

Setting up a modem is so easy a 65-year-old retired male doctor could do it. The following sections tell you how.

- The best way to use a modem is with its own phone line. Just about every house or apartment has the ability to have a second line added without paying for extra wiring. If so, have the phone company hook that line up and use it for your modem. Why? Because . . .

✔ You can't use your phone while your modem is talking. In fact, if somebody picks up another extension on that line, it garbles the signal, possibly losing your connection — not to mention that he or she hears a horrid screeching sound. By the way . . .

✔ To disable Call Waiting, you must prefix every number the modem dials with *70, (or whatever the command is to disable Call Waiting for your phone company). That's asterisk, 70 and a comma. So if you're dialing 555-1234, you need to enter *70,555-1234 as the phone number. (The comma provides a pause in the dialing command, so if you need a longer pause just add a second or third comma.)

Hooking up your modem

In the best of worlds — the one where blue birds help get you dressed in the morning — someone else has installed your modem. Your job is merely to connect it to the wall.

Figure 15-1 shows what the back of the internal modem may look like. Two phone jacks are there. Plug one end of the phone cable into the Line hole. Plug the other end of the phone cable into the wall jack.

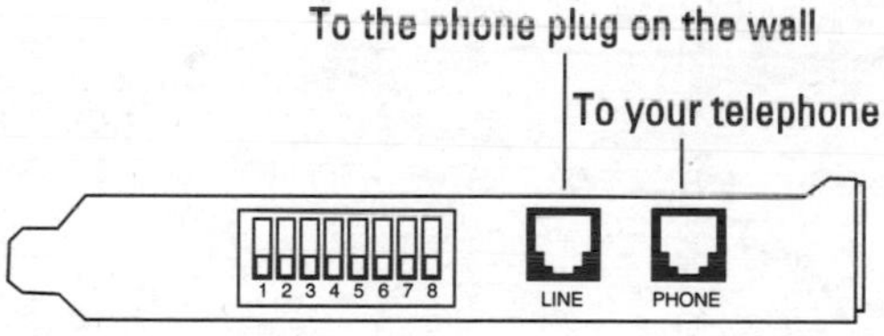

To the phone plug on the wall

To your telephone

Figure 15-1:
Important
stuff on the
back of an
internal
modem.

LINE   PHONE

If the internal modem has only one phone jack, well then by-golly it plugs into the wall.

It doesn't matter which end of the phone cord goes into the wall or modem; plugging in a modem is just like plugging in a phone. If a phone is already plugged into the wall, unplug it. Then plug it into the Phone hole in the back of your modem.

✔ How do you know you got things right? Try it! If the modem doesn't dial out, then just swap the cords.

✔ These instructions apply to a standard modem. If you have a cable modem, DSL, or other fancy modem, then you'll most likely have someone else set it up for you.

✔ External modems also require that you connect the modem to the computer's COM1 or COM2 port using a serial cable (which you have to buy extra). Additionally, the external modem must also be plugged into a wall socket.

Telling Windows about your modem

After setting up your modem, you must tell Windows about it. This task isn't as painful as it used to be; Open the Control Panel's Modems icon. You'll see the Modems Properties dialog box, as shown in Figure 15-2.

Click the Add button and then work through the wizard to have it detect and install your modem. My advice is to *not* have Windows automatically detect your modem; just select it from the list of manufacturers and models.

In addition to running the wizard, you also need to install your modem's software. This comes on a CD that accompanied the modem in the box. Stick the CD into the CD-ROM drive and heed whatever instructions it offers.

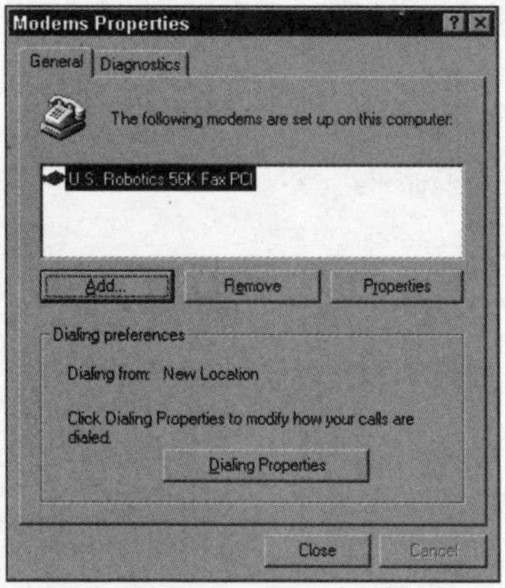

Figure 15-2:
Tell
Windows
all about
your new
modem in
the Modems
Properties
dialog box.

In continuing its fine tradition of doubling the typical number of steps to accomplish anything, Windows XP has you get to the Modems Properties dialog box via this strange path: Choose the Control Panel from the Start menu. Click the Network and Internet Connections item. Click Phone and Modem Options. Click the Modem tab in the Phone and Modem Options dialog box. From there you can click the Add button to add a new modem. (And Windows XP is supposed to make things easier. Yeah. Right.)

Some Modem Hints

People who tell you that they don't have any problems with their modems are either lying or trying to sell you one (or both). There's probably a specific psychological term called *modem woe*. I'm certain of it.

The following sections should provide you with some instant modem relief. If not, refer to Chapter 27 for information on running the Modem Troubleshooter in Windows.

Making the modem appear even when Windows doesn't see it

If Windows ever loses track of the modem (which happens often), don't despair. Just try again and Windows will magically seem to find the modem.

- ✔ Don't blame yourself when this happens.

- ✔ If you have an external modem, double-check to make sure that it's turned on before you dial. (Sometimes this "modem's not there" problem happens when you turn an external modem off and on again.)

Dealing with "local" long distance

The phone companies seem to delight in forcing us to dial our own area codes for *local long distance*. This requirement goofs up some modem programs, which assume that because the number is in your area code, it's not long distance!

To get Windows to believe local long distance isn't local, open the Modems Properties dialog box as described earlier in this chapter. Click the Dialing Properties button, and then click the Area Code Rules button. You'll be presented with the Area Code Rules dialog box, where you can tell stupid old Windows when to dial the area code, when to prefix 1 to a "local" long distance number, and other mayhem.

In Windows XP, click the Dialing Rules tab in the Phone and Modem Options dialog box. Use the Edit button to change the rules for dialing long distance and local long distance numbers for the highlighted location in the dialog box.

It dials too fast!

Modems dial phone numbers all by themselves. They can dial slow. They can dial fast. But that's not a problem. What can be a problem is when you need to dial a 9 or an 8 before the phone number to get an outside line. That means Mr. Modem should wait after the 9 or 8 before dialing the number, or you end up connecting with the nice lady who tells you that if you can't use a phone, you may as well run away from civilization and start herding yaks.

To slow down your modem after it dials an 8 or 9 to get an outside line, add a comma after the 8 or 9 in the number you dial. For example:

```
8,11-202-555-7892
```

The preceding number is what I would dial to connect with the Pentagon's war room. But because my hotel in Minsk has a slow connection, I stuck a comma after the 8.

Changing your location for a laptop

If you use a laptop PC on the road, you need to tell Windows about your new location so that it can dial the modem properly from wherever you are.

1. **Display the Modems Properties dialog box.**

   Instructions for doing this are listed earlier in this chapter.

2. **Click the Dialing Properties button.**

3. **Click the New button.**

   The words New Location appear in the I Am Dialing From text box.

4. **Type in a name for wherever you are.**

   For example, when I visit San Diego, I have a separate entry for the Hilton (out by the beach) and my mom's house (in El Cajon).

5. **Type the area code, the country, and other vital stats for your remote location.**

   Here you're telling Windows just how to dial different phone numbers from that new location. (Windows is smart and knows about long distance and the like.)

6. **Click OK to save the information to disk.**

The next time you use the Dialing Properties dialog box, you can select any of your locations from the I Am Dialing From drop-down list. That way you don't have to reenter information every time you're on the road.

✔ Okay, Windows XP again. To set a new location, summon the Phone and Modem Options dialog box, described earlier in this chapter. Then, you can continue with Step 3 above.

✔ You use the Dialing Properties dialog box whenever you use Windows to dial the modem. This can be for an Internet connection or a local system.

✔ By telling Windows the area code and location from which you're calling (plus the other information), you save yourself from having to re-input that information each time you visit that location.

✔ Save the Default Location item for wherever your laptop is most of the time.

Chapter 16

The Hills Are Alive with the Sounds of PC

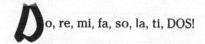o, re, mi, fa, so, la, ti, DOS!

Even though the first IBM PC had a speaker, it could only *BEEP*. Games could play silly songs but nothing symphonic. Fortunately, a few companies began creating *sound cards,* mostly so game players could hear music and primitive space grunts. Then, over time, the sound circuitry became part of the motherboard. Throw in a pair of stereo speakers and a subwoofer, and you have the melodic PC of today.

This is your PC sound chapter. Face it, sound is *fun!* Of course, you can tut-tut yourself and claim that you use sound for *business presentations* and *educational uses,* but what you really want to hear is the *THWOK!* as the club makes perfect contact with the ball in the famous Microsoft Golf game.

Sound in Your PC

All PCs have built-in sound circuitry. You'd have to set the Way-Back-Machine for 1993 or so to find a soundless PC. And the sound circuitry offered today is good stuff. The only time you'll need better sound equipment is if you plan on doing professional, studio-quality audio. Even then, all you need is a professional-level sound card (and the expensive software to drive it).

"How can I tell if my PC has sound?"

Too many people write me questions about whether or not their computer can bleep and squawk with a sound card. How can you tell if your sound card is installed? Easy: Look 'round back.

Your PC should have sound connectors on its rump if it has a sound card installed. You should be able to find three tiny jacks — called mini-din; they accept tiny ⅛ inch audio plugs. The jacks are labeled Mic, Line In, Line Out, or Speakers.

If your PC has the jacks, then it can produce sound. Whether the sound is working at that point is a software problem. (You should check with your computer dealer if you still can't hear the sound.)

If there are two sets of sound jacks, then the second set usually appears on an expansion card, either a high-octane music card or the DVD expansion card. Use that set.

The sound card

When your PC has a sound card, either an expansion card or circuitry on the motherboard, it's capable of doing more than beeping through the speaker.

The first thing the sound card does is to play *wave sounds,* which are the recorded sounds you hear when you turn on the computer or run a program. These are also the sounds you hear when you play a computer game: a ding-dong for a correct answer, the sound of your opponent going "ouch," or the sound of spent 9mm shells hitting a concrete floor. They're all wave sounds.

The second thing most sound cards can do is play music. Included with the basic audio circuitry is a complete musical synthesizer. You can use this synthesizer to play MIDI files, which produce near-realistic music over the PC's speakers.

Finally, sound cards amplify and play music from your computer's CD-ROM drive.

- With a microphone and the proper software, you can also use the PC's sound card to record your own voice. See the section, "Recording your voice," later in this chapter for more information.

- To use the sound card you need to have sounds to play. Most of these sounds are included in game programs, which take the best advantage of your PC's sound hardware. Otherwise, you can create your own sound files or download them from the Internet.

✔ By the way, sound files takes up huge amounts of room on a disk. That's why most digitized sounds are limited to short bursts like golf swings and grunts.

✔ Wave sounds are saved as WAV files.

Speakers

Your computer needs speakers so that you can hear the sounds the sound card makes. Most PCs come with speakers or offer them as options. If not, buying a set of speakers with a subwoofer costs $80 or more at your local computer or office supply store.

✔ The quality of the speakers really isn't important. Unless you're a die-hard audiophile, I see no point in spending too much money on PC speakers. However, I do recommend external speakers over the built-into-the-monitor type. The quality is better.

✔ It's best to run your speakers electrically instead of through batteries. If your speakers didn't come with an AC power adapter, you can usually buy one.

✔ Subwoofers? These boxes sit on the floor beneath your PC and amplify sounds at the low-end of the spectrum. They really give oomph to the bass in music, and the thud of your enemy dropping in a game has all the more impact. I recommend them!

✔ If you put speakers on your desk, remember that they contain magnets. If any stray floppy disks come too close, especially behind the speakers, then they will lose data.

Having Fun with Sound in Windows

If you have time to waste, you can turn your smart business computer into a goofy business computer by adding sounds to Windows. I'm not going into any detail here, because this is an area wide open for play. But I will show you the playground.

The sound playground

Sound central in Windows is the Sounds and Multimedia Properties dialog box, which you can get to from any Control Panel near you. Here's how:

1. **Open the Control Panel's Sounds and Multimedia icon.**

   From the Start menu, choose Settings➪Control Panel. Then double-click to open the Sounds and Multimedia icon.

In Windows 98, the icon is named Sounds.

In Windows XP, click the Sounds, Speech and Audio Devices link, and then click the task "Change the sound scheme."

However you get there, a sound-setting dialog box is revealed, which looks similar to Figure 16-1.

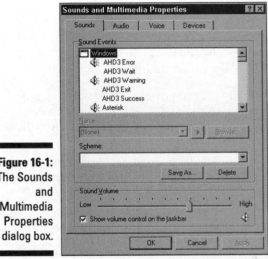

Figure 16-1:
The Sounds
and
Multimedia
Properties
dialog box.

2. **Mess around.**

The dialog box sports a list of events, which are various things done by Windows or your applications. You can apply a specific sound to any of those events.

For example, scroll down to the New Mail Notification item. That's where you can tell Windows to play a sound when you have new mail (in Outlook Express). To assign a new sound, highlight that item and use the drop-down list to pluck out a new sound, or use the Browse button to hunt for a sound in a specific location on the hard drive.

The little triangle "play" button is used to play the sound.

To remove a sound from an event, choose (None) from the top of the scrolling list.

3. **Fiddle and have fun!**

4. **Click OK to get back to work.**

Windows comes with several sets of preassigned sound schemes. You can choose them from the Scheme drop-down list, or you can save your own custom sound scheme by using the Save As button.

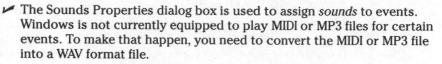

- ✔ If you can't find an event in the list, you cannot assign a sound to it.

- ✔ The Sounds Properties dialog box is used to assign *sounds* to events. Windows is not currently equipped to play MIDI or MP3 files for certain events. To make that happen, you need to convert the MIDI or MP3 file into a WAV format file.

- ✔ The best source for sounds is the Internet, where there are Web page libraries full of sound samples.

- ✔ Don't be embarrassed when you call tech support for some reason, and each time that they tell you to open this or that window, Mary Poppins says, "Spit-spot?"

- ✔ See the section "Recording your voice" for more information about recording sounds.

- ✔ When you eventually have your own set of eclectic-but-important-to-you sounds, save them as a Scheme. That way you can instantly restore the sound settings by using the Scheme drop-down list, where your scheme shows up in the list along with Windows' own schemes.

Playing sounds

It's easy to play any sound file in Windows, whether it's a WAV, MIDI, MP3 file or whatever: just double-click to open the file and the sound plays.

The program that plays the sounds is the Windows Media Player, unless you've installed anything better than that on your own. Figure 16-2 shows the Windows Media Player, which may look different on your computer. (It's one of the most changeable programs in Windows; use the Skin Chooser button to see what I mean.)

I won't go into any detail here on the Media Player or any of its several hundred options; it's one program that truly encourages play.

- ✔ Consider creating Playlists of music (or sound files) you like to hear. Click the Media Library button and heed the instructions to create your own library list.

- ✔ Some versions of Windows keep music files in the My Music folder, which can be found inside the My Documents folder. This is where most of the music files you download from the Internet will be saved, although I do encourage you to create even more folders within the My Music folder for specific categories or "albums" of music.

- ✔ MP3 is a special wave file format that plays high-quality music on your PC's speakers. See Chapter 25 for information on obtaining MP3 files from the Internet.

✔ MIDI stands for Musical Instrument Digital Interface. It's the standard for recording electronic music.

✔ MIDI files don't contain recorded music. Instead, the files contain notes plus information about the instruments that play those notes. In a way, the MIDI file "plays" the synthesizer on your PC's sound card.

✔ Using the proper software, plus maybe some MIDI musical instruments, you can create your own MIDI files.

Recording your voice

If you hook up a microphone to your PC, you can record your voice. Aside from the microphone, you need software. Recording software may have come with your PC or sound card, or you can use a Windows program called Sound Recorder.

For most versions of Windows, start the Sound Recorder from the Start menu by choosing Programs⇨Accessories⇨Entertainment⇨Sound Recorder.

In Windows XP, from the Start menu choose More Programs⇨Accessories⇨ Entertainment⇨Sound Recorder.

The Sound Recorder's window appears, as shown in Figure 16-3.

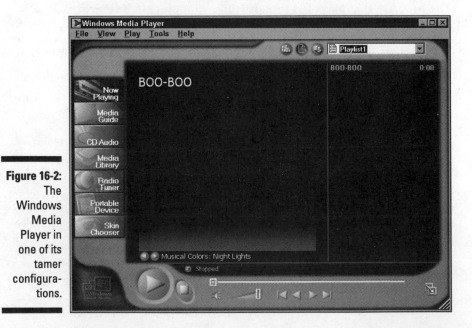

Figure 16-2:
The Windows Media Player in one of its tamer configurations.

Why are MP3 files so big?

Q: There is something that I don't understand. Why are MIDI files smaller than MP3 files, even though the MIDI files play about as long as the MP3 files? Isn't MP3 newer and more compressed? So why is it so big? A three-minute MP3 file is about 3MB, but a similar MIDI file is only 30KB. I am very confused.

A: A MIDI file merely contains instructions to play the PC's internal synthesizer. You know:

"Play D# for .125 seconds," which is only about four bytes of code. The MP3 files, however, are compressed audio recordings that play back through the speakers. Typically MP3 files are 1MB for each minute of sound — which is actually fairly good when compared with other sound file formats.

Figure 16-3:
The Sound
Recorder.

 Get ready at the mic and then click the record button. Start talking or singing. If you're uninspired, say "Sanky Winkervan makes the best meat cakes."

 To stop, click the stop button.

To hear yourself, click the Play button.

Save your work to disk by choosing the File⇨Save As command, just as you would any file in any application.

- ✔ If you can't find Sound Recorder on the Start menu, use the Find command (covered in Chapter 7) to find the file named SNDREC32.EXE.

- ✔ If the Find command can't locate Sound Recorder on your computer, you can add it from the Windows CD. Your favorite book on Windows should have this information in it, or you can visit the following Web page at www.wambooli.com/help/PC/Sounds/ for more information.

- ✔ Better, more sophisticated sound-recording programs than Sound Recorder often come with your PC's sound card.

- ✔ Sound files are huge! Although playing and collecting sounds is fun, be aware that they occupy lots of space.

✔ If you have a Zip drive, know that Zip disks make excellent storage for sound files.

✔ Sound Recorder can also record sounds from the Line-In jack on your PC. Just click the Record button and play the sound.

Adjusting the Volume

Setting how loud your PC plays sounds is done in two places. The first place is a hardware place: the sound volume knob on your PC's speakers. Sometimes the knob may also be on the subwoofer, if you have one of those. And some cheapie PC speakers lack a volume knob altogether.

 The second spot for adjusting the volume is the Volume Thing in the System Tray, as shown in Figure 16-4.

Figure 16-4:
Set the PC's
volume
here.

In Windows XP, you might need to click on the << arrows to see the Volume Thing in the System Tray (which Windows XP calls the "Notification Area").

To set the volume, click on the Volume Thing once. Use the slider in the pop-up window to increase (up) or decrease (down) the volume.

To get an idea of how loud the sound is now, just click the slider bar and Windows makes some sort of noise.

To mute the sound, click to put a check mark in the Mute box.

Click anywhere else on the desktop to make the pop-up window go away.

The Volume Thing is more of a general control. To specifically control the volume or individual sound-producing devices, double-click the Volume Thing. This displays a whole window full of squeaking and squawking things in Windows, each with its own volume setting slider and Mute button, as shown in Figure 16-5.

For example, if you detest having MIDI music play while you're on the Internet (or anywhere), just mute that one item. All other sounds in your system continue to play, but MIDI sounds will be muted.

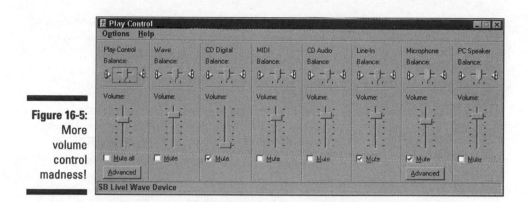

Figure 16-5:
More
volume
control
madness!

(Use the Options⇨Properties command to set which sound-producing devices in your PC appear in the window.)

"Where did the volume thing go?"

Fret not if the speaker suddenly splits from the System Tray. Restoring it to view depends on your version of Windows:

In Windows 98, open the Control Panel's Multimedia icon. Put a check mark by "Show volume control on the taskbar," and click OK.

In Windows Me/2000, open the Control Panel's Sounds and Multimedia icon. Put a check mark by "Show volume control on the taskbar," and click OK.

In Windows XP, the Volume Thing disappears along with any other items in the Notification Area, providing you haven't used them recently. But if you click on the << arrows to see the full Notification Area and notice that the Volume Thing still isn't there, open the Control Panel and click the Sounds, Speech and Audio Devices link. Then click the Sounds and Audio Devices link to display the Sounds and Audio Devices Properties dialog box. In the middle of the Volume panel, put a check mark by the item "Place volume icon in the taskbar notification area." Click OK and you're done.

Can It Talk?

Only Windows XP contains talking software, where the computer can dictate the contents of a Window or dialog box. This is done through the Accessibility Options link in the Control Panel. After choosing that item, look in the See Also area of the window to find the Narrator. Click that item to activate the Narrator in Windows.

Keep in mind that the Narrator is really a tool for the visually impaired. In that perspective, it isn't the kind of desktop companion you could use to, say, read your e-mail aloud while you're making coffee in another room. But for serving those with vision problems, it's a handy tool.

✔ If you don't have Windows XP, then your computer's sound card may have come with speech synthesis software. SoundBlaster once came with a program called *Texto'LE,* which could read text files aloud using one of several voices. I'm not aware whether this software is still included with Sound Blaster hardware.

✔ Other talking software may be available on the Internet or at your local software store.

Dictating to Your PC

I'll be brief here: There are programs available that let you talk to your PC. You can dictate to the PC, for example, and the program fairly accurately interprets your speech into text right on the screen. The technology is available, but it's still very crude in my opinion.

One milestone in speech recognition is Microsoft Office XP. Its applications will let you use speech recognition, providing that you configure it properly within the Word program.

Until speech recognition directly becomes a part of Windows, I recommend that you refer to the documentation that came with the speech recognition software for the most accurate and up-to-date information. (I briefly cover dictation for Microsoft Word in *Word 2002 For Dummies.*)

✔ If you have Office XP, then you'll notice two new icons in the Control Panel: Speech and Text Services. Each one controls how the PC communicates, either reading text or accepting audio input.

✔ Speech recognition extracts a high toll from your computer: You need at least a 166MHz Pentium PC with 32MB of RAM for most speech recognition software to work properly.

✔ For a fast typist such as myself, talking software doesn't really work. I find talking mode and typing mode to be two different things. Also, I change my mind a lot, which means I'm always editing my own text as I write it, something the dictation software is rather poor at.

✔ If you do want to take a turn at dictation software, I recommend Dragon Naturally Speaking. It's inexpensive and comes with a nifty microphone headset. Setting up and configuring the program does take a few hours, but it works rather well at taking proper dictation.

Chapter 17

The Scanner and Digital Camera Chapter

1 believe that photography developed because too many people wanted to paint, and face it, they were all really bad painters. Think of the throngs massed before the Eiffel Tower, hundreds of families and couples standing still, stifling in the Paris sun with plastic smiles, waiting for their brush-wielding relatives to finish the damn portrait. No, photography was designed to save us all from such peril.

Enter the computer age, especially this graphical world of Windows. Sure, painting programs exist. But despite their boasted ease-of-use, painting programs are best put to work by those already blessed with a talent for the brush and easel. That leaves the rest of us foraging in the digital soup, looking for some graphical form of expression. And, lo, it's here: Enter the scanner and digital camera. They are beacons of hope to a dark, formless world. Now anyone can "do graphics" on the computer.

Here's Your Scanning Hardware

The hardware part of doing graphics involves getting the image from out there in the real world, where things are alive and colorful and full of life, to inside the computer, where it's dark and filled with pointy electronics, most of which would electrocute you if the lid were to suddenly pop open. To make a digital copy of the real world, you need a hardware device called a *scanner*.

Scanners come in two types. The first is the traditional scanner, which looks like a teensy copy machine. The second is a digital camera, which is a portable, hand-held scanner.

✔ Yes, a digital camera is really a hand-held scanner. Internally, it contains all the electronics that a scanner has, though a lens is used to focus the image as opposed to using a reflected image as a scanner does.

✔ Things inside the computer are digital. Things in the real world are *analog*.

Scan this, Mr. Spock!

Scanners are nifty little devices that work like photocopiers. Instead of copying, the scanner converts the image into a graphics image in your computer. From there, you can modify the image, save it to disk, add it to a document, or send it off as an e-mail attachment. That's the big picture.

Figure 17-1 illustrates the typical computer scanner, not because you might be unfamiliar with them but more because I really like that illustration.

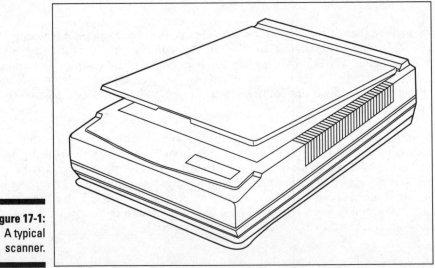

Figure 17-1:
A typical
scanner.

There are a few important points to consider when getting a scanner. Here's the short list:

- ✔ How does the scanner connect to the computer? The best and fastest scanners use a FireWire (or often SCSI) connection. Most scanners, however, use the USB or Printer ports.

- ✔ Scanners are judged by their resolution, which is measured by the number of dots-per-inch (dpi) the scanner can read. The higher the dpi resolution, the better the scanned image.

- ✔ Scanners come with software. There are usually three packages. The first is a utility that lets you use the scanner to scan in an image. The second is typically some type of photo-editing program, such as Adobe PhotoDeluxe. The third is an OCR program, which is used to translate written documents into editable text. OCR stands for Optical Character Recognition.

- ✔ Typical scanner prices range from $100 to over $1,000. You pay more for higher-quality scanners, but those are mostly used by graphics professionals. Also, high-priced scanners contain options such as transparency adapters (for scanning slides or negatives) and sheet feeders (for law offices or other outfits that need to scan in large quantities of text).

- ✔ Don't bother with a SCSI scanner unless your PC has a SCSI port.

- ✔ If your PC has a USB port, get a USB scanner!

- ✔ Don't let anyone fool you into believing that adding a scanner can turn your PC into a photocopier. True, you can scan an image and then print that image. But the process takes more time than it would to drive to the copy store and make a few copies. (Well, maybe not that long, but scanning and printing isn't the fastest thing the PC does.)

Everyone say, "Megabyte!" (Digital cameras)

The latest PC craze is the digital camera. Not only have these wonderful toys come down drastically in price, but the quality of the images they take is rivaling traditional cameras.

Digital cameras range in price from you-don't-want-it cheap to well over $1,000 for professional set ups. The average price for a decent digital camera is between $600 and $800. The prices do come down, but that's because this new technology is constantly leaping forward. So I don't expect anything to settle any time soon.

There are three things to look for in a digital camera: Resolution, how the image is stored in the camera, and how the image gets from the camera to your computer.

Resolution. A digital camera's resolution is measured in horizontal-by-vertical pixels — the more pixels, the better (and pricier) the camera. Don't get anything with a resolution less than 1024 x 768 pixels. Average resolution is about 1280 x 1024, and some of the *nice* digital cameras have a resolution of 1600 x 1200 pixels. The higher these values are, the sharper the image will appear when printed, especially if that image has to be enlarged.

The number of images the camera can store varies depending on the resolution. If you're just shooting images for the Web, then your camera will most likely store 100 or more pictures. But taking higher resolution images cuts down on the number of pictures that can be stored. An interesting thing to note, however, is that you can delete images to make room for more. The camera is like a computer, so if you don't like one shot, you can remove it to make room for another try. (Or if you take that embarrassing picture of your spouse, you can safely delete it later to avoid sleeping on the couch.)

Image storage. All digital cameras have some type of internal storage or "digital film." Some cameras use a standard floppy disk for storage. When you're done with the disk, you simply shove it into your PC and read the images. Most cameras, however, use a special storage card or memory stick. The advantage of the memory card is that it holds much more information than a standard floppy disk, typically several megabytes.

Beaming the image to the computer. A final, most important thing to consider when selecting a digital camera is how the image is transferred from the camera into the computer. If your camera uses floppy disks, then you just have to stick the disks into the PC. Otherwise, the camera most likely comes with a cable (such as a USB cable) you use to send the images to the computer. Or you can get an adapter to read the camera's storage card and access the images that way.

Here are some other digital camera points to ponder:

- ✔ Most cameras use LCD viewfinders, which means you must hold them away from your face to get an image — like those camcorders that have LCD viewfinders. Same thing.

- ✔ Beware of digital cameras with too many confusing and poorly labeled dials and buttons.

- ✔ If your camera uses storage cards then buy more of them! The more cards you have, the more images the camera can take.

- ✔ The easiest way to get digital images into the computer is to buy a storage card adapter so that you can plug the storage cards directly into the PC.

Getting the Image from out There to inside the Computer

Scanners and digital cameras are merely methods of collecting images. The real useful part is getting the images from the scanner or digital camera and into your computer, where you can edit them, save them to disk, print them, e-mail them, or whatever. Thus begins the software side of your digital imaging adventure.

First, something to totally ignore in Windows

All versions of Windows (well, not Windows 98 or earlier) come with a special Control Panel thingy called Scanners and Cameras. This is the barn where Windows stores information about any digital cameras (including video cameras) or scanners attached to your computer.

In Windows XP, go to the Scanners and Camera item from the Printers and Other Hardware link.

Honestly, you can ignore the Scanners and Cameras item. Even though there is an option there for adding a scanner or digital camera to your computer's hardware inventory, you don't need it. All scanners and digital cameras come with their own setup software. Use it instead of Windows.

After setting up the hardware, you'll use the photo-editing programs that came with your scanner or digital camera. The Scanners and Cameras icon in the Control Panel doesn't really do squat.

The quick-and-dirty overview of how to scan an image

A scanner can take anything flat and convert it into a graphic image. Oh, I suppose you could scan the cat if it would sit still long enough, but that's not the device's true design. If it's flat or can fold that way, you can scan it. Here's an overview of how it works:

1. **Activate the scanner.**

   This may be an automatic step. Some scanners pop on when you raise their lids or use the scanning software. Other types must be switched on.

2. **Start your photo-editing software.**

   Most scanners come with photo-editing software, such as Adobe PhotoDeluxe. This program is where your scanned image will end up. (Other programs can be used to activate the scanner, but most of the time you'll need the power of a photo-editing application to complete the operation.)

3. **Place your image facedown in the scanner.**

   Most scanners scan from the back to the front, and they'll tell you which corner is the *upper right*. Try to place your image snugly against that corner — though this is not a hard and fast requirement.

4. **Choose the proper command to get a scanned image.**

   The command depends on the program. There could be a scan button on the toolbar, for example. Or you may have to choose File⇨Acquire or File⇨Scan from the menu. However you get there, this program runs a special scanning utility that controls the scanner directly. Figure 17-2 shows such a utility.

5. **Preview the image.**

   Use the scanning utility to preview the image. This allows you to see what you're going to get without having to scan in more than you need. For example, if you're scanning Uncle Richard's boat but don't want Uncle Richard in the picture, you can tell the scanner not to scan him in.

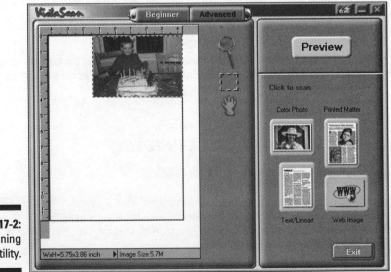

Figure 17-2: A scanning utility.

6. **Select the part of the image you really want.**

Use the scanner's selection tool to lasso only that part of the image you want scanned. Drag the lasso over the image, or use the mouse to drag the lasso's edge in or out.

You may need the magnifying glass tool to inspect the image in detail, ensuring that you're getting only what you want to scan.

7. **Make adjustments for the type of image.**

In Figure 17-2 (the *beginner* mode), four options are available: Color Photo, Printed Matter, Text/Line art, and Web Image. Some scanner programs may list options for scanning in black and white or color. Some may list resolutions. Whatever. Select the options that best describe the image you're scanning.

Some scanning utilities have an Auto Adjust button. Use it to have the computer make its best guess as to the settings you need.

8. **Scan the image.**

Click the Scan button to do this.

In Figure 17-2, in the beginner mode, you click the button associated with the type of image you're scanning. For example, to scan the photograph of Jonah, I would click the Color Photo button (the one with the lady and the stupid hat on it).

The scanner may take a few moments to warm up or calibrate itself.

Scan . . . scan . . . scan. . . .

(I apologize for not having an appropriate scanner noise to insert here.)

9. **Place the image into your application.**

Some scanner programs have an OK button. If so, click it. That action puts the image into the application for editing, saving, or printing.

Your scanner may automatically place the image into the application. If so, you don't have to click anything!

10. **Fuss with the image.**

Now you're ready to edit, print, or save the image.

For more information on editing an image, see the section on photo-editing software at the end of this chapter.

- ✔ You may be able to scan several photographs at once: Scan the lot and then use the photo-editing software to crop out and save each individual photograph. This technique takes less time than scanning each image individually.

- ✔ Special hardware is needed to scan slides. This hardware is either a special slide-scanning device or an attachment to a traditional scanner. You cannot, unfortunately, put your slides of that Bermuda trip into a flatbed scanner and have them appear as anything other than a black rectangle.

✔ TWAIN is an acronym associated with scanning graphics. It stands for Technology Without An Important Name. No, I'm not making that up.

Snapping a digital picture

Grabbing an image with a digital camera is yet another way to soak graphics into the PC. The method of delivery depends on how the camera connects with your computer.

Those cameras that use a cable to connect to the PC come with a special picture-reading utility, one that can be activated inside a photo-editing program or used on its own. The picture-reading utility lists the images inside the camera and lets you select one or several to beam into the computer.

For cameras with removable storage, such as a floppy disk, you merely stick the storage into the proper device on your PC, and then access the images as you would any other file on your computer.

Of course, the next step you most likely want to take would be to run a photo-editing program on the images. You may want to resize them, crop them, or save them in special graphics file formats for sending as e-mail attachments. That's all covered in the next section.

✔ After beaming the images into your computer would be a good time to erase them from the camera. You're not losing the images, because a copy is kept on the computer's hard drive.

✔ If Windows hasn't created one already, then I recommend using the My Pictures folder inside the My Documents folder as the main place to store your graphics images. Create additional subfolders within the My Pictures folders for various albums.

✔ Despite the existence of the My Pictures folder, also consider saving images on Zip disks or, over time, stocking the images on a CD-R disk. Remember that graphics images take up oodles of disk space. A few rounds with the digital camera, or an event like a wedding or graduation, may fill up your disk quicker you'd expect.

Using Photo-Editing Software

Most scanners and digital cameras come with photo-editing software that lets you modify or edit the image you've just created. Some, such as Adobe PhotoDeluxe, are quite easy to use.

Entire books have been written on photo-editing software, and I encourage you to check them out if it's something you're into. Otherwise, you probably only want to do a handful of things with the image, some of which I cover in the following sections.

Cropping the image

Cropping is the same as trimming — what you would do with a pair of scissors to a photograph. It allows you to clip the image to contain only the part you want.

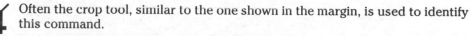 Often the crop tool, similar to the one shown in the margin, is used to identify this command.

In PhotoDeluxe, the command is called Trim, which is shown in Figure 17-3. To crop the image, select the Trim tool and drag over the part of the image you want to keep. Complete the command by clicking in the image or pressing the Enter key.

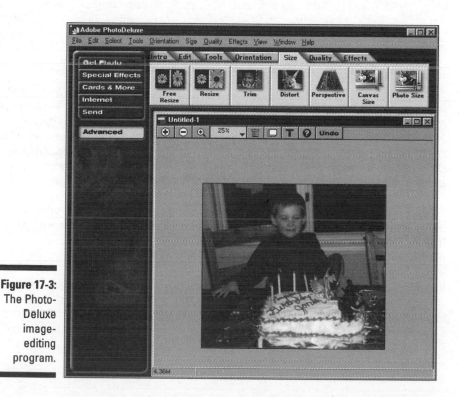

Figure 17-3: The Photo-Deluxe image-editing program.

How do I print an image that's larger than the screen?

Q: I've been trying to print out a copy of the map that I found on a Web page but haven't had any luck. The map is larger than my screen, and my printer will not print it all. Is it possible for me to print it out even if it takes several sheets?

A: Right-click on the map to display a pop-up menu. Choose the Save Image As command

from that menu, which saves the image from the Web page to your PC's hard drive. You can then open the image using a graphics program on your computer, such as the Microsoft Imager. Once there, you can resize the image to fix on a sheet of paper.

Changing the image's dimensions

If you're new to photo-editing software, you might assume that scanned images are *huge*. That's not the case. An image's size is measured by its horizontal and vertical resolution, say 1024 x 768 pixels. That image may fill your screen (especially if your monitor is set to that same resolution), but when you print it on a 600 dpi printer, then the image may end up being only 4 by 6 inches. It's all this crazy resolution stuff. . . .

Fortunately, most image-editing programs have tools that let you calculate exactly how large the printed image will be. (What you have, after all, is a computer, which is good at such things.) Figure 17-4 illustrates PhotoDeluxe's Photo Size dialog box, which you can see by clicking the Photo Size button on the toolbar. Note that the image is scanned at 4 x 3-something inches — but that's a whopping amount of pixels — 3.96MB according to the figure.

To change the image size, enter a new value in the dialog box. The value can be in inches, centimeters, or pixels. Use inches for the stuff you plan on printing. For Web page and e-mail images, use pixels. A good width for an e-mail image is around 300 pixels wide.

If you're saving the image to be used as your Windows desktop wallpaper, make it the same size as the desktop: Right-click on the desktop and choose Properties from the shortcut menu. In the Settings tab of the Display Properties dialog box, note the size of the Screen area. Resize your image to those exact dimensions.

Figure 17-4:
The resizing
dialog box in
Photo-
Deluxe.

Saving the image in a specific format

The final chore for your scanned image, edited or not, is to save it to disk.

If you choose just to use the Save command — watch out! Most photo-editing programs use their own formats for the images. For example, if you save an image in PhotoDeluxe format, not only will it be very large on the hard drive, but only people who have PhotoDeluxe will be able to view the image. No, it's best to select a file format best suited to what you're doing with the image.

- ✔ The best format for sending photographs through e-mail, or saving photos to a Web page, is the JPEG file format.

- ✔ If the image contains artwork, such as an illustration, kid's drawing, signature, or anything that isn't a photograph, use the GIF format. GIF images can also be e-mailed or posted to a Web page.

- ✔ If you're going to place the image into another program, such as a desktop publishing program, word processor, or other application, save the file as a TIFF. This format uses a huge amount of disk space, so while it stores the image very well it's impractical for sending via e-mail. (TIFF images will not display on a Web page, either.)

- ✔ If you're going to use the image as Windows wallpaper, save the image as a bitmap file, BMP. That's about the only time you want to mess with bitmap files.

To save in these formats, use the Save As or Export command.

If you use the Save As command, select the proper file type from the Type drop-down list. (See Chapter 5 for more information on the Save As command.)

The Export command, called *Send To* in PhotoDeluxe, usually displays a sub-menu full of file formats. Select the proper one from the list.

If you quit after exporting, the program may warn you that the image is not saved. That's okay! The program means that the image is not saved in its own format. You're not required to do that if the image was saved in another format (and I wish the program would wake up and realize that, but I'm only a small voice in the wilderness).

Chapter 18

More Stuff for Your PC (Peripherals)

Scientists claim that the universe is expanding, constantly growing outward in all directions. My doctor tells me that my belly is doing the exact same thing. At last, I have something in common with the universe! And with you, if you're like most PC users.

No, I'm not talking about how PC users typically gain weight while eating chips and surfing the Internet. I'm talking about your PC itself and its ever-expanding universe of gizmos and gadgets. Those extra parts are called *peripherals,* which you can add to your computer to make it more useful or more fun — and certainly more expensive. This chapter takes a look at some of the more popular peripherals that attach to a PC.

The Wide, Wide World of Peripherals

Peripheral refers to anything outside of the main. For example, the *peripheral nervous system* is made up of all the nerves in your body outside of your brain (which is called the *central nervous system*). *Peripheral vision* includes things you can see without looking directly at them. And *peripheral nervous vision* is what first-time computer buyers get when they enter the store. With a computer, however, a *peripheral* is any accessory or auxiliary equipment you may buy and connect to the computer.

The variety of peripherals you can buy for your computer is endless. Common peripheral items include scanners, tape drives, CD-Rs, digital cameras, video cameras, and numerous other toys you can connect to the typical PC.

- ✔ Peripherals enable you to expand your computer system without having to buy a totally new computer. You can add these extra hardware devices yourself or have a guru, computer consultant, or some other overpaid individual do it for you.

- ✔ All peripherals are hardware.

- ✔ Although the word peripheral refers to things outside of a computer, you can also add peripherals internally — inside the PC's console. (In a way, peripheral refers to anything beyond what comes standard in the computer.)

- ✔ If your PC sports a USB port, always check for a USB version of whatever peripheral you're buying: speakers, joystick, scanner, whatever. USB hardware is hands-down the best and easiest to install.

- ✔ Well, actually some FireWire devices are better than USB devices. For example, FireWire storage devices (hard drives, CD-Rs, and so on) and FireWire scanners are much faster than their USB cousins.

Installing a peripheral

The hardware side of adding a peripheral is really cinchy. Most peripherals sit outside the PC. All you need to do to connect them is find the proper hole and plug the thing in.

Well, granted, you need to follow other instructions when adding a peripheral, but plugging the thing into the proper port is most important.

Because peripherals can also live inside the PC, installing one may involve opening the console and plugging in an expansion card. Again, this process isn't that tough, but it's not the sign of a PC wimp if you pay someone else to do it.

- ✔ Most peripherals plug into standard connectors on the back of every PC. See Chapter 8 for a review.

- ✔ Generally speaking, whenever you install hardware inside of or onto your PC you should first turn off the computer. See Chapter 2 for the official turning-off instructions.

- ✔ USB peripherals are the easiest by far to install. You don't even need to turn off your PC; just plug in the USB cable, and you're on your way.

- ✔ Sometimes you must install the peripheral's software *before* you install the peripheral. For example, the Zip drive and modem I just installed both required that I first install their software, and then plug in the hardware. However, sometimes it works the other way around; you need to install the hardware doohickey first, and then install the software. Always refer to the manual to see which way to do it.

Telling Windows about your new hardware

All peripherals come with software. The software side of the installation happens either before or after you install the hardware; the manual that comes with the peripheral will tell you which way to go. So heed that manual's instructions!

After the hardware is attached, Windows detects it and adds the device to Windows secret internal list of hardware. If not, then you must manually add the device yourself. Again, the device's manual will tell you whether or not Windows will recognize it.

For example, Windows may not recognize some modems. To finish modem installation, you need to open the Modems icon in the Control Panel and click the Add button to add your modem. Ditto for joysticks: open the Gaming Options icon in the Control Panel and click the Add button to manually add your joystick.

- ✔ The Gaming Options icon is called Game Controllers in Windows 98 and Windows 2000.

- ✔ In Windows XP, Gaming Options can be found in the Printers and Other Hardware link.

- ✔ Windows' capability to instantly recognize new peripherals is known as *Plug and Play:* When you restart your computer after installation, Windows instantly recognizes the new hardware (unless it's a USB peripheral, in which case you don't have to turn the PC off in the first place).

- ✔ The software that controls your hardware is called a *driver*. So when someone says, "Windows needs a new driver," he's not insulting you as the computer operator.

- ✔ Plug and Play isn't foolproof. For that reason, many in the industry have dubbed it "plug and pray."

"Windows is stupid and doesn't recognize my new peripheral!"

In some rare cases, Windows may not recognize your new hardware. The problem could be that the hardware isn't Plug and Play compatible, or it could be that you're installing something that doesn't grab the computer's attention directly, such as a new external modem.

Add New
Hardware

When Windows refuses to recognize the new hardware, you should run the Add New Hardware Wizard. Open the Control Panel and then double-click the Add New Hardware icon to run the wizard.

Follow the steps in the driver. Read the screen. Click the Next button or select options as necessary. In mere moments, your new hardware should be up and running, and everything will be groovy.

 - ✔ In Windows 2000, the icon is named Add/Remove Hardware.

 - ✔ In Windows XP, click the Printers and Other Hardware link in the Control Panel. Then look for the Add Hardware link in the See Also part of the dialog box.

 - ✔ The Big Decision point in the Add New Hardware Wizard is whether to let Windows look for the new hardware or select it yourself from a list. Sometimes it's tempting to taunt Windows: "Go ahead! Find that hardware! I dare you to find it! Double-dog dare you!" Other times plucking the device from a list on your own is easier and quicker.

 - ✔ Windows cannot (or refuses to) find tape backup units, especially the internal models. If you've just added one, don't fret if Windows seems mute to its existence. Instead, run the backup software that came with the tape backup unit. It should locate the device, no problem.

Some Popular Peripherals

This chapter gets shorter and shorter with each edition of this book. Back in 1992, modems and CD-ROM drives were considered peripherals. Today the list is short — and may grow shorter still.

The most popular PC peripheral today is the scanner, but it became so popular that I put it off into Chapter 17 along with digital cameras. So that leaves the most popular peripherals as external disk drives (Zip disks, CD-R/RW drives), tape backups, and video cameras.

External disk drives

It's easy to expand your system's storage; just plug in another disk drive! Adding a CD-R, CD-RW, hard drive, DVD, Zip disk, or multiple combinations of each is a snap.

The best way to add external storage is via the USB port. (And if your PC lacks a USB port, then buy a USB expansion card for $20 and you're in business!) With the USB port, you can add as many external storage devices as your VISA card can afford.

The second best way to add external storage is to use the PC's Printer port. Unfortunately, that allows you to add only one device, so if the Printer port is already used for a scanner or some device, then you cannot daisy-chain in another device.

✔ Actually, FireWire peripherals are better than USB, though not every type of external storage device comes with a FireWire version.

✔ If you have FireWire, buy FireWire devices!

✔ One major bonus for external storage devices is that they can survive your current computer setup. For example, my external FireWire hard drive may outlive my current computer and end up plugged-in to next year's model. That way I don't have to copy over my software; instead I just plug in the Firewire drive.

Tape backups

A tape drive is a device used to create backups, or duplicates, of all the information on your PC's hard drive. Everything. It's an emergency copy. A safety copy. A just-in-case copy.

Choosing a peripheral for backing up

Q: You say nothing about backing up to floppy disks. I thought that was the original purpose of the floppy disk.

A: No, the original purpose of the floppy disk was to provide a disk environment to people who couldn't afford $15,000 hard drives in 1978. Consider that you would need hundreds of the 1.4MB floppy disks to backup the data on a typical PC hard drive. That would cost you more than a tape backup unit, so why not just buy the tape backup? I won't even mention that floppy disks are highly unreliable, nor that it would take you about a week of inserting and removing floppy disks to complete the operation.

Adding a backup drive to your PC is simple. Some can be added internally, piggy-backing themselves onto your PC's floppy drive (actually taking over the position of drive B). Others can be added externally, often plugging into the printer port or a USB port.

After you install your tape backup drive, use it! Make a backup copy of your work *at least* once a month. I make backup copies of the books I write *daily*. And the backup software automates everything. All I did was tell it what to backup and when. Oh, it's times like this that computers really fulfill everything the brochure promised.

- ✔ A tape backup drive costs anywhere from under $100 to over $1,000 for the fancy, super-duper network backup drives.

- ✔ Tape backup drives come with one tape. Buy more. You need about three to rotate your backup copies.

- ✔ The amount of information storable on a backup tape varies. Some tapes store only 500MB, others over 8GB. Buy a tape backup unit that uses tapes equal to or greater than the capacity of all your PC's hard drives.

- ✔ You can also back up to CD-R or CD-RW drives, and those drives usually come with software to assist you in backing up. However, those disks hold maybe 650MB maximum, which is far less than a single backup tape.

- ✔ I recommend using your tape backup's software and not Windows own software for backing up your hard drive. Windows backup software stinks (or in the case of Windows Me, it doesn't exist). Your tape backup drive probably comes with something better anyway.

It's live, and it's living on top of your monitor!

An interesting toy to add to your PC is a video camera. These little mechanical eyeballs perch near your PC, usually on top of the monitor. You can use them to record movies or single images, or to send live images over the Internet — it all depends on the software that comes with the camera.

- ✔ My camera appears to be broken. So much for including a live action shot of me writing this book. . . .

- ✔ If you want one of those cameras that sends pictures to the Web, what you want is a *Webcam*. I have such a device in my office (actually, it's a *wireless* Webcam), which you can view by visiting www.wambooli.com/Live/.

- ✔ Make sure the software you need is included with the camera. For example, videoconferencing is possible only with the proper software. The camera is just a device; you need software to really play with it.

"I Have Some Money, and I Want to Upgrade My Hardware"

Most people don't trade in their cars each year. TVs, VCRs, blenders, and clock radios usually stay put until they break, and then you buy a new one. It's the Bic lighter theory: Why repair something that's cheap, when you can just buy a new one? The same thing applies to most pets. For example, why incur a $35 vet bill on a $1.59 mouse? Toss it out and buy the kid a new one! But I digress. . . .

The computer world, being bizarre and different as we know it, offers updates and upgrades on a monthly basis, if not weekly. It's technology! There's something new and better! And you still have $1,500 credit on your VISA!

What to buy first

Instead of buying a new computer, upgrading the old one may be cheaper. Or, rather, have somebody else upgrade your old computer for you. But where do you spend your money first? Too many enticing things can get in the way of a sane decision. Let me help.

Memory: Your first upgrading priority should be memory. It's not that expensive, and installation isn't a major headache. Just about all your software will enjoy having more memory available.

- ✔ Increased memory can make these programs work faster and handle larger chunks of information. It also lets the computer handle more graphics and sound.

- ✔ More memory is the best thing you can buy for your PC.

- ✔ For more information about memory stuff, read Chapter 10.

Hard drive: Buy a second hard drive. Make it a big one. Most PCs can handle two hard drives internally (and dozens externally). And by the time you need another one, you'll know exactly how many more gigabytes of storage you need.

- ✔ The best way to add hard drives is via the FireWire (preferred) or USB port. You can add dozens of hard drives to your computer this way.

- ✔ If you have a UPS, then plug any external hard drives into it. Otherwise the computer may not be able to save your documents should the power go out. (See Chapter 2 for more information on a UPS.)

- ✔ By the way, larger hard drives don't take up any extra room in the computer's case, so don't worry about needing a bigger case.

Monitor: Buy a big monitor, like a 21-inch jobbie. These things are *great*. You can really see a lot of windows on the screen at once without feeling crowded. Oftentimes, just replacing the old monitor is easy. In fact, you can do the whole operation yourself but have someone with an expendable back hoist the thing up for you.

✔ Go nuts and buy an LCD monitor. I love them! They're much better on the eyes, but are still rather expensive.

✔ Consider that Windows will let you install multiple monitors on a PC. (Well, the "Personal" edition of Windows XP doesn't let you.)

✔ For more information on monitors, see Chapter 11.

Microprocessor: Upgrading the microprocessor is something I don't recommend. Generally speaking, it's just better to buy a whole new computer. That way you get *all* new components at a cost cheaper than buying a new PC one bit at a time.

My opinion is that you're better off adding more memory to your system or installing a bigger hard drive. These two upgrades give you instant results, whereas a faster microprocessor may or may not be noticeable right away. Of course, this is my opinion, and if you're dead-set on doing an upgrade, go for it.

When to buy a new computer

Plan on this: Every four or five years, replace your PC. By then, the cost of a new system will be cheaper than any upgrading you do.

Your PC is essentially out of date the moment you purchase it. Somewhere right now in Silicon Valley, they're devising new microprocessors and better motherboards that will cost less money. Maybe not the *minute* you purchased your PC, but sooner or later your leading-edge technology will be yesterday's kitty box.

But do you really need to buy a new computer? Maybe not. Look at the reasons you bought it in the first place. Can the computer still handle those needs? If yes, you're doing fine. Upgrade only when you desperately need to. No sense in spending more money on the monster.

✔ Computer technology grows faster than fly specks on a clean windshield. But, unless your computing needs have changed drastically, your computer can still handle the tasks you bought it for.

✔ Most people buy newer computers for the increase in speed. Yet speed doesn't always mean increased productivity. For instance, most word processing time is spent pondering the right choice of words. A faster computer can't help there. Faster computers do help those applications that need the extra horsepower, such as graphics, animation, desktop publishing, and programs of that ilk.

- ✔ Compare the price of a new computer with the amount of time you'll save at a faster processing speed. If you spend a lot of time waiting for your computer to catch up with you, an upgrade may be in order.

- ✔ Avoid the lure and seduction of those techy computer magazines that urge you to Buy! Buy! Buy! the latest PC. Remember who most of their advertisers are.

Part IV

The Non-Nerd's Guide to Computer Software

The 5th Wave   By Rich Tennant

"Okay, Darryl, I think it's time to admit we didn't load the onboard mapping software correctly."

In this part . . .

Computer software makes the computer hardware go. It's the real brains of the operation, even though it comes later in this book than computer hardware. Why? Because you must have one before you can use the other. Software needs hardware like a symphony needs an orchestra. After all, what's the point of a bassoon without music to play? And isn't the word *bassoon* fun to say?

Bassoon.

I would love to go on and on about the bassoon and how I believe it was inspired by an attempt at amateur indoor plumbing in the seventeenth century, but this part of the book is about PC software and not musical instruments. So enjoy your PC software and learn to play the bassoon if you have the time.

Chapter 19

Software 101

- -

In This Chapter

▶ How to buy software

▶ Stuff in the software box

▶ Installing software

▶ Uninstalling software

▶ Updating software

▶ Whether or not to upgrade Windows

▶ Learning software tips

- -

*W*hen you use your computer, you're really using software. Even something as hardware-like as ejecting a disk is really software in action. You tell the software to eject the disk and the disk drive hardware obeys the software and (hopefully) ejects the disk. Yea, verily, software hath the power.

There's no need for this book to go into gross detail on how all your computer's software works. I consider *PCs For Dummies* to be a hardware book for the most part. So I've distilled the essence of software down into the most necessary nuggets. The first of them is the chore of installing and updating software, which is something you may not do often but which typically leads to trouble.

A Few Words on Buying Software

"Software? Son, you in the wrong place! This here is Big Earl's Ace Hardware Store, and I should know 'cause I am Big Earl. We ain't got no E-Z-calc here. We have caulk. We got paint. We got power tools. Things men 'ud use. Or would you know anything 'bout that? Nope. Didn't think so. Yup. You in the wrong place, son."

Buying software is part of the computer buying process. If you heed my advice in *Buying a Computer For Dummies*, then you know to pick out your software *first* and then the hardware to match. Even so, you probably won't buy all your software at once. No, eventually you'll wander into the computer store (not the hardware store) and sift through the selection. When you do, keep these things in mind:

- ✔ If you're utterly unfamiliar with something, try to get recommendations from friends on which programs to use. For example, if you want to get into genealogy, then hound someone who's already into genealogy about what they use.

- ✔ Try before you buy software. If the store won't let you do this, then find a store that does. They are out there!

- ✔ Always check out a store's return policy on software. If the store won't let you return opened software, then basically they're saying that you cannot return the software at all. Watch out for that.

- ✔ Check the software's requirements. They should match your computer's hardware inventory. For example, you don't want to buy the DVD version of a program when your PC has only a CD-ROM drive.

What's That Stuff in the Box?

Surprisingly, many large software boxes contain air or cardboard padding to make the boxes look bigger and more impressive in the store. I suppose the idea is to push the competition off the shelf. Or it could be to justify paying $279 for what ends up being a CD and a pamphlet.

The most vital things inside the software box are the discs. Nearly all software comes on one (or more — many more!) CDs. Some stuff still does come on floppy disks, however. And you'll occasionally see a DVD disc, especially in packages with multiple CDs.

After the disks you may find one or more of the following:

The Hideous Manual: Most programs toss in a printed manual, typically the size of a political pamphlet and about as interesting. More than one manual may be included. Look for the "Getting Started," "Installation," or "Setup" section of the manual first. (Gone are the days of finding a thick manual, and never were the days of finding a useful manual.)

Registration card: Resembling a postcard, though it could be larger, this is what identifies you as a user of the product to the manufacturer. Fill in the blanks on the card and then mail it back to the company. The company then (supposedly) notifies you of any defects, including nonfunctional commands or air-bag problems. Some companies require you to fill out the registration card before they'll offer technical support over the phone.

Quick reference card: The manual works fine for explaining everything in great detail, but you'll find yourself continually repeating some commands. A quick reference card contains those useful commands; you can prop it up next to the keyboard for quick sideways glances. Not all software comes with these cards, however.

Quick installation card: Computer users thrive on instant gratification: Push a button and watch your work be performed instantly. Nobody wants to bother with slow, thick manuals, especially when installing the software. A quick installation card contains an abbreviated version of the manual's installation instructions. By typing in the commands on the card, you can install the software without cracking open the manual. Victory!

License agreement: This extensive batch of fine print takes an average of 3,346 words of legalese to say four things: 1) Don't give away any copies of this program to friends — make them buy their own programs. 2) If you accidentally lose any data, it's not the developer's fault. 3) If this software doesn't work, that's not their fault, either. 4) In fact, you don't even own this software. You merely own a license to use the software. We own the software. We are evil. We will one day own the world. Ha-ha!

Read me first: When the company finds a mistake in its newly printed manual, it doesn't fix it and print out a new manual. It prints the corrections on a piece of paper and slaps the headline "Read Me First!" across the top. Staple that piece of paper to the inside cover of your manual for safekeeping.

Unsolicited junk: Finally, some software comes with company catalogs and *free* offers from related companies for their stuff. You can toss all this stuff out if you like.

Some additional, meandering thoughts:

Never toss out the CD-ROM or floppy disks! I keep them in the box they came in, especially after installation, which makes finding the disks easy should I ever need them again in the future.

- ✔ Sometimes a manual isn't included. You may find an installation card or pamphlet. The manual is *on the disk.* Egads!

- ✔ If your software comes on a CD but your PC lacks a CD-ROM drive, then you can order the floppy disk version of the product. Stand back! The program can be anywhere from 2 to 36,000 floppy disks.

✔ Sometimes the licensing agreement is printed on a little sticker on an envelope; you have to tear apart the agreement before you can get to the disks inside. Whether or not this means you accept the agreement is up to a battalion of attorneys to discover.

✔ In addition to the registration card, many products let you register online using your modem. Or you can print out a list of information to fax to the company, if you prefer not to modem anything.

✔ Thank goodness software boxes aren't junky like those magazine publisher sweepstakes things. You can never find the things you need to fill in, stickers to place over the TV set or on Ed's head, or options to clip. What nonsense! Software boxes are much neater by comparison.

Software Installation Chores

Anyone who's owned a computer for more than a month has had to install some new software. It's a chore we all have to put up with. The following sections help make it easier for you.

The easiest way to install software

Get someone else to do it for you.

The way most of us end up installing software

Follow these steps to install your new software. I'm assuming that you've already experienced the ecstasy of ripping off the shrink-wrap and the thrill of smelling the industrial plastic odor of the box's insides. Sift through the junk and get ready to start.

1. **Read the *Read Me* blurb.**

   When you first open the box, scrounge around for a piece of paper that says "Read Me First!" and follow the first instruction: Read it. Or at least try to make some sense of it.

   Sometimes the Read Me First sheet contains a sentence or two left out of the manual's third paragraph on page 127, "Dwobbling your shordlock by three frips." If you don't understand the sheet, don't throw it away. It may come in handy after you've started using the program.

2. **Set the manual(s) aside.**

   Say, "There," when you do this.

3. **Put the Installation disk into your disk drive.**

   Find the disk marked with the words *Installation* or *Setup* or *Disk One,* (or the only disk if there is just one) and place that disk in the disk drive where it fits.

   If you're installing from floppy disks, put them in a neat stack, in order, first disk on top. That way you can easily feed them, one after the other, into the disk drive without having to rummage for the next disk later.

4. **Start the Installation program.**

   If you're lucky, the installation program runs automatically when you insert the CD into the CD-ROM drive.

Add/Remove
Programs

   If the installation program doesn't start automatically, you need to run it yourself. You can do this by opening the Add/Remove Programs icon in the Control Panel. Use the dialog box that appears to help you hunt down your program.

5. **Read the screen carefully; click the Next button as necessary.**

   Watch the instructions carefully; sometimes they slip something important in there. My friend Jerry (his real name) just kept clicking the Next button instead of reading the screen. He missed an important notice that said an older version of the program would be erased. Uh-oh! Poor Jerry never got his old program back.

6. **Choose various options.**

How do I quit all other programs?

Q: The installation program tells me to be sure that I've quit all other running programs. How do I know what's running and what's not? And why bother quitting in the first place? Would something bad happen?

A: This is a guess, but I believe the reason you must quit other programs is to be sure that you don't lose any unsaved documents. For example, if the installation program resets the computer, you might lose an unsaved file. By forcing

you to quit all other programs, this risk is reduced.

To make sure no other programs are running press the Alt+Tab key. If Windows switches you to another program, quit it. If you're switched to another window, close it. Keep pressing Alt+Tab until the only program you see is the installation program.

The software asks for your name and company name, and maybe for a serial number. Type all that stuff in.

Don't freak if the program already knows who you are. Windows is kinda clairvoyant in that respect.

When asked to make a decision, the option already selected (called the *default*) is typically the best option. Only if you know what's going on and *truly care* about it should you change anything.

You can find the serial number inside the manual, on the CD-ROM case, on the first disk in the stack of 3½-inch disks, or on a separate card you probably threw away even though I told you to keep everything in the original box. Don't lose that number!

7. **Files are copied.**

Eventually, the installation program copies the files from the CD-ROM drive onto your hard drive for full-time residence.

If you're unlucky enough to be installing from floppy disks, keep feeding them, one after the other, into the floppy drive. Make sure that you get them in the proper order (they're numbered). Make sure that you remove one disk and replace it with the next disk.

8. **It's done.**

The installation program ends. The computer may reset at this point. That's required sometimes when installing special programs that Windows needs to know about. (Windows is pretty dumb after it starts.)

Start using the program!

- These steps are vague and general. Hopefully your new software comes with more specific instructions.

- You can get software from the World Wide Web on the Internet. This process is known as *downloading,* and Chapter 25 covers it.

- Keep the quick reference card next to your computer immediately after installing the program; it's more helpful than the manual.

- Some programs require you to disable your antivirus software before installation can begin. This is a good idea generally; antivirus software, though necessary, tends to slow down and interrupt regular computer processes more than necessary. Read more of my rants on this subject in Chapter 26

- If the software has a serial number, keep it! Write it down in the manual. Don't lose it! With some software, such as Adobe PageMaker, you cannot order the upgrade unless you have a proper serial number.

Uninstalling Software

To remove any newly installed program, you use an uninstall program. This program is not a feature of Windows. Each software program must come with its own uninstall feature. Otherwise removing unwanted software is dern tough (see the sidebar, "Out software, out!").

You uninstall software by running the uninstall program. Typically you can find that program on the Start menu right by the icon where you start the program. Figure 19-1 shows such an arrangement; the Norton AntiVirus software is shown in a submenu on the Start menu. Right there, you see the Uninstall Norton AntiVirus option, which removes the software.

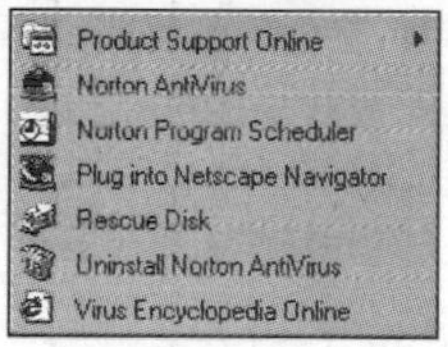

Figure 19-1: The Norton AntiVirus submenu on the Start menu.

If your software lacks an obvious uninstall program, you can attempt to use Windows to rid yourself of it. You can open the Control Panel's Add/Remove Programs icon to try to uninstall software. Opening the Add/Remove Programs icon displays the Add/Remove Programs Properties dialog box, as shown in Figure 19-2.

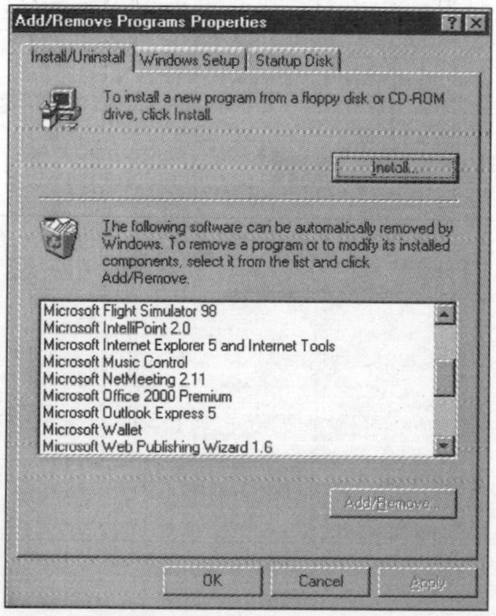

Figure 19-2: The Add/ Remove Programs Properties dialog box.

The list of programs that Windows knows about and can uninstall is listed at the bottom of the dialog box (refer to Figure 19-2). Click one of those programs, the one you want to uninstall. This selects the program for action. Then click the Add/Remove button.

A warning dialog box appears before Windows yanks the cord on your program. Click Yes to zap it to Kingdom Come.

✔ In Windows XP, click the Add or Remove Programs link in the Control Panel to access the Add/Remove Programs dialog box.

✔ Do not attempt to uninstall any software by deleting it from your hard drive. You should never delete any file you did not create yourself. (You can, however, delete any shortcuts you create.)

✔ The Norton AntiVirus is a third-party program that I paid for and installed on my own computer. It does not come with every Windows computer, so you may not have such a menu on your PC.

✔ You can also use the Add/Remove button to add individual components to your programs. For example, you can click Microsoft Office to add a new component or piece of that software, something you didn't choose to install way back when.

✔ For adding components missing from Windows, click the Windows Setup tab in the Add/Remove Programs Properties dialog box.

Updating Your Software

After a novel's written, it's finished. Subsequent reprints correct a few misspellings, but that's about it. But software's never finished. It's too easy to change. Most software packages are updated about once every year or two.

Out software, out!

The best way to remove unwanted programs — especially those without uninstall programs — is to get a third-party disk-cleaning program. I recommend CleanSweep, currently available from Peter Norton/Symantec.

CleanSweep searches your hard drive for every possible component installed with a program. It gives you a list so you can check and uncheck which components you really want to delete.

Further, it creates a backup copy of the uninstalled program so you can *undo* what CleanSweep does.

CleanSweep and other third-party uninstall programs work best when they monitor a program's installation. This way they know exactly what to remove and what to reset to bring your PC back to the state it was in before you installed your software.

The reason software is updated used to be to fix problems or to introduce new features. But, honestly, most of the reason new versions of programs appear today is to make more money for the software developer. Upgrading means that everyone who owns the software might buy a new version and generate revenue for the company. Yup, it's greed.

My advice: Order the update only if it has features or makes modifications you desperately need. Otherwise, if the current version is doing the job, don't bother.

- ✔ "Software never gets obsolete." — Bill Gates

- ✔ Consider each upgrade offer on its individual merits: Will you ever use the new features? Do you need a word processor that can print upside-down headlines and bar charts that show your word count? Can you really get any mileage out of the *intranet version* when you're a sole user sitting at home?

- ✔ Something else to keep in mind: If you're still using DoodleWriter 4.2 and everybody else is using DoodleWriter 6.1, you'll have difficulty exchanging documents. After a while, newer versions of programs become incompatible with the older models. If so, you need to upgrade.

- ✔ In an office setting, everybody should be using the same software version. (Everybody doesn't have to be using the *latest* version, just the *same* version.)

TIP

What about upgrading Windows?

Upgrading Windows is a *big deal*. Why? Because everything else in your computer relies on Windows. Therefore it's a major change, something to think long and deep about.

Often the newer version of Windows has many more features than the older version. Do you need those features? If not, don't bother with the update.

One problem you may have if you decide to upgrade is that your software may not work properly. None of my Adobe applications worked with Windows 95 when it first came out. I had to wait months and pay lots of money for upgrades before things got back to normal. When Windows 98 came out, I opted not to upgrade so I wouldn't have to go through the same hassle and expense. Windows XP? It just has too many changes that I deem unnecessary, so I'll skip that upgrade as well.

After a time, you may notice newer software packages coming to roost on the newest version of Windows. The new stuff will be better than your current stuff, meaning you'll need to upgrade if you want to take advantage of it.

So where does this leave you? *Don't bother updating Windows!* Just wait until you buy a new computer, and that PC will have the newest version of Windows, all preinstalled and set up nicely.

Some Tips for Learning a Program

Using software involves learning its quirks. That takes time. So my first suggestion for learning any new software is to give yourself plenty of time. Sadly, in today's rush-rush way of doing everything, time isn't that easy to come by. It's a big pain when the boss sends you down to the software store expecting you to come back and create something wonderful before the end of the day. In the real world, that's just not possible (not even if you're an expert).

Most software comes with a workbook or a tutorial for you to follow, which is a series of self-guided lessons on how to use the product. It also tells you about the program's basic features and how they work. I highly recommend going through the tutorials. Follow the directions on the screen. If you notice anything interesting, write it down in the tutorial booklet and flag that page.

Some tutorials are really dumb, granted. Don't hesitate to bail out of one if you're bored or confused. You can also take classes on using software, though they may bore you as well. Most people do, however, understand the program much better after the tutorial.

After doing the tutorial, play with the software. Make something. Try saving something to disk. Try printing. Then quit. Those are the basic few steps you should take when using any software program. Get to know it and then expand your knowledge from there as required.

- ✔ Some businesses may have their own training classes that show you the basics of using the in-house software. Take copious notes. Keep a little book for yourself with instructions for how to do what.

- ✔ Take notes whenever someone shows you something. Don't try to learn anything; just note what's done so you won't have to make a call should the situation arise again.

- ✔ Never toss out your manual. In fact, I recommend going back and trying to read the manual again several weeks after you start to learn a program. You may actually understand things. (Consider that the fellow who wrote the manual knew the product about as well when he first sat down to write about it.)

- ✔ Computer books are also a good source to learn about programs. They come in two types: references and tutorials. The tutorial is great for learning; references are best when you know what you want to do but aren't sure how.

- ✔ This book is a reference. All *For Dummies* books are references.

Chapter 20

Software Galore!

• •

In This Chapter

▶ Personal finance software

▶ Game and entertainment software

▶ Educational software

▶ Word processing

▶ Spreadsheets

▶ Databases

▶ Programming software

▶ Utility programs

▶ Shareware and freeware

• •

*I*t used to be that you could have just one computer, and on that computer, you could have a sample of every type of software on the market. Not anymore. Programs have grown so complex and occupy so much disk space — not to mention they get downright grumpy with each other from time to time — that having them all just isn't possible. You can try but probably won't succeed.

This second, and yes, last chapter in the software part of the book wraps up the discussion with the whirlwind tour of software tips: Loose ends of software, which all happen to be programs that computer nerds really enjoy! Maybe you will, too, should you have the time or desire.

Software for the Home

Who would have thought that a computer would become part of a home's furnishings? When you speak of furniture in the home, you typically use words like ottoman, chinoiserie, or credenza. But a computer desk? And just what is a credenza anyway? It's fun to say. Not as fun as bassoon, but close.

Home users have different interests than business users, which is why some software is written specifically for "home" things, such as education, entertainment, and personal finance software. People also do work at home, but the work stuff is covered in the section "Software for Business" because work is business, even home work.

Personal Finance

The old reasons for getting a computer were quaint and impractical: You could balance your checkbook, keep track of your recipes, and create a Christmas mailing list. Sheesh. They should have said: You can meet the mate of your dreams, dial up the Pentagon and launch a weapon, or kill a million space gremlins without getting blood on your tunic.

Even so, one of the most popular software packages of all time is called Quicken (see Figure 20-1). It's essentially a home (and business) accounting package that makes keeping track of your money easy and fun — yes, fun, in that most people actually sit down and balance their checkbooks because it's so dern easy.

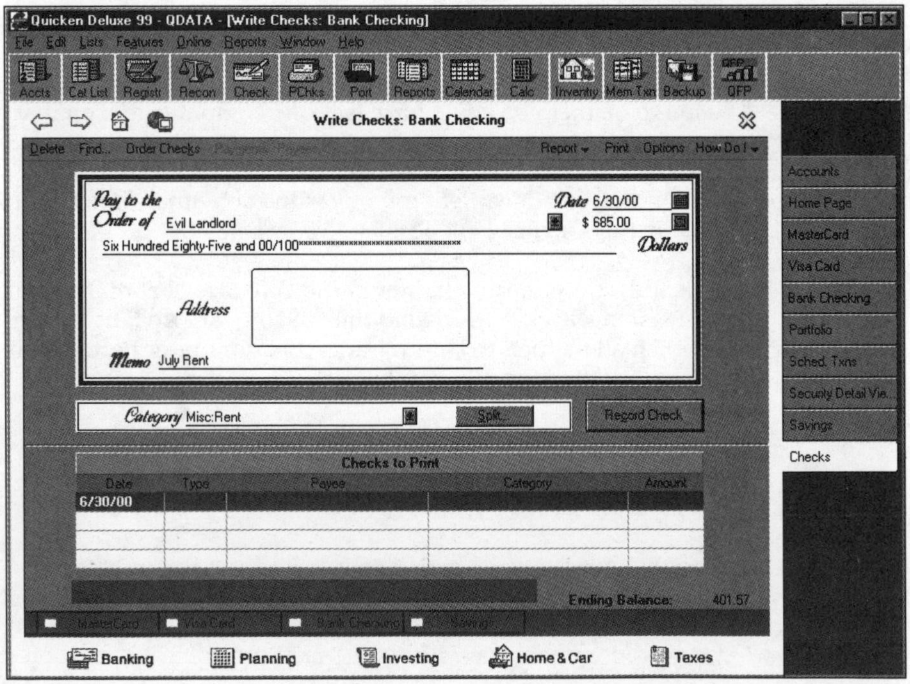

Figure 20-1:
Quicken helps you write checks.

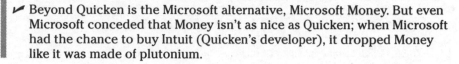

✔ Quicken can also do finances for a small or home business. For larger businesses, other financial software is available.

✔ Beyond Quicken is the Microsoft alternative, Microsoft Money. But even Microsoft conceded that Money isn't as nice as Quicken; when Microsoft had the chance to buy Intuit (Quicken's developer), it dropped Money like it was made of plutonium.

Games and entertainment

When it comes to leading edge, power-hungry, and top technology innovations you need look no further than the arena of computer games. Believe it or not, gaming software makes more demands on PC hardware than all other types of software combined. This is because the PC is just the most excellent gaming platform ever developed. Look in the PC game magazines and you'll find the most advanced computer available. The games need that hardware; they demand it.

To play a game on your PC in the best possible way, your computer should be equipped with the latest and best of everything:

✔ The most current, fastest microprocessor.

✔ A large, roomy hard drive.

✔ A CD-ROM or DVD drive. Nearly every game comes on a CD, although I predict that games will be the first software category to require DVD drives.

✔ A powerful graphics card. 3-D graphics is better. More memory on the graphics card (upwards of 8MB) is even better.

✔ A sound card. Gotta hear the crunch of your enemy's skull under the tank treads.

Optionally you might also need a joystick, though you can play many games using some combination of the mouse and the keyboard. If you do buy a joystick, ensure that it's fully compatible with the game. Many flight-simulator games are geared to work best with a specific brand of joystick. If you know that before you buy, you'll get the best possible configuration.

✔ See, Dad? I'm not making this up. When your kid begs you for the latest, bestest hardware for playing games, he's not joking around.

✔ The game lord's dream: a high-octane PC connected to a wall-sized video projector, stereo surround sound, and a large, cushy armchair to sink into. Disconnect the phone. See you in a week.

✔ Another popular way to play games is online. Plenty of sites allow you to play interactive games online with one or more other folks.

Rating the games

Nothing can be as disappointing as buying what you think is a nice, engaging computer game for your nine year old, only to find him frothing at the mouth as he controls a character on the screen who's ripping the spine from its electronic opponent. To prevent such shock (to the parent, not to the electronic opponent, who really doesn't feel a thing), two rating systems have evolved to allow parents or any PC game buyer to know what to expect before buying anything.

The Entertainment Software Review Board (ESRB) uses a five-level scale similar to movie ratings for its games (I'd show you the graphics here, but they're trademarked, and I'm too lazy to get permission):

✔ **EC:** Early Childhood means the game is designed for young children and would probably bore a teenager to tears.

✔ **K–A:** A G-rated game for kids to adults.

✔ **T:** A teen game with some violence and language, but nothing too offensive.

✔ **M:** Mature audiences only, preferably 17 years old or older. This is the type of game the teenager actually *wants*.

✔ **AO:** Adults only, with strong sexual content or gross violence.

Competing with the ESRB is the Recreational Software Advisory Council (RSAC). Unlike ESRB, which reviews software submitted to it, the RSAC is a voluntary rating decided by the software developer. It has three categories: Violence, Nudity/Sex, and Language. For each category, a tiny thermometer rates the content at four levels, with level 4 being the most offensive. (I'm personally striving for a level 5 in any category.)

As an example, a game I purchased recently has an RSAC Advisory label proclaiming that the game has a Violence rating of 3 and a Language rating of 2. The explanations given on the software box are, for Violence, "Blood and gore" and for Language, "Profanity." (Now please don't draw any conclusions about what type of game I like to play based on my "research." Ahem.)

You can get more information from the following Web sites:

✔ **ESRB:** www.esrb.org/

✔ **RSAC:** www.rsac.org/

Teach me something new today

Computers have always had educational software. It may not have been as flashy or as animated and noisy as it is today, but it's a grand old tradition. And don't just think identifying shapes or learning ABCs is all that educational software can do; it can teach you anything from typing to reading music to connecting a 24,000-volt transformer to your cell phone.

Like games, educational software comes in different types. Mavis Beacon (oh, Mavis!) teaches typing through a series of drills cleverly disguised as games. Dr. Seuss's ABCs is a read-along computer book that educates as it entertains.

✔ The best way to find good educational software is to ask around. Discover what others are using. Ask what the schools and preschools recommend. Family magazines, both computer and noncomputer, offer reviews and recommendations as well.

✔ Try to avoid game software that masks as educational. A hefty chunk of software designed for young children is really silly games, puzzles, and painting software with some educational bits tossed in as an after-thought. Your kids may have fun, but they won't be learning as well as they would otherwise.

✔ If you ever find yourself justifying a computer game with the catch-phrase *hand-eye coordination,* then be aware that something better is probably available. In fact, the best way for your kids to develop hand-eye coordination is to play catch or hit a ball with a bat.

Software for Business

Most software sold is for business use, probably because computers are still essentially office equipment. This doesn't mean you can't use the software at home; for example, Microsoft Word is a "business" word processor, but just about everyone uses it on their home computers for writing letters, diaries, and political manifestos. Still, I had to dream up a different category for this stuff, something to separate a serious product like Microsoft Word from Putt-Putt Wins the Race.

The following sections mull over some of the more popular categories of computer "business" software. Actually, I should call it "productivity" software, which includes all the workhorse stuff you use to get things done on your PC.

The wordy stuff

Just about everybody wants to use the computer to write something. Whether it's a thank-you note to Aunt Sally, a letter to the wacko liberal editor of your local paper, or a 500,000-word sweeping romance novel about two entomologists in Bolivia, computers make the writing process much easier.

Writing on a computer is officially known as *word processing.* The word processor is the most popular program on any computer. And why not? The best part about writing on a computer is that you can change what you've written without messing up the printed page. Editing on the screen means that each printed page will be perfect. Or as near perfect as you and the computer can make it.

There are three levels of word processing software: text editors, word processors, and desktop-publishing programs.

Text editors. A text editor is a bare-bones word processor. It won't let you set the margins, and forget about formatting the text or using different fonts. That's because text editors are designed to be fast and easy, for creating simple plain text files that computers use all the time. The point is that you often don't need the full power of a word processor, so the text editor neatly fills the gap.

- A text editor is basically a no-frills word processor.

- In Windows, the text editor is called Notepad.

- Text editors save their documents as plain text or ASCII files. No fancy-schmancy stuff.

- Actually, any word processor can be a text editor. The secret is to save the file as a *plain text* or *text only* type of file. Refer to Chapter 5 for more information on saving files of a certain type.

- Why should Freon cost anything?

Word processors. The word processor is the natural evolution of the type-writer. No longer are words written directly on paper. Instead, they're *words electric,* which you can toss around and fiddle with on the screen to your heart's content. Editing, fixing up stuff, spell checking, formatting — computers were made for this stuff. It's no wonder IBM sold off its typewriter division.

- Word processors work with text just like text editors, but they add formatting, styles, proofing, and a whole grab bag full of features that no one ever takes the time to learn.

- The files that word processors save are commonly called *documents*.

- In the early part of this century, Vladimir Nabokov wrote by hand while standing up. In the latter part of this century, he probably would have used a word processor — but standing up anyway.

- Windows has a word processor called WordPad. It's like an early version of Microsoft Word. In fact, WordPad has features that people would have drooled over ten years ago. Today, it's considered ho-hum. (But it's free with Windows, and besides, people don't drool as much as they used to.)

- The most popular word processor sold today is Microsoft Word.

- Another popular word processor can be found in the Microsoft Works productivity program. Be careful to note that Microsoft Works is not the same program as Microsoft Word.

Desktop publishing. The pinnacle of word processing achievement is desktop publishing, or DTP if you're in a hurry. It's where words and pictures are combined to produce professional-looking documents and publications.

With desktop publishing, you use a word processor to compose the text. Then you use one or more graphics programs to create images. And finally you put them all together by using a desktop publishing program.

✔ Yes, some word processors can also mix text and graphics. But if you've ever tried, you may notice that the word processors tend to slow down and crash when you get too fancy. That won't happen in desktop publishing programs, which are designed to mix text and graphics.

✔ Desktop publishing software is expensive. Cheaper, *home* versions are available. But the stuff the pros use is some of the spendiest software in the biz.

The numbery stuff

Word processors deal with words, but for numbers you need software called a spreadsheet, such as Microsoft Excel (see Figure 20-2).

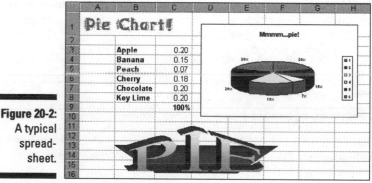

Figure 20-2:
A typical spread-sheet.

A spreadsheet uses a large grid of box-like *cells* on the screen (see Figure 20-2). Into those cells, you can put text, numbers, or formulas.

The formula part is what makes the spreadsheet so powerful: You can add various cells, compare values, and perform any number of odd or quirky mathematical operations or *functions*. The whole spreadsheet is instantly updated, too; change one value and see how it affects everything else. Millions of dollars have been embezzled this way.

✔ For adding up simple numbers, Windows comes with a calculator program. It can be found in the Accessories menu off the Start thing's Programs menu.

✔ More than numbers, spreadsheets can really handle any information that fits into a grid. For example, when doing my vacation schedule, I often use a spreadsheet because its grid is easier to work with than the tabs in Microsoft Word.

✔ Spreadsheets are also quite adept at doing graphics. The pie chart in Figure 20-2 took maybe 20 seconds to create, after answering some simple yes-or-no questions. Amazing stuff. Good pie, too.

✔ Don't be shy about using color in a spreadsheet — especially if you have a color printer!

✔ The files saved by spreadsheets are called *worksheets*. A worksheet is created by a spreadsheet. Even so, many people refer to worksheets as spreadsheets. Ain't no crime in that.

✔ Most spreadsheets can convert the numbers into graphs and charts, making it easier to visualize how much money the CEO is *really* making.

✔ The worksheets you create are blank, ready for you to fill them in. Some worksheets are not blank. They're called *templates* and have been pre-designed and customized to do specific tasks.

✔ Number crunching = using a computer to work mathematical problems.

The databasey stuff

Because the word and number processing chores are snapped up by word processors and spreadsheets, database programs are required to mangle every other type of data out there.

Two important things about *data* first: It's pronounced *day-tuh*. It's not *dat-uh*. Think *day-tuh*. The second thing is that *data* is just Latin for our word *stuff*. A database contains stuff, information mostly. (Data can also mean information, but I like *stuff* better.)

Databases do two things: sort and report. They handle any type of information,, whether it's words, numbers, or little-known bits of trivia (the *Lawrence Welk Show* was originally called the *Dodge Dancing Party,* or the scientific name for a gorilla is *Gorilla, gorilla*).

✔ Like spreadsheets, databases can be customized to match specific needs. Rather than toil on your own, you can hire a programmer to create a database perfectly suited to your line of work.

✔ Oh, heck, just put the programmer on the payroll; those guys never finish their work.

✔ Databases and spreadsheets can sometimes replace each other's jobs. If the fields in a database contain mostly numbers, a spreadsheet may work better. If a spreadsheet contains more labels and text, a database may be in order.

✔ Of all the computer software, databases are about the slowest. Especially if you have particularly huge files, fetching information from the database takes a lot of time.

✔ The designation *Gorilla gorilla* is a tautonym.

Those Office-Type Programs

To make even more money, the software developers have come up with so-called *office suite* types of programs. These suites are actually several software programs sold as a single unit. You can buy them cheaper that way, plus the software company makes oodles of money selling you upgrades from time to time. (You can find more on upgrading in Chapter 19.)

Office packages are great when you're starting out. But you might not consider one if you're buying it for just one piece of pie. For example, if you're just buying Microsoft Office XP to run Excel or Word, consider buying them separately. I see no point in junking up your hard drive with stuff you'll never use.

✔ Most people buy a version of Microsoft Office to run Word. That's it! They pay for the other programs but never use them.

✔ I might also mention that installing programs you don't plan on using is a waste of disk space.

✔ Most office programs allow you to select which of their applications you want to install when you set them up. You always have the option of adding the other applications later, so at first you should just select what you need.

✔ A good office program should offer: a word processor, spreadsheet, database, and graphics or presentation program, plus — and this is most important — the ability to integrate each of those items. Everything should work together smoothly.

Software for Nerds

Of course, I use the term *nerds* fondly. And so do they, when you get to know them. There is a certain delight in being enamored with a computer. Those who love their PCs call themselves nerds or geeks. They're terms of pride.

Do you need a database?

No, you don't need a database. You could probably benefit from one, but fewer people use databases than use spreadsheets.

If you want to mess with a database, then visit the local Software-O-Rama and pick up a simple mailing list database program. That's something you can probably use for managing the various lists of people you have (Holiday cards, Relatives, Baseball team members, Crime lords, and so on). The mailing list type of database can print out mailing labels or even create e-mail lists. Useful.

One day, you may become a computer nerd. Maybe not. If you do, you may end up programming the computer. Or you may just enjoy ogling over utility software, which I also cover in the sections that follow.

- ✔ Remember, computer nerds *create* the hardware and software you use. You can be quick to blame them when things are hard to understand, but be just as quick to thank them when you find something easy or enjoyable.

- ✔ Just because software is branded for one type of person doesn't mean you shouldn't try it. For example, graphics software can be fun and the results amazing, even if you don't wear a hemp beret.

Tell the stupid thing what to do with itself (programming)

To tell the computer what to do with itself, you must speak a language that the computer understands — a programming language. It's actually quite easy. (I have 9-year-olds who read my *C For Dummies* books and send me the programs they've written.)

The simplest programming language to learn is BASIC. Microsoft distributes a product called Visual Basic that makes building programs as easy as cut and paste. The BASIC language is easy to learn as well; most of the words are English, so the instructions read like commands you'd give a dog, for example:

```
PRINT "I am stupid"
```

And the computer diligently displays I am stupid on the screen. (It doesn't send the text to the printer, which would make sense. Throw me a bone.)

- ✔ Before you set out to program, understanding what a variable is and how it's used helps. For that, a wee bit of algebra is good.

- ✔ When you program, the computer does the math. You merely tell it the problem, and the computer solves it.

- ✔ BASIC is an acronym for Beginner's All-Purpose Symbolic Instruction Code.

- ✔ C is another good programming language to learn. Most programs sold today are written in the C language or in the C++ variation of the C language. (About 95 percent of the C++ language is basic C.)

- ✔ If you want to program for the Internet, then learning languages such as Perl or Java is beneficial.

The utility stuff

Most software is designed to help you get to work. Utility programs help your computer get to work. Basically, a utility helps a computer accomplish a chore, whether it's organizing the hard drive or figuring out why the computer isn't working right. In fact, most utilities are disk utilities.

Windows comes with most of the utilities you'll need. To see its portfolio of disk utilities, right-click on a disk drive in the My Computer window and choose Properties from the pop-up menu. Click the Tools tab, and you see three disk utilities you can (and should) run from time to time. Figure 20-3 shows the Tools tab in the disk drive Properties dialog box.

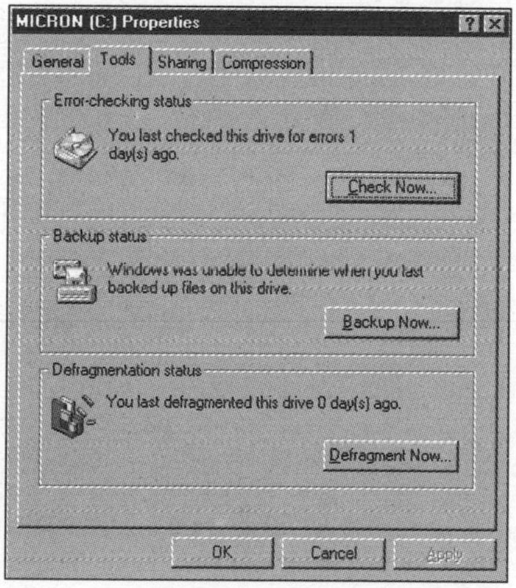

Figure 20-3: Windows disk utilities.

- ✔ On the Start menu, you can find Windows utilities in the Programs⇨Accessories⇨System Tools submenu. (In Windows XP, choose More Programs⇨Accessories⇨System Tools.)

- ✔ Windows comes with a few handy utilities, but that doesn't mean you shouldn't buy any more. A lot of the third-party utilities are tons better than the stuff Windows has.

- ✔ One utility that Windows doesn't come with is a virus checker. These utilities scan your hard drive for any evil programs and wipe them out before the viruses try some nasty trick. Virus checkers are mondo important if you download lots of files from the Internet. See Chapter 25.

- ✔ Even though Windows can, supposedly, uninstall software, you may consider buying an uninstall program. These programs do a much better job than Windows by itself, often saving you lots of disk space in the process. I recommend CleanSweep from Norton/Symantec as an excellent uninstall program.

Software for (Almost) Free

Frustrated by the system, some programmers give away their programs for free. Or almost free. Or sometimes free-with-strings-attached. Here's a breakdown of the several types of this freebie software available, each of which has its own cutsie name:

Public domain software. This is absolutely free stuff, written for the good of the people. No charge is ever made for the software, and you're free to do whatever you like with it.

Freeware. This software is also free for the taking, but the author retains ownership. You cannot modify the software or repackage it without permission.

Shareware. This is software you can try free. The software may have a special startup screen begging for money, or some feature may be disabled. After you pay for the software, you get the full program.

You can find most free or near-free software on the Internet, which I cover in Chapter 25. You may also be able to find the software at a computer store, a swap meet, or a user's group.

- ✔ Always get your software from a reputable source. Avoid programs sent to you at random and given by "friends." These programs often contain viruses. See Chapter 26 for more information on viruses.

- ✔ If you use shareware, pay for it. I do.

- ✔ Software will state that it's public domain or freeware. If it doesn't say so, it ain't free.

Part V
The Non-Nerd's Guide to the Internet

The 5th Wave   By Rich Tennant

[Cartoon: A man stands on a sidewalk holding a cup, wearing a sign that reads "NO INTERNET ADDRESS". A sign on the ground reads "PLEASE." with a hat in front of it.]

In this part . . .

The Internet has become such a big thing that its growth threatens to consume us. Eventually phone wires will encircle the globe to a degree that vacationing space aliens will go out of their way to visit the galaxy's largest ball of cable. It probably won't be that bad, but when you sit in a movie theater and everyone there gets a joke about something-dot-com, you know the Internet is a big deal. And its jokes are more effective than all those "hard drive" puns I made in the '80s.

This part of the book covers the Internet. It's the Web! It's e-mail! It's pictures of your Chihuahua sent to everyone you know! Well, that and a whole lot more. These chapters give you the whirlwind tour. (Refreshments will be served in the lobby at intermission.)

Chapter 21

Introducing the Internet

● ●

In This Chapter

▶ What the Internet is all about

▶ Things you need to get on the Internet

▶ Finding an Internet service provider (ISP)

▶ Setting up Windows for the Internet

▶ Connecting to the Internet

▶ Saying bub-bye to the Internet

● ●

There is a point in the space-time continuum where your telephone, TV, and computer collide. That point is the Internet.

The Internet has grown from a way for computer scientists and researchers to share information to a way for your teenage daughter to type at her friends for hours on end. Seriously, the Internet brings the world of communications and information to your desktop computer. Just about everyone you know is either on the Internet or thinking about getting on the Internet. And if they aren't, why then those reactionary fools shall suffer the have-not consequences of their perilous decisions! Ha!

A-hem.

Taking things one at a time, this chapter is your basic Internet orientation. It starts with getting on the Internet, then describes what you can do next, and finally gets you off the Internet — which always seems to be the hardest step!

The 1¢ Description of the Internet

It's easy to describe the Internet by what it's not:

The Internet is not a piece of software.

The Internet is not a single computer.

No one person owns the Internet, though Bill Gates is trying as hard as he can.

The Internet is really thousands and thousands of computers all over the world. The computers send information. They receive information. And, most importantly, they store information. That's the Internet.

- The idea behind using the Internet is to get at that information.

- The best way to get at the information stored on the Internet is by using a piece of software called a *Web browser*. I cover browsers in the next two chapters.

- Information is also exchanged via e-mail, which is used by more people than the Web. (Believe it or not, e-mail is number one, and using the Web is a distant second.)

- Chapter 22 covers e-mail. Actually Chapter 24 does as well. E-mail is a big topic.

You Have Almost Everything You Need to Get on the Internet

There are six things you'll need to access the Internet, five of which you probably have and one of which you'll have to go out and get.

Here are the five things you most likely have already:

Your computer. Enough said.

Your modem. Rare is the PC without a modem. If yours is one of the rare ones, then go out and buy an external modem today. (See Chapter 15 for more modem mayhem.)

A way to talk to the Internet. This is commonly done through the phone line, though there are DSL, Cable modems, and other ways to access the Internet.

Internet software. Windows comes with nearly all the software you need.

Money. This is perhaps the toughest thing to come by; access to the Internet costs you, just like cable TV. Expect to pay anywhere from $5 to over $100 a month to get on the Internet, depending on which type of service you get. The average cost is about $20 a month.

Here is the final thing you need to get on the Internet — the one you probably don't have right now:

An *Internet Service Provider* or **ISP.** Obtaining an ISP is covered in the next section.

- Though I hate using acronyms, ISP is becoming popular enough that I feel I must. Not only is it easier to type, but many people today say "ISP" and don't even know that it stands for Internet Service Provider.

- Though the Internet isn't a program, you do need special software to access the Internet and to send or retrieve information.

- Windows comes with Internet software, but other alternatives are available. These alternatives are covered in the appropriate chapters that follow.

- It's best to access the Internet through a separate phone line. Do your computer a favor and buy it its own phone line.

- If you work for a large company, it may already give you Internet access through the network at your office. Ditto for universities and some government installations.

What to look for in an ISP

The best way to get on the Internet is through an ISP. ISPs give you a direct connection to the Internet, plus they may offer 24-hour help or classes to get you started.

The S in ISP stands for *service*. For the money you pay, the ISP must provide you with service. This includes the following items at the least:

- Internet access from your computer using a modem. This is the most basic thing.

- A local phone number to dial.

- An e-mail account. Some ISPs offer more accounts in family or office plans. Every person needs an e-mail account. Get the login names and passwords, too.

- A *getting started* booklet, class, software, or other information to ease you onto the Information Superhighway.

- A toll-free help line, classes, or some other form of *human* help. This is key, especially for beginners.

I rave about ISPs that offer those *getting started* pamphlets. The pamphlet should contain everything you need to know about connecting to the Internet, all the secret numbers you need, plus the phone number and your passwords and other information. This is a must.

What about AOL as an ISP?

I'm not a big AOL fan. Believe me, I've tried. I used it back in the '80s on my Macintosh when it was called AppleLink. And I've had several accounts since then. For me, in the world of high-speed ISPs, AOL is a throwback. But can 20 million users be wrong?

Pro: AOL is great if you're just starting out. The software is free, and it's easy to set up. Access is available all over, which means you can get your mail and go online when you travel. And AOL is widely supported by many companies, news organizations, and online retailers.

Con: Using AOL is *slower* than directly connecting to the Internet through an ISP. You're limited by the AOL software, through which Web pages are funneled, as opposed to viewing them

directly with a true Web browser. Also, AOL's e-mail is non-standard, meaning some attachments cannot be received (see Chapter 25). Though AOL's phone lines may not be as busy as in days past, AOL is still subject to outages. And AOL's help system is impersonal.

I favor a local ISP because you often get hometown service and the fastest Internet access possible. All of your Internet software works, and you're not restricted to certain places or prevented access because the system is busy.

My advice: If you use AOL chiefly for e-mail, great! But if you use AOL for Internet access, consider moving to an ISP in the future. The price may be cheaper, and you may end up with better access to the Internet.

Beyond the basics, try to find an ISP that offers most of the following:

- **Unlimited access time.** Some ISPs charge by the hour. Avoid them. If they charge by the block of time, get a plan where you can have 100 or more hours a month. Only the very sturdy can be on the Internet for more than 100 hours in a month.

- **Web space or disk storage space.** This is a small amount of the provider's disk storage you can use for whatever. If the provider offers it, you can use the space to create your own Web page at some point in the future.

- **Web support tools.** These include mostly advanced goodies used for Web publishing, such as FTP access, Real Audio/Video abilities, CGI programming, Web page statistics, and even programmers for hire.

- **Other stuff.** The list of items an ISP can offer is endless, including high-speed DSL or Cable Modem access, Newsgroups, plus even more and even stranger goodies that are way too complex to get into now. The more they offer, the merrier.

- Don't get a shell account unless you enjoy using UNIX.

Finding an ISP

Most cities and even towns and hamlets have their own ISPs. I highly recommend that you go with a local outfit, not some large impersonal organization like, well, Verio. No, service is important in an ISP, and nothing beats the local Ma-and-Pop Internet Shop.

If your area is blessed with more than one ISP, shop around. Find the one that gives you the best deal. Oftentimes, the cheapest ISP lacks a lot of features that other ISPs offer (but it won't tell you that unless you know what you're missing). Also, paying quarterly or annually (if you can afford it) is cheaper than paying monthly. These places can wheel and deal with you — providing that you know a bit about what you want.

  ✔ Don't be afraid to change ISPs if yours doesn't work out. I've done this twice. Please don't put up with crummy service; change ISPs if you need to.

  ✔ Most communities have several ISPs offering access to the Internet. You can find them in the yellow pages under *Internet.* Some of them even advertise on TV, usually late at night along with the 1-900 psychic babe hotlines.

  ✔ I might add that ISPs with 24-hour service rank high on my list. If your e-mail dies at 11:00 p.m., and you need to get online, it's nice to have someone there who can help you.

Configuring Windows for the Internet

Setting up your PC to do the Internet is not all that hard, provided you have the following three things:

  ✔ A silver bowl
  ✔ A ceremonial knife, preferably bejeweled
  ✔ An unblemished goat

No. Wait. You needed those things in the *old days,* back before Windows came with the Internet Connection Wizard. Now all you need is some information from your Internet service provider, and the Internet Connection Wizard does the rest.

Here's what you need to run the Wizard:

- ✔ The phone number to call.

- ✔ Your ISP's domain name — the blorf.com or yaddi.org thing.

- ✔ Your Internet login ID and password.

- ✔ Your Internet e-mail name, address, and password (if different from your login ID and password).

Additionally you may also need the following, so have them handy:

- ✔ The number for your provider's DNS (Domain Name Server). This is a four-part number separated by periods, like this: 123.456.789.0.

- ✔ The name of your ISP's e-mail server, which involves the acronyms POP3 or SMTP.

- ✔ The name of your ISP's news (NNTP) server.

Fortunately, your ISP probably provided you with *all* of this information when you signed up. It should be handy on a sheet of paper for you or located inside a booklet. All you need to do is tell the Internet Connection Wizard about the numbers. It does the rest.

Running the Internet Connection Wizard

The easiest way to start the Internet Connection Wizard is to look for the Internet Connection Wizard shortcut icon on the desktop. If you see it there, open it: click-click. That gets things rolling. Otherwise, finding the Internet Connection Wizard on the Start menu varies with your edition of Windows:

From the Start menu choose <u>P</u>rograms⇨Accessories⇨Communications⇨ Connection Wizard. (In Windows XP, choose More Programs, then Accessories, and so on.)

Run the Wizard and answer the questions using the information provided to you by your ISP. Read the screens. Click the Next button to move on.

Dial-Up
Networking

After everything is done, and you click the Finish button, your Internet connection will be saved in a special folder. This folder contains the icon representing the settings you've just made, and you can use that icon to connect to the Internet if you like (though running any Internet program, such as Internet Explorer, makes the connection automatically).

- ✔ The name of the special folder in Windows 98 is Dial-Up Networking. You access it from the My Computer window.

- ✔ In Windows Me, you can access the Dial-Up Networking folder from the Control Panel.

✔ In Windows 2000, the special folder is named Network and Dial-Up Connections, which you can access from the Start menu, Settings sub-menu.

✔ In Windows XP, open the Control Panel and choose Network and Internet Connections, then click the Network Connections icon. This displays the Network Connections window, where the Internet and local area network icons reside.

✔ To set up AOL, just install the AOL software from the CD. You're done.

✔ You need to run this wizard only once. Well, if you change or add ISPs, you need to do it again.

✔ Never toss out the booklet or sheet of information your ISP gave you! You may need those numbers later.

✔ Your Internet login ID and password will be different from the user ID and password you use to get into Windows. You need a different ID and password for each system you access.

✔ $111,111,111 \times 111,111,111 = 12,345,678,987,654,321.$

Connecting to the Internet

Connecting to the Internet is cinchy; simply run any Internet program on your computer. Windows is smart enough to connect automatically for you. Here's how things go most of the time:

1. Start your Web browser.

In Windows, the browser is Internet Explorer. Double-click the Internet Explorer icon on the desktop, or choose Programs⇨Internet Explorer⇨ Internet Explorer from the Start menu.

2. Fill in the connection dialog box (if it appears).

After the Internet software starts (the Web browser in this case), the Connect To dialog box may appear. Figure 21-1 shows one version of that dialog box. There is a second version of the dialog box that displays an additional list of messages ("Dialing" and so on). Both dialog boxes work the same.

Enter your Internet username.

Enter your password.

Click the Connect button.

Click in the Save Password box if you don't want to be troubled to type in the password each time you log on. However, for laptops and in open office environments, I recommend deselecting that item.

To connect automatically without seeing a dialog box first, just start any of your Internet programs, such as Internet Explorer or Outlook Express. To make that happen, click in the Connect Automatically box.

Clicking the Connect button is optional; if you've configured Windows to connect automatically, you don't need to click anything. The modem just dials by itself: *Boop-beep-doop-dap-dee-dee-dee*.

Hopefully you're connected and logged into your ISP, ready to do the Internet. If not, Windows gives you a few more tries to make the connection. After that, you have to start all over.

3. Waiting while the modem dials.

Doh-dee-doh.

4. You're connected!

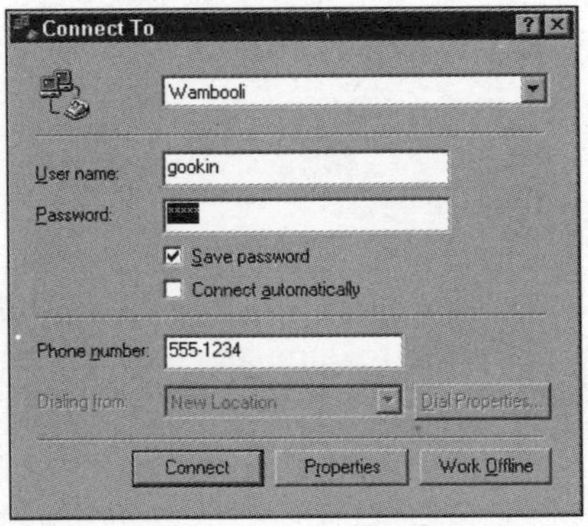

Figure 21-1:
The
Connect To
dialog box.

After you're connected, you may see the Connection Established dialog box, shown in Figure 21-2. You're there! Welcome to the Internet. Read the dialog box. Click in the Do Not Show This Dialog Box in the Future check box if you want. Then click Close.

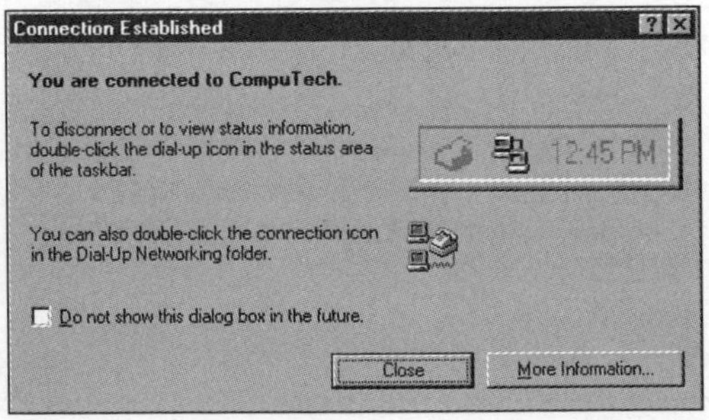

Figure 21-2:
The
Connected
to Whatever
dialog box.

"But I always have to enter my password!"

Q: You say it works one way in your book, but on my computer screen I always have to enter the password to connect to the Internet. Always. And the Save Password item is gray, so I cannot select it. Why is this happening?

A: It could be for a number of reasons. First, you may have a laptop and therefore would be unable to save the password for security reasons. Second, you probably didn't log in properly to Windows. If you click Cancel in the password dialog box displayed when Windows first starts, then Windows won't remember any passwords that you've previously typed. You must log into Windows properly for it to remember the passwords.

After closing the Connection Established dialog box — or even if it doesn't appear — you should notice a new teensy icon in the system tray (on the right end of the taskbar), looking like the graphic in the margin. That's your Connected To Whatever teensy icon indicator, telling you that you're online with the Internet and ready to run your Internet software.

Continue reading in the next section.

- ✔ To connect to AOL, start the AOL software. Choose your screen name and type in your password in the Welcome dialog box. Click the Sign On button to connect. See? Simple.

- ✔ If you have a DSL or cable modem, then you're probably on the Internet all the time already. In that case, you don't need to manually connect to the Internet, nor do you need to disconnect. Simply run any Internet program and — ta-da! — there you are.

- ✔ Some DSL or cable modems may disconnect you, depending on how your ISP sets things up. In that case, you will need to go through the connection procedures described in this section.

- ✔ Use the Work Offline button to tell Windows not to connect to the Internet. That way you can use your Web browser to view documents on your computer or read your e-mail without connecting.

- ✔ If it bugs you later that Windows connects automatically to the Internet, you can always turn off that option. When the Dialing Progress dialog box appears (automatically), click the Cancel button. That action redisplays the connection dialog box (Figure 21-1), where you can un-check the Connect Automatically check box.

- ✔ Keep an eye out for the Connected To Whatever teensy icon indicator on the taskbar! It's your reminder that your PC is talking with the Internet.

Doing Something on the Internet (Using Internet Software)

After you've made the connection to your ISP, you're ready to run any or all of your Internet software. Fire up your Web browser, e-mail package, or any of a number of applications designed for fun and folly on the Internet.

✔ As long as you have the Internet connection, you can run any program that accesses information on the Internet.

✔ Yes, you can run more than one Internet program at a time. I typically have three or four of them going at once. (Because the Internet is slow, I can read one window while waiting for something to appear in another window.)

✔ You can also stay on the Internet while using an application program like Word or Excel. Just don't forget you're online.

✔ Close your Internet programs when you're done with them.

Adios, Internet!

To wave bye-bye to the Internet, follow these steps:

1. **Quit all of your Internet programs.**

   This step isn't a must, but it's a starting point. If you want to keep your programs open (say, to read a long Web page), that's okay too; just don't close that window, and move on to the next step.

2. **Tell Windows to hang up the phone.**

   Chances are Windows will want to hang up automatically when you quit your Internet programs. A dialog box appears, such as the one shown in Figure 21-3. Click the disconnect button, Disconnect Now (or it may be labeled only Disconnect). You're disconnected.

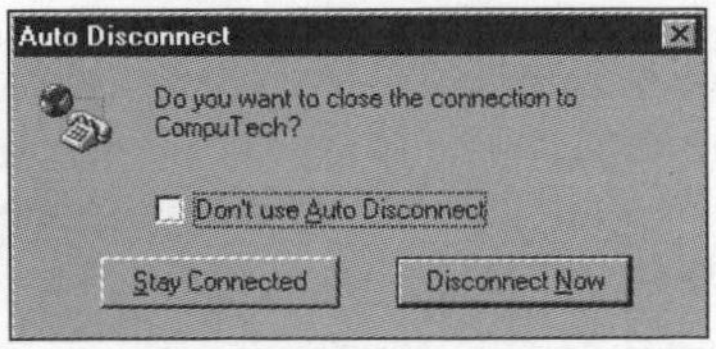

Figure 21-3:
A disconnect dialog box.

Auto Disconnect

Do you want to close the connection to CompuTech?

☐ Don't use Auto Disconnect

[Stay Connected] [Disconnect Now]

If a disconnect dialog box doesn't appear, such as when you want to keep a window or two open, then you must *manually* disconnect. To do this, double-click the Connected To Whatever teensy icon indicator in the system tray. A window appears, looking like Figure 21-4. Click the Disconnect button. You're done.

- ✔ On AOL, you can choose Sign Off⇨Sign Off from the menu to disconnect but continue using the AOL program. Choosing File⇨Exit disconnects as well as quits the AOL program.

- ✔ Never forget to disconnect from the Internet.

- ✔ Big hint that you're no longer connected to the Internet: The little Connected To Whatever teensy icon indicator disappears from the system tray on the taskbar.

- ✔ You can keep track of how much time you've spent online by viewing the Connected To Whatever dialog box. This information is important when you eventually grow to spend several more hours on the Internet than you originally intended. Just double-click the Connected To Whatever teensy icon indicator in the system tray. View the time. Exclaim, "My goodness, that's a long time!" and then click the OK button.

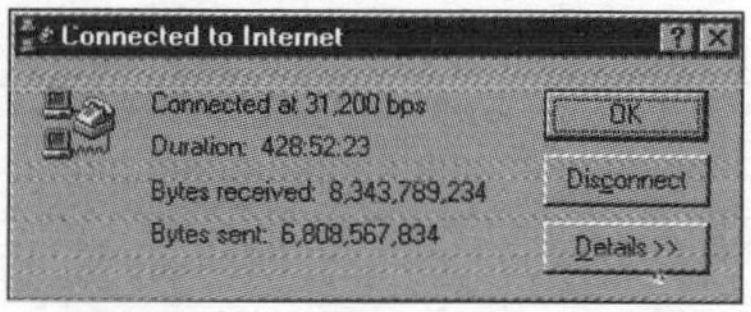

Figure 21-4:
Click the
Disconnect
button to bid
farewell to
the Internet.

Connected to Internet

Connected at 31,200 bps
Duration: 428:52:23
Bytes received: 8,343,789,234
Bytes sent: 6,808,567,834

OK

Disconnect

Details >>

Chapter 22

Basic Internet Stuff

• •

• •

*T*he World Wide Web is directly responsible for making the Internet as popular as it is today. The Web introduced the Internet to graphics and text. And after the ugly and intimidating Unix-like nature of the Internet was removed, everyone wanted to "surf the Web."

Beyond the Web, there's e-mail, which is actually more popular. E-mail is as old as the Internet itself, but with the popularity of the Web, Internet e-mail use has exploded. And nothing beats the joy of getting new e-mail. For some people, it's all they live for every day.

This chapter covers the Web and e-mail. They are the two things you'll waste time, er, spend time doing on the Internet more than anything else.

Say Hello to the Web

Prepare to dip yourself into the cool waters of the Internet. . . .

The chief piece of software used to access information on the Internet is a Web browser, or *browser* for short. Fortunately for all mankind, Microsoft has deemed that Windows is, in fact, a Web browser. That means you don't really need to buy any more software to access information on the Internet. Aren't we all lucky?

> ✔ Though other Web browsers exist, this book assumes that Internet Explorer (IE) is your Web browser.
>
> ✔ You can also browse the Web in AOL, though there are restrictions and limitations to browsing the Web in AOL not covered in this book.

Starting Internet Explorer

Open the Internet Explorer icon on the desktop to start your Web browser. If you're not already connected to the Internet, you will be (refer to Chapter 21). And soon, Internet Explorer's main window fills with a *page* of information from the World Wide Web (see Figure 22-1).

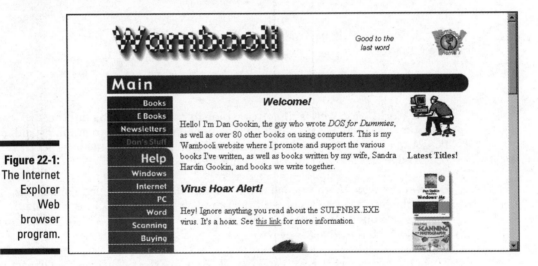

Figure 22-1:
The Internet Explorer Web browser program.

The first page you see is called the *home page*. It's merely the first page you see when you start your Web browser. (It's not your own personal page on the Web, but you can change it to that page if you like; see the section "Take me home!" later in this chapter.)

You should notice a few things in the Web browser window:

Button bar. Below the menu bar, you find a series of buttons. You use these buttons to visit various places on the Web and do basic things with your Web browser.

Busy thing. The far right of the button bar has what I call the *busy thing*. The busy thing becomes animated when the Web browser is doing something, which usually means that it's waiting for information to be sent from the far parts of the Internet. That's your signal to sit, wait, and be patient; the Web is busy.

Address box. As in the days of DOS, you can type in various commands to make the browser visit certain places on the Web. These commands are officially known as *URLs,* though I call them Web page addresses. Either way, what you type is cryptic, but you can get used to it.

Web page. The contents of the Web browser (what it displays) is a page of information on the Web. In Figure 22-1, you see the home page for *Wambooli,* my company's home page on the Web (`http://www.wambooli.com`).

Scroll bars. What you see on the Web may often be larger than your browser's window. So you don't miss out, scroll bars allow you to move the Web page's contents hither and thither.

The Web browser shows you how simple it is to view information on the Internet. What you see are graphics and text — almost like a magazine. In addition, some Web pages may have animation on them. Many Web pages also play music while you're viewing them (which can be annoying). Also, you do most of your input with the mouse. Only rarely do you have to type anything. I suppose that's why it's called *browsing* and not *hunting and pecking*.

- ✔ The busy thing will be busy a lot. It's often said that the World Wide Web should be WWWW, the fourth W being Wait.

- ✔ You pronounce only the letters in URL: *You Are El.* It's an acronym for Uniform Resource Locator. Essentially it's a command that you give the Web browser to go out and find something on the Internet.

- ✔ Most URLs you type start with http://. That cryptic doodad is actually an Internet command. The text that follows http:// is the address of that information — its location on some computer somewhere in the world. Think of it as the *location* of a file on the Internet, much like the location of a file on your hard drive.

- ✔ Only rarely will you type in a Web page address. Normally, you can do most of your navigation on the Web by clicking various *links* located on a Web page or by choosing a Web page from your list of bookmarks or favorites. More on that in a sec.

- ✔ In AOL, type a Web page address into the navigation bar just below the row of buttons just below the menu bar. Click the Go button to open the Web page.

- ✔ Web pages can be wider and very often longer than what you see displayed in your browser's window. Don't forget to use the scroll bars! Better still, maximize the browser window to get the full-screen effect.

Visiting somewhere webbish

An estimated 100,000,000 pages of information are on the World Wide Web. Why not visit them all?

To visit a Web page, you have two choices. First, you can manually type in the address of some page somewhere on the planet — you know, all those http://www-slash-dot-com-dot-slash-dash things you see all over the place. Second, and more easily, you can click a *link,* which is a piece of text or graphic on one Web page that takes you to another Web page.

The manual way. To manually visit any Web page in the known universe, type in its address in the Address bar near the top of the Internet Explorer window.

Type in the address *exactly.* Upper and lower case mean different things; it must be exact.

Use the backspace or delete keys to erase or edit any text already in the Address bar.

When you're ready to visit that Web page, press Enter. For example, to visit the CNN Web page (`http://www.cnn.com`), you type **http**, a colon, two forward slashes, **www**, a period, **cnn**, another period, **com**. You don't need to type a final period at the end of that address. Just type it in like it looks, weird stuff and all. Press Enter and you'll (eventually) see the CNN Web page, displaying the latest news from around the world (with an American slant, of course).

✔ If the Web page doesn't load, you may see some type of error message. First thing you should do is try again! The Web can be busy, and oftentimes when it is, you get an error message.

✔ If you get a *404* error, then you probably didn't type in the Web page address properly. Try again!

✔ The keyboard shortcut for getting to the address box is Ctrl+L. When you press that key combination, a dialog box appears into which you can type a Web page address.

✔ In the Now He Tells Us Dept.: The http:// part of a Web page address is optional. The browser automatically assumes you mean to type in http:// even when you forget.

✔ On the other hand, if a Web page address starts with ftp:// or gopher://, then you're required to type in those commands.

The automatic way. It's called a *Web* because nearly every page has a link to other pages. For example, a Web page about the end of the world may have links to Web pages about Nostradamus or that guy who walks around with a sandwich board that says, "Doom is near." Click the link to see more information.

Most links on Web pages are text. The text appears underlined and usually in a different color from other text on the screen.

Links can also be graphical; some pictures are links. The only way to know for certain is to hover the mouse pointer over a link. If the pointer changes to a pointing hand, then you know that it's a link you can click to see something else.

- Clicking a link takes you to another Web page, just like typing in a new address but without typing in a new address.

- Quite a few Web pages are simply collections of links.

- Any good, informative Web page will have links relating to other topics. You find most links at the bottom of the Web page, though some Web pages have the links laced throughout the text.

- Link is short for *hyperlink* — yet another bit of trivia to occupy a few dozen neurons.

Going back, way back, forward, and stop

Following links can be fun. That's the way most people waste time on the Web. For example, I found a Web page recently that explained all the lyrics to Don McLean's *American Pie*. I don't know how I got there; I just ended up there after clicking a few dozen links. Unlike Hansel and Gretel, I neglected to leave breadcrumbs along the Information Superhighway. Fortunately, the Web browser does that for you.

To return to the Web page you were just ogling, use your Web browser's Back button. You can continue clicking the Back button to revisit each Web page you've gawked at, all the way back to the first page you saw 18 hours ago.

If you really need to dig deep, click the down arrow by the Back button. A list of the last several Web pages you've visited appears. (In Netscape, you can also use the Go menu to see the past few pages.)

And if you need to return from going back, you use the Forward button. Back. Forward. It's like learning to drive, but no hills.

Finally, if you accidentally click a link and change your mind, click the Stop button. The Internet then stops sending you information. (You may need to click the Back button to return back to where you were.)

- These buttons are also found on AOL's navigation bar.

- The American Pie link:

```
http://urbanlegends.com/songs/american_pie_-
          interpretations.html
```

Ah! How refreshing

Your browser's Refresh button serves a useful purpose in the world of ever-changing information. Refresh merely tells the Internet to resend you the information on a Web page. That's it!

The reasons for clicking the Refresh button:

Changing information. Many Web pages have updating information on them. Clicking the Refresh button always gets you the latest version of the Web page.

Missing pictures. Occasionally a graphic image may not appear. In that case, a *blank* icon shows up, telling you the image is missing. Oftentimes, clicking the Refresh button works some magic that causes the image to reappear.

Accidental click of the Stop button. Oops! Click Refresh to unstop and reload the Web page.

Take me home!

To visit your home page, click the Home button. This action takes you back to the first page you saw when you connected with the Internet.

The beauty of the home page is that you can change it. For example, I use Yahoo! as my home page. (Yahoo is a portal site, like an airport terminal for connecting to other places on the Internet.) To set a home page, follow these steps:

1. **Visit the page you want to call home.**

   For example, Yahoo is at `http://www.yahoo.com`. Type that into the Address box to visit that page.

2. **Choose Tools⇨Internet Options.**

3. **Click the Use Current button in the Home Page area of the General tab.**

   See Figure 22-2.

4. **Click OK.**

The new home page is now set. And you can change it again at any time. After all, it's *your* home page!

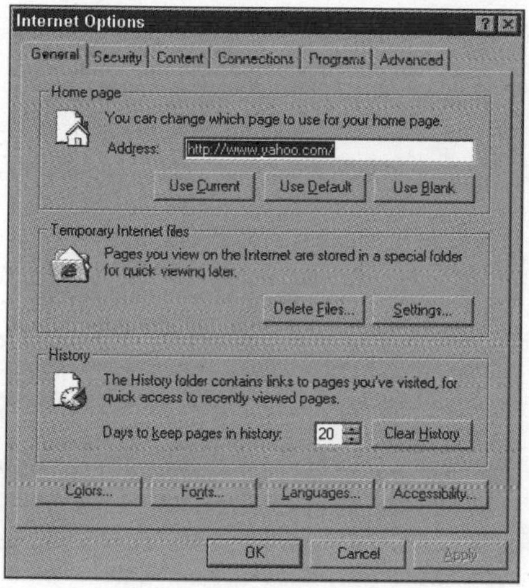

Figure 22-2:
The Internet
Options
dialog box.

Quitting Internet Explorer

After you're done browsing the World Wide Web — meaning that it's 4:00 a.m. and you need to get up in 90 minutes to get ready for work — you should quit Internet Explorer. This is easy: Choose File⇨Close from the menu.

Quitting Internet Explorer does not disconnect you from the Internet. If you're using a modem connection, then you must manually disconnect if Windows doesn't automatically prompt you. See Chapter 21 for more information on disconnecting from the Internet.

Mail Call!

Nothing perks up your Internet day like getting fresh e-mail. If you have AOL, then you get the mellifluous, "You've got mail!" greeting at the start of a productive day. *Ahhhh, people care enough about me to write! I'm loved!*

The following sections deal with e-mail, which can be an obsession for some folks. In fact, if you're like most people, you'll probably run both your Web browser and e-mail program at the same time. That way you won't "miss anything" while you're on the Internet.

- This book assumes that you have Outlook Express (Version 5), the Windows e-mail package.

- Outlook Express is *not* the same program as Outlook, which is another e-mail program made by Microsoft and distributed with Microsoft Office.

✔ Oh, and this chapter mentions AOL, though the subject here is really Outlook Express.

Starting Outlook Express

Outlook Express

Start Outlook Express by opening the Outlook Express icon on the desktop (shown in the margin). You may also find the icon on the Quick Launch bar.

If you aren't already connected to the Internet, starting Outlook Express connects you. If not, refer to Chapter 21 for information on connecting to the Internet.

REMEMBER

You cannot send or receive e-mail unless you're connected to the Internet.

The first thing Outlook does is check for new mail. Refer to the section "Reading e-mail," later in this chapter, if you *really* can't wait to get started. Outlook also sends any mail you have waiting.

Figure 22-3 details the Outlook Express screen. It consists of three parts:

Folders list. On the upper left of the window is the list of folders where sent, received, trashed, and filed mail goes.

Contact list. On the bottom left is a list of *contacts,* people with whom you may normally communicate.

Message summary. On the right is a "home page" of sorts for messages, newsgroups, and stuff. You may or may not see this screen. Instead, you may configure Outlook to display your Inbox whenever you switch it on: Click in the When Outlook Express Starts, Go Directly to My Inbox check box.

The opening screen for Outlook Express is something you really don't want to see. No, you want to get that mail! Click the Inbox link to see any old or new messages you've received.

When you go to the Inbox (Figure 22-4), the right side of the screen splits into two parts. The top part shows the queue of e-mail in the Inbox. Bold text indicates unread mail; normal lines indicate read mail (and the open/closed envelope icon confirms this information).

The bottom-right part of the window shows a preview of the message's contents, such as the advertisement in Figure 22-4.

TIP

Between the left and right side of the window is a separator bar. You can drag that bar with the mouse, making either side larger. My advice is to drag the separator bar to the left, making the Inbox and preview windows larger.

Folders list   Unread messages

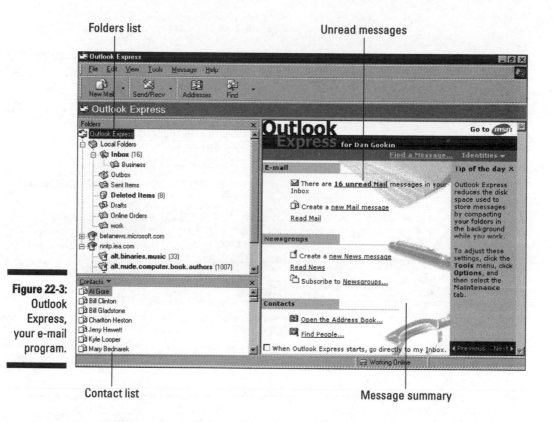

Figure 22-3:
Outlook
Express,
your e-mail
program.

Contact list   Message summary

That's it for your introduction! If you have mail waiting, jump forward to the section "Reading e-mail." Otherwise, continue with the next section on composing a new message.

> ✔ Most e-mail programs look similar to Outlook Express. Often an Inbox displays pending messages in bold type and read messages in normal type. A list of folders is off to the side.

> ✔ You probably won't have any mail waiting for you right away. Oh, you may have a welcome message from Microsoft. Like it cares. . . .

Sending e-mail

In order to get e-mail, you must first send it.

Naturally you're popular. People love you. And you give out your e-mail address to everyone you've ever met. Even so, to get a lot of e-mail you have to send a lot of e-mail. Occasionally some people will send you spontaneous stuff, but keep in mind that communication is a two-way street.

Envelope icon   Read mail   Unread mail

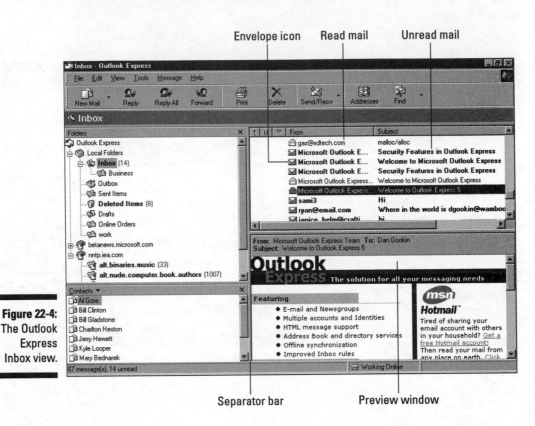

Figure 22-4:
The Outlook
Express
Inbox view.

Separator bar   Preview window

To create a new message in Outlook Express, click the New Mail button. The New Message window appears, as shown in Figure 22-5. Your job is to fill in the blanks.

To. Who are you sending the message to? Type the person's e-mail address into the To field.

- ✔ To compose an e-mail epistle, you need to know the e-mail address of some other person on the Internet. Your friends and coworkers can give you this information, and it's extremely trendy to put your e-mail address on your business card and résumé.

- ✔ Do not put spaces in the e-mail address. If you think it's a space, then it's probably an underline.

- ✔ You must enter the full e-mail address: blah@wambooli.com. Note the single exception: If you have e-mail nicknames set up, you can type the nickname into the To field instead of the full e-mail address. (See Chapter 24 for information on nicknames.)

Type subject here

Type e-mail address here

Send button

Click this to check your spelling

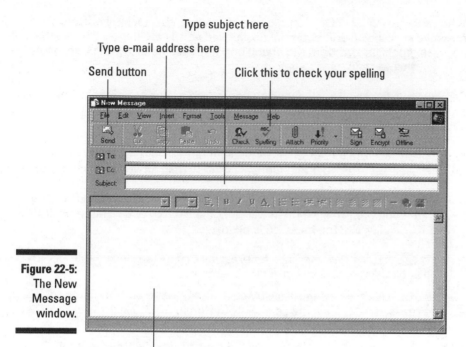

Figure 22-5:
The New
Message
window.

Message contents go here

✔ You can type in more than one address in the To field. If so, separate each with a semicolon, as in:

```
president@whitehouse.gov;first.lady@whitehouse.gov
```

✔ If you type in the wrong e-mail address, the message *bounces* back to you. This is not a bad thing; just try again with the proper address.

Cc. The carbon copy field. This field contains e-mail addresses of people you want to carbon copy the message to. Those people receive the message, but they also know that the message was not intended for them.

Subject. Type in the message's subject. What is the message about? It helps if the subject is somehow related to the message (because the recipients see the subject in their Inboxes, just like you do).

The message itself. The last thing to fill in is the contents.

```
Actually, I didn't suspect that Joyce had her eyes "done."
          I just assumed that she was very surprised all
          evening.
```

When you're done, check your spelling by clicking the Spelling button. Your message is scanned, and potential misspelled words are flagged. Select the properly spelled word from the dialog box — the same drill you go through with your word processor's spell check.

Review your message! Spell checking doesn't check for grammatical errors or potentially offensive outrageous statements. Remember, you can't recall e-mail after it's sent!

Finally, you send the message. Click the Send button, and it's off on the Internet, delivered cheaper and more accurately than any post office on earth.

If you don't want to send the message, close the New Message window. You'll be asked if you want to save the message. Click Yes to save it in the Drafts folder. If you click No, the message is destroyed.

- ✔ You can start a new message by pressing Ctrl+N or choosing File➪New➪Mail Message from the menu bar.

- ✔ In AOL, create a new message by clicking the Write button on the toolbar, or press Ctrl+M. Click the Send Now button in AOL to send your message, well, *right now!*

- ✔ An e-mail message is sent instantly. I sent a message to a reader in Australia one evening and got a reply back from him in less than 10 minutes.

- ✔ Please don't type in ALL CAPS. To most people, all caps reads LIKE YOU'RE SHOUTING AT THEM!

- ✔ Spell checking in Outlook Express works only if you have Microsoft Word or the entire Microsoft Office package installed. Otherwise you will not be able to spell-check in Outlook Express.

- ✔ Be careful what you write. E-mail messages are often casually written, and they can easily be misinterpreted. Remember to keep them light.

- ✔ Ignore people who write you nasty messages. It's hard, but you can do it.

- ✔ Don't expect a quick reply from e-mail, especially from folks in the computer industry (which is ironic).

- ✔ To send a message you've shoved off to the Drafts folder, open the Drafts folder. Then double-click the message to open it. The original New Message window is then redisplayed. From there, you can edit the message and click the Send button to finally send it off.

Reading e-mail

To read a message, select it from the list in the Inbox. The message text appears in the bottom of the window, as shown earlier in Figure 22-4. You can read any message in the list like this, in any order; selecting a new message displays its contents in the bottom part of the window.

Of course, you're not stuck viewing the message in the crowded jail of Outlook Express' multiple window inferno. No, if you like you can open a message window by double-clicking the message in the Inbox. A special message-reading window opens, which is similar to the one shown in Figure 22-6.

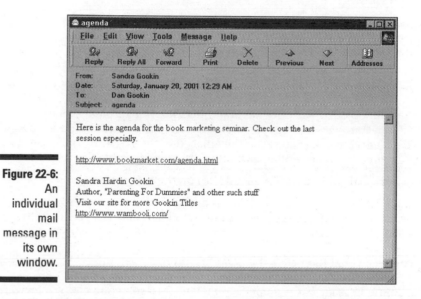

Figure 22-6:
An individual mail message in its own window.

Being its own window, you can resize or drag around the message anywhere on the screen. And you can open more than one message-reading window at a time, which helps if you need to refer to more than one message at a time (those he-said-she-said type of things).

The message-reading window also has two handy buttons: Previous and Next.

Why does my real name appear in my e-mails?

Q: Why is it that when I send e-mail, my real name appears? I got an e-mail today from someone that did not show that person's real name. How do I know who it is REALLY from?

A: Your e-mail program is configured to display your real name. You filled out this information when you set up the program. That name appears in the From line of every message you send.

Click the Previous button to read the previous message in the Inbox, the one before the current message.

 Click the Next button to read the next message in your Inbox. If you're reading the last message in the Inbox, then clicking the Next button makes an annoying sound.

After reading a message, you can do one of many things to it:

 To print an e-mail message, choose File➪Print from the menu. The Print dialog box appears; click OK to print. You can also print a message by clicking the Print button on the toolbar.

 To send an answer or follow-up to an e-mail message, click the Reply button.

Note that Outlook Express does several things for you automatically:

- ✓ The sender's name is automatically placed in the To field. Your reply goes back directly to the sender without your having to retype an address.

- ✓ The original subject is referenced (Re) on the Subject line.

- ✓ Finally, the original message is *quoted* for you. This feature is important because some people receive a lot of e-mail and may not recall the train of the conversation.

Type your reply and then click the Send button to send it off.

 Forwarding a message is the same as remailing it to someone else. To forward a message, click the Forward button. The forwarded message appears *quoted* in the body of the new message. Type in any optional comments. Fill in the To field with the address of the person to whom you're forwarding the message. Finally, click the Send button to send it off.

To delete the message you're reading, click the Delete button. Poof! It's gone. (Well, to be accurate, the message is merely moved into the Deleted Items folder on the left side of the Outlook Express window.)

- ✓ Actually, you don't have to do anything with a message after reading it; you can just keep it in your Inbox. There's no penalty for that.

- ✓ New e-mail messages appear in your Inbox in bold text.

- ✓ You can edit the quoted text when replying or forwarding a message. The quoted text isn't "locked" or anything. I typically split up quoted text when I reply to e-mail, so I can address topics individually.

- ✓ You can also edit away quoted text by deleting it, if you so desire.

✔ Use the Reply All button when you reply to a message that was carbon-copied to a number of other people. By clicking Reply All, you create a reply that lists *everyone* the original message was sent to so that they can all read the reply.

✔ After replying to a message, the envelope icon in the Inbox changes (shown in the margin). This change is your clue that the message has been replied to.

✔ Deleted mail sits in the Deleted Items folder until you clean out that folder. To clean it out, choose Edit⇨Empty Deleted Items Folder from the menu.

Quitting Outlook Express

To quit Outlook Express when you're done, close the program's window. Or choose File⇨Exit from the menu.

How do I resend bounced messages?

Q: After typing an inaccurate address on an e-mail letter and having it returned with the message user unknown, can I correct the address and resend the letter?

A: You can forward the returned e-mail to the proper address. The forwarding command is Ctrl+F. Then type in the proper address and maybe an explanation of how you goofed or something. Or you can copy the message and paste it into a New Message window that has the proper e-mail address.

Chapter 23

General Advice for the Web Weary

● ●

In This Chapter

▶ Finding things on the Web

▶ Shopping online

▶ Buying and trading at a Web auction

▶ Organizing your Favorites

▶ Learning from your Web History

▶ Using Internet Explorer tips and tricks

● ●

*S*o much time, so little to do. . . . — Willy Wonka

One reason the Web is so successful is that it doesn't really take a lot to figure out how it works. It might have once, but thanks to well-designed Web pages and a simple point-and-click interface, using the Web isn't tough for anyone. So rather than give you the Big Web Tour, and waste your time reading about buying airline tickets on-line or how to phone the Chinese restaurant down the block for take-out, I've decided to dedicate this chapter to various Internet Explorer tips, tricks, and general advice for the Web weary. This will save you tons of time, and give you something to read while you wait for your General Tso chicken.

Finding Things

The Web is like a library without a librarian. It doesn't have a card catalog, either. And forget about finding something on the shelves: Web pages aren't organized in any fashion, nor is the information in them guaranteed to be complete or accurate. Because anyone can put anything up on the Web, well, anyone does.

You find something on the Web by using a *search engine*. That's a Web page that contains a huge catalog of other Web pages. You can search through the catalog for whatever you want. Results are displayed, and you can click those *links* to eventually get to the Web page you want. It's all very nifty.

Whenever I search for stuff on the Internet, I start at Yahoo. It's perhaps the oldest and most traditional of all the search engines. Visit Yahoo at www.yahoo.com. (Figure 23-1 illustrates what Yahoo sort of looks like.)

With Yahoo you have two choices for searching: Type in something to search for in the Search text box or browse the categories by clicking those links with your mouse.

In mere moments, Yahoo displays a list of found items for you. The list may include Category Matches (which are like finding what you find in a library's card catalog) or individual Web pages. These results are all displayed on the next screen you see.

Yahoo is not alone. Many search engines are available, as well as all-in-one "Web portal" sites, which offer news, web-based e-mail, games, chat, and other goodies all designed to enhance the whole web experience. Table 23-1 lists the gamut of search engines/web portals.

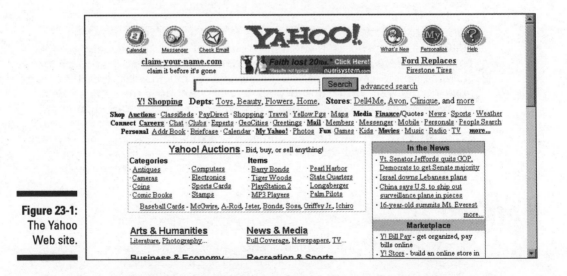

Figure 23-1:
The Yahoo
Web site.

Table 23-1	Popular Portal Sites, But Not All of Them
Site	**Address**
CNET	www.cnet.com
CNN	www.cnn.com
Dogpile	www.dogpile.com
Excite	www.excite.com
Lycos	www.lycos.com
Microsoft	www.msn.com
Yahoo!	www.yahoo.com
ZDNet	www.zdnet.com

✔ Google is considered by many to be the ultimate search engine, though it's not truly a portal site. Visit Google at www.google.com/.

✔ If the search engine finds more than one page of information, you see a <u>Next 20 Matches</u> link (or something similar) at the bottom of the page. Click that link to see the next list of Web pages found.

✔ The more information you give in the Search text box, the more accurate the Web page results.

✔ Of all the searches on the Internet, finding people is perhaps the least successful. You'll find that most people-searching Web pages require a TON of information about the person you're trying to find. Even then, they don't always find that person.

✔ For a sample people-finding site, visit people.yahoo.com.

✔ Don't freak out when you find yourself (and your address and your phone number) listed. Most people-searching places let you un-list yourself quite easily.

✔ A portal is a great thing to have as a home page. That way you can always quickly return there by clicking the Home button. See Chapter 22 for information on setting your home page.

Proper Disposal of Your Income

Shopping on the Web is currently *the thing* to do with a computer. You can buy computers, books, clothes, knickknacks, even real estate from the comfort of your orthopedically designed computer chair. All it takes is a few clicks of the mouse and a credit card number.

Online shopping Q&A

Belay your fears: Shopping online is fast, easy, and "safe." You're just a few clicks away from maxing out your Visa card. . . .

Q: What can I buy online?

A: Anything and Everything.

Q: Isn't it a little weird that they sell computers online?

A: Not really. When radio first became popular, the commercials all advertised new radios.

Q: How do I shop?

A: You find a Web page that sells something. The most famous is Amazon.com (`www.amazon.com`), which started as an online bookstore but now sells other goodies.

Q: How do I pick out something?

A: You pick out a product by adding it to your *virtual shopping cart*. You click a button, which places the item into a *bin* that you can check out later.

Q: How do I pay for it?

A: Just as you pay for items at a store, you open your shopping basket window (usually by clicking a shopping basket link) and review the items listed there. Follow the instructions on the screen for checking out, which usually involve filling in personal and shipping information, as well as a credit card number.

Q: Is my credit card information safe?

A: Very safe. Most shopping sites and Web browsers use special encryption technology to ensure no one snags your credit card on the way to the store. (This process is much safer than, for example, handing your credit card to a waiter in a restaurant.) You can tell you're at such a site by seeing `https` in the address bar instead of the standard `http`.

Always pay by credit card. That way if you don't get what you want, or get nothing, then you can easily cancel the debt. A credit card is a good form of protection in case the online retailer turns out to be a phony.

Q: What about returning things?

A: This is very important: Check the store's return policy. Some places are very good and quick to accept returns. If possible, try to find a place that has a no-questions-asked return policy. But watch out! Some places are cryptic and hide return information. Always check!

Some other advice tidbits I could not fit into the Q&A format:

✔ Check for a real phone number or an address for the online retailers you deal with. There has never been a major online scam; companies doing business online are legitimate. Those that aren't probably won't have a phone number or address listed.

✔ Some online retailers offer payment alternatives if you fear paying online. You may be able to phone-in an order or direct the company to phone you for confirmation. Some places may let you print out and fax an order.

✔ The big online retailers have search engines that search their sites for the stuff you need. So you can either browse for that perfect hammock, or you can type **night vision goggles** into the Search box and see what comes up.

✔ Many online retailers have lists of best-selling products. Check them out! Also refer to comments from other users on the products sold, if available. Don't forget the specials! I buy *Web-only* specials all the time. Save money!

Auctions without the auctioneer

Two types of auctioneers exist. First there's the rapid-fire auctioneer who spews out numbers like a machine gun, *budda-budda-budda-budda.* Then there's the Sotheby's or Christy's type of auctioneer, very polite: "I'm bidding $35-point-2 million for the Van Gogh. Do I hear 35-point-3? Mr. Gates?"

Online auctions don't have auctioneers, per se. In most cases, the auctioneer is the Web page itself. It works like a combination search engine and online retailer.

The search engine lets you look up whatever trifle you're trying to buy, say that 1977 vintage Darth Vader action figure still in the box. The seller offers a price and you bid on it, sending off how much you want to pay to the Web page. Hundreds of people bid on it every hour, so the price goes up and up. Eventually you get your trifle, and the seller gets money.

One of the most popular online auction sites is eBay (www.ebay.com). It lets you buy or sell just about anything. After registering, you can enter the fray, searching for some tchotchke you want to buy or posting information about one you want to sell.

- The online auction site makes its money off commissions collected from the seller.

- After a given time, if you hold the winning bid, you and the seller decide on payment and shipping terms (or they may be dictated in advance).

- To avoid being ripped off, many of the better online auction sites offer information about the seller, including comments from other buyers.

- You can also use an online escrow service if you want to hold your payment until you receive the merchandise. One such service is I-Escrow at www.iescrow.com.

We All Have Our Favorites

Often you'll find some Web place you love and want to visit again. If so, drop a *bookmark* on that page. That way you can visit it any time by selecting the bookmark from a list.

To drop a bookmark, use the Ctrl+D command. D for drop.

This command places the bookmark on the Favorites menu in Internet Explorer. That way you can revisit the Web page by plucking it from the Favorites menu. Cinchy.

- Never fear to add a Web page to your favorites! It's better to add it now and potentially delete it later than to regret not adding it in the first place.

- To add a Web page (or any place in AOL) to your AOL favorites list, click the *heart* button located in the window's upper-right corner. In the dialog box, select the Add It to My Favorite Places item.

- If you forget to drop a bookmark, then use the drop-down list on the Address bar to locate a Web site you've visited recently. Or you can use the History list; see "History 101" later in this chapter.

- I really wish Microsoft would call *favorites* by their proper name: bookmarks. Every other Web browser uses bookmarks instead. That name is just so much more descriptive than *favorites*.

Organizing the Favorites

The Favorites menu can get messy quickly. The solution to that, or any mess on the computer, is to organize. You can organize the favorites menu by deleting unwanted bookmarks or by creating submenus and sub-submenus. It's all quite easy.

To organize the Favorites menu in Internet Explorer, choose Favorites⇨Organize Favorites. The Organize Favorites dialog box appears, as shown in Figure 23-2.

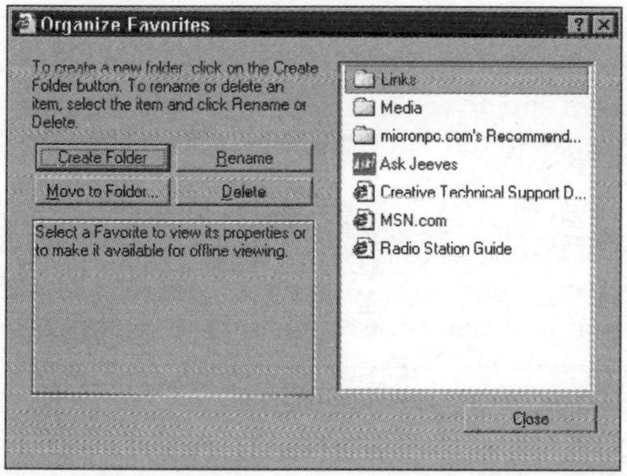

Figure 23-2:
The
Organize
Favorites
dialog box.

To create a new folder, click the Create Folder button. The New folder appears, named "New Folder," though you can type a new name for it at that time.

To move a selected bookmark into a folder, you can drag-and-drop the bookmark with the mouse or use the Move to Folder button.

Renaming a bookmark can be done by selecting the bookmark and then clicking the Rename button. This is a good idea, especially for long bookmark names, which make the Favorites menu very wide. For example, I changed the quite-long-name of my local weather Web page to read only "weather," which is all I need to know when choosing that link from the Favorites menu.

And, of course, to delete unwanted bookmarks, select them with the mouse and click the Delete button.

✓ I try to keep only as many bookmarks on the Favorites menu as will fit on the screen. So if I open the Favorites menu and it starts to scroll off the screen, I know I need to go in and do some organizing.

✓ Create folders for specific categories of bookmarks: news, weather, sports, music, movies, fun stuff, computer reference, or whatever you're into.

- You can use submenus to further organize your topics.
- Feel free to delete any favorites that Microsoft preinstalled on the Favorites menu. Those bookmarks are from companies that paid money to have their products advertised there. Feel free to delete them.

Using the Links folder

One special folder that comes already set up inside the Internet Explorer's Favorites menu is the Links folder. The items that appear in that folder also appear on the Links toolbar in Internet Explorer, which makes those links even handier to get at.

To make the Links toolbar appear, choose View⇨Toolbar⇨Links from the menu. The toolbar displays whatever links are saved in the Favorites\Links folder. Submenus in the Links folder appear as menus on the Links toolbar.

On my computer, I went into the Organize Favorites dialog box and deleted all the preinstalled links in the Links folder. I then created submenus for the places I like to visit every day: News, Daily (for Web pages updated daily), Computer, Reference, Shopping, and others. Then I moved my bookmarks into the appropriate submenus inside the Links folder. That way I always have my favorite places handy on the Links menu.

History 101

Internet Explorer keeps track of every Web page you've visited, today, yester-day, and sometimes for the past several weeks. Many people like this feature; it lets them review where they've been and re-visit those places. Many more people hate this feature because it lets anyone else snoop on where they've been on the Internet.

To see the History list, click the History button on the Internet Explorer tool-bar. The History panel appears on the left side of the Internet Explorer window, as shown in Figure 23-3. The panel is divided into areas by date: Today, Last Week, 2 Weeks Ago, and 3 Weeks Ago. Beneath each date are fold-ers representing the Web sites you've been to. Open a folder to view the list of individual pages.

Close the History list when you're done with it: Click the X (close) button on the History panel, or just click the History button on the toolbar.

- The History button in Internet Explorer 6 is not labeled "History." It's there, it just looks like a clock with an arrow pointing counter-clockwise. Oh, never mind: Just press Ctrl+H to see the History list.

✔ To re-visit a page, simply choose it from the History list. For example, open the Last Week item, then choose the Obscene Arbor Day Humor Web site, then choose an individual page from that site that you visited last week.

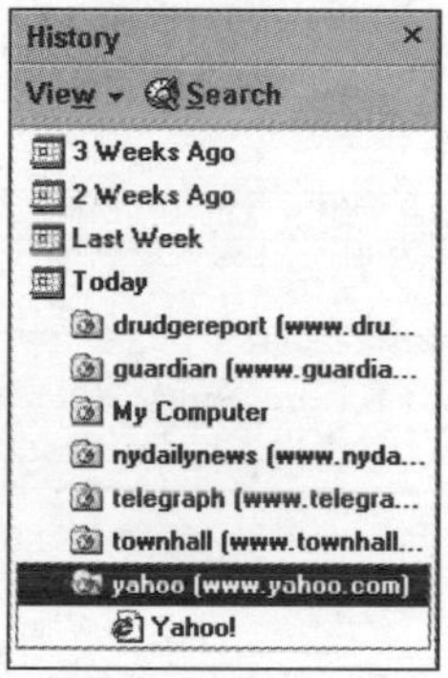

Figure 23-3:
Internet
Explorer's
History list.

History	×
View ▾ ⓖ Search

🗐 3 Weeks Ago
🗐 2 Weeks Ago
🗐 Last Week
🗐 Today
   ⓖ drudgereport (www.dru...
   ⓖ guardian (www.guardia...
   ⓖ My Computer
   ⓖ nydailynews (www.nyda...
   ⓖ telegraph (www.telegra...
   ⓖ townhall (www.townhall...
   ⓖ yahoo (www.yahoo.com)
      🗐 Yahoo!

✔ To remove a page or Web site from the list, right-click on that item. Choose Delete from the pop-up shortcut menu.

✔ You can utterly disable the History list if you detest it: Choose Tools➪Internet Options to display the Internet Options dialog box. In the General tab, locate the History area. There you can reset the "Days to keep pages in history" item to zero, which disables Internet Explorer's History. Click OK.

✔ You can also clear all items in the History list by clicking the Clear History button, also found in the Internet Options/General dialog box.

The Web Tips and Tricks Grab Bag

Finally, I'm tying up this chapter's loose ends with a grab bag of advice and knowledge tidbits to help you better conquer the Web. These are culled from hundreds of questions I get from this book's readers, as well as insights I have after using Internet Explorer for the past few years.

The following sections highlight only a few of the more common tips, tricks, and suggestions. If you have any further comments or would like some insights, feel free to send e-mail to dgookin@wambooli.com, or visit my Web page for additional information: www.wambooli.com/.

How do I delete those pesky adult sites?

Q: Uh, I recently visited one of those adult sites. It wasn't my fault! But anyway, I followed your advice and deleted it from the History list. But yet it still comes up in the Address bar sometimes when I type part of the name. Any help?

A: I don't know of anyone who hasn't accidentally fallen into one of those annoying adult sites, so don't worry about it. But to utterly remove the site from the computer's memory, you need to use the Windows Registry. This is a scary thing, so you might consider having some-

one who knows the Windows Registry do this. Basically, the offending URL is found in the following Registry entry:

HKEY_USERS\.Default\Software\Microsoft\Internet Explorer\TypedURLs.

The offending address can be removed from the list that appears for that entry. But keep in mind that doing such editing in the Registry is not something I recommend.

Don't enable the Content Advisor

Internet Explorer comes with a thing called the Content Advisor. It's designed to control the Internet content you view by preventing certain sites from displaying on the screen. This sounds like a good idea, because I know of no one who really wants to be surprised or shocked by suddenly seeing some porn they weren't expecting.

Alas, the Content Advisor is not the best way to protect your eyes from seeing porn on the Internet. In fact, it can really mess up a lot of plain harmless Internet sites — not to mention that the Content Advisor is truly a pest that is hard to remove once it's been activated. For that reason, I heartily recommend *not* using it.

> ✔ Instead of the Content Advisor, consider some of the other anti-porn or safe-surfing programs available, such as Net Nanny (www.netnanny.com) or Cybersitter (www.cybersitter.com). They offer better service and do a far superior job than the silly Internet Explorer Content Advisor.

> ✔ Most of the problems people have with the Content Advisor deal with setting *and forgetting* the Supervisor Password. If you're going to mess with the Content Advisor *do not forget that password!*

Printing Web pages

To print any Web page, choose File➪Print from the menu. No tricks.

Some Web pages, unfortunately, won't print right. Some are too wide. Some are white text on a black background, which doesn't print well. So my advice is to always use the Print Preview command to look at what you're printing before you print it. If you still have trouble then consider one of the following solutions:

- ✔ Consider saving the Web page to disk; choose File➪Save As. Ensure you choose "Web Page, complete" from the Save as type drop-down list. Then you can open the Web page file in Microsoft Word or Excel, or any Web page editing program, and edit or print it from there.

- ✔ To print large graphics on a Web page, download the graphic image to disk (see Chapter 25). Then use an imaging application or the Paint program to resize the image to something that can print on a single sheet of paper.

- ✔ Use the File➪Page Setup program to select landscape orientation for printing wider-than-normal Web pages.

- ✔ Use the Properties button in the Print dialog box to adjust the printer. These settings depend on the printer itself, but I've seen printers that can reduce the output to 75 or 50 percent, which ensures that the entire Web page prints on a single sheet of paper. Other options may let you print in shades of gray or black-and-white.

"What is a plug-in?"

Plug-ins are small programs that expand the power of Internet Explorer. Most of them are multimedia plug-ins, which let Internet Explorer play animation files, view 3-D images, hear sounds and other multimedia-ish things.

The two most common plug-ins are Flash and Real Player.

Flash is a graphic tool that lets you play animations and hear sounds. The animations and sounds load quickly, which makes Flash incredibly popular.

Real Player lets you hear sounds, including "live" audio, as well as view video clips.

Obtaining these plug-ins is easy: simply visit any Web page that employs the technology and there is often a link that lets you download the plug-in program. There is nothing wrong with this, and nothing bad happens if you choose not to download and run the plug in; you'll just not see the animation or hear the sound.

✔ Most plug-ins are free. You can download and install the software without paying a nickel.

✔ Web pages that use plug-ins offer alternative Web pages for those who don't have or don't want to use the plug-ins.

✔ I am leery of the Real Player plug in, which seems to take over the entire computer. It also begs to be updated or upgraded or something way too often, which I find annoying.

Oh! Those annoying pop-up windows

Some Web pages use special windows that seem to pop-up on the screen, usually displaying some ad. You may find this annoying, especially when you try to scroll through the window only to find that the tiny advertisement is bullying its way to the front again.

What can be done? Nothing, unfortunately. What you're seeing are the effects of a Web page programming language called *JavaScript*. This language causes your Web browser to open new windows and display information at times you may find irritating. All you can do is try to close the windows as they pop up.

✔ The worst offenders for these pop-up windows are those accidental porn sites you may crash into from time to time. Trying to close their windows or use the Back button results in even more Windows displayed. You just have to keep closing them, or quit Internet Explorer.

✔ Consider e-mailing the "webmaster" if you'd prefer not to have pop-up windows appear. One e-mail may not help, but if everyone e-mails then the Web site may dispense with the pop-up windows.

✔ Pray that Microsoft will allow this feature to be disabled for future editions of Internet Explorer.

Chapter 24

E-Mail and Beyond

*N*o one seems to have a problem with e-mail any more. In the olden days, I suppose, e-mail was an alien thing. But visit any quilting bee today and you'll see the grannies exchanging e-mail addresses more often than they show pictures of newborns. E-mail isn't all that alien any more.

To wrap up the *PCs For Dummies* e-mail discussion, I've created this chapter full of various odds and ends, tips and tricks, and various bonus informational bonbons to wrap-up your e-mail journey. This isn't the final word, of course, but it should inspire you to become a more efficient and knowledgeable Outlook Express user.

 ✔ Basic e-mail is covered in Chapter 22.

 ✔ Also see Chapter 25, which covers e-mail file attachments.

Personalizing Your E-Mail

All e-mail is text. All of it! Letters, numbers, punctuation symbols, that's the basis of all the e-mail sent all over the world. Despite that, there are ways of sprucing up and individualizing your e-mail, which are covered in the next two sections.

Composing messages in style

Outlook Express has the ability to let you compose prettymail. I call it prettymail because the mail looks better than plain-old boring text.

To make prettymail, you can start a new message by clicking the down arrow next to the New Mail button. A list of stationery appears, as shown in Figure 24-1. Select a type from the list, and Outlook Express displays a new message window with a special background pattern, picture, or design. You then proceed to create your new message.

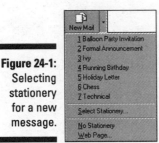

Figure 24-1:
Selecting
stationery
for a new
message.

After entering the To, Cc (if necessary), and Subject fields for the message, you can begin typing in the newly styled message body. You can use the buttons on the formatting toolbar to change the message's font, size, color, and other formatting attributes. The buttons on the toolbar are similar to buttons you find in your word processor, and they have the same effect on your text.

✔ Click the Send button to send your heavily formatted e-mail epistle.

✔ To create your own stationery, choose the Select Stationery command from the New Mail drop-down menu (refer to Figure 24-1). In the Select Stationery dialog box, click the Create New button to run the Stationery Setup Wizard.

✔ Not every e-mail program will receive the message formatted the way you see it. If you get a reply claiming that the message looked like jumbled text, then consider composing messages *without* the fancy formatting and stationery.

Creating a signature

Another way to personalize your messages is to create a signature. That's a bit of text that gets appended to every message you send. For example, my signature is

```
Cheers!
DAN
```

That text is automatically appended to each e-mail message I compose or reply to. Setting it up is a snap in Outlook Express:

1. **Choose Tools⇨Options.**

   The Options dialog box is displayed.

2. **Click the Signatures tab.**

3. **Click the New button to create a new signature.**

4. **Enter the text you want to appear in the bottom of the dialog box.**

   Figure 24-2 shows how I created my signature. You can type multiple lines into the Text box, just as if you were typing those lines at the end of an e-mail message. Note how I added a line of hyphens and my Web page address to the signature in Figure 24-2.

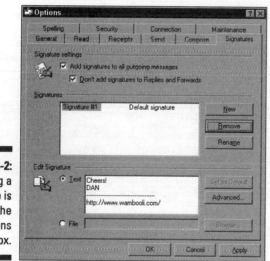

Figure 24-2: Creating a Signature is done in the Options dialog box.

   Another option is to use a file on disk as your signature, in which case you click on File and use the Browse button to locate the signature file.

5. **Click to put a check mark by "Add signatures to all outgoing messages."**

   You want Outlook Express to append your signature to the messages. Optionally un-check the "Don't add signatures to Replies and Forwards" box if you'd like your signature to go out all the time.

6. **Click OK.**

The signature is ready for use.

The next time you create a new message you'll see your signature appear in the message area. Ta-da! Automatic typing.

  ✔ It's possible to have several signatures. To set the one you prefer to use, select it in the Options dialog box and click the Set as Default button.

  ✔ To switch signatures in a new message, choose Insert⇨Signature and then choose the proper signature from the submenu that appears.

Managing Your Messages

Vinton Cerf — Father of the Internet and the creator of the @ in all your e-mail messages — said that e-mail can be like barnyard manure; it accumulates if you don't take care of it.

To help you take care of your e-mail, Outlook Express has the Folders window (refer to Figure 22-3). It has five standard folders:

Inbox. This is where all your unread mail messages sit and also where read mail sits until you delete those messages or move them elsewhere.

Outbox. This folder contains messages waiting to be sent. If you're online, then this folder is empty most of the time.

Sent Items. A copy of all messages and replies you've ever sent is stored here.

Deleted Items. Messages you've deleted are kept here.

Drafts. Any messages you decide not to send are stored here.

In addition to these folders, you can create your own folders for storing and organizing your messages. The following sections detail the process.

  ✔ Folders with blue numbers in parentheses by them contain unread mail. The number indicates how many messages are unread.

  ✔ To remove a message from the Drafts folder, open it. Once open, you can view or edit the message, but click the Send button to send it off. Or you can drag a message from the Drafts folder to any other folder in the list.

Creating a mail folder

To create your own mail folder, a place for specific types of messages, follow these steps:

1. **Choose File⇨New⇨Folder from the menu.**

   The Create Folder dialog box appears, as shown in Figure 24-3.

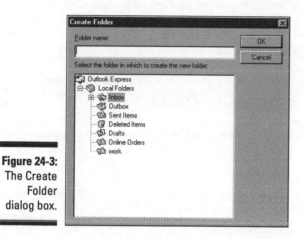

Figure 24-3:
The Create
Folder
dialog box.

2. **Enter a name for the new folder.**

   Type the name into the Folder Name box.

   For example, I have a folder named *Online Orders* for e-mail receipts sent to me when I order things on the Web. Another good folder to create is a *Jokes* folder for humorous things people send you.

3. **Select where you want the folder created.**

   Click the folder in which you want the new folder to be placed. If you select the Local Folders item, Outlook places the folder on the *main level*. Selecting another folder creates a subfolder.

   I keep my folders on the main level, so I select the Local Folders item from the bottom of the Create Folder dialog box.

4. **Click OK.**

   The new folder is created, appearing in the Folder list on the left side of the window.

You manage the folders you create by right-clicking on them. A pop-up menu materializes with commands for renaming or deleting the folders.

To view the contents of a folder, select it from the Folders list. Click once to highlight the folder, and any messages stored there are listed on the left side of the window.

The folders Outlook Express uses for mail are *not* the same as the folders you use in Windows to store files. Technically, each folder is a text file on disk, a file that Outlook Express indexes and chops up to reflect the individual mail messages within that huge text file. And it's much better to use Outlook Express to manage those folder/text files than it is to try and hunt them down in Windows and manage them yourself.

Moving a message to a folder

I try to keep my Inbox empty of all read mail. After reading a message, I simply drag it off to the proper folder. This works just like dragging any icon in Windows.

From the Inbox, for example, you can drag a message over to the Jokes folder: Click the envelope icon next to the message and drag it to the proper folder on the left side of the window.

Note that you can delete messages by dragging them to the Deleted Items folder.

Deleting (and un-deleting) messages

Generally speaking, I do not recommend that you delete any of your e-mail. Instead, consider moving it to a folder. I do this with all my e-mail; a copy of it goes to a related folder: friends, family, business, fan mail, hate mail, and so on. I only delete mail messages not specifically directed to me, such as junk e-mail, which is known in the Internet universe as "spam."

If you do delete e-mail, then it goes into the Deleted Items folder. And there it sits until you empty the Deleted Items folder. Or, if you like, you can un-delete a message by dragging it from the Deleted Items folder back to your Inbox or some other, custom folder.

To empty the Deleted Items folder, choose Edit⇨Empty "Deleted Items" Folder from the menu. Note that this *permanently* erases all your mail messages contained in the Deleted Items folder. You cannot recover them after they've been deleted from the Deleted Items folder.

✔ Deleted mail does not go to the Recycle Bin! Don't go looking in the Recycle Bin for any deleted e-mail. It's not there.

✔ You cannot recover e-mail that has been deleted from the Deleted Items mail folder.

The Valued Address Book

Whenever you get e-mail from someone new, or when you learn a friend's new online address, you should note it in the Outlook Express Address Book. Not only does the Address Book let you keep the addresses in one spot, but you can easily recall an address for sending mail later.

Adding a name to the Address Book

You can add an e-mail name to the Address Book in one of two ways: manually or automatically.

Manually. To manually add a name, choose File⇨New⇨Contact from the menu. Outlook then creates a new Address Book entry (shown in Figure 24-4), which you fill in.

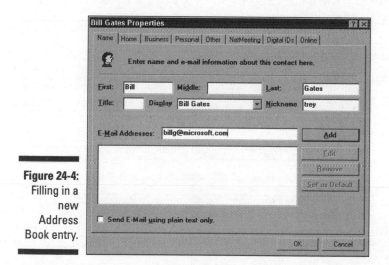

Figure 24-4: Filling in a new Address Book entry.

The dialog box has many tabs and gizmos for you to work, but you really need to fill in only four items in the Name tab: First, Last, Nickname, and E-Mail Addresses.

The Nickname item is optional, though it can be handy. For example, you can type **goober** into the To field of a new message instead of your brother's full e-mail address. Outlook Express recognizes the shortcut and replaces it with the proper, full e-mail address.

After filling in the four fields (or more, if you're entirely bored), click the Add button and then click OK.

Automatically. To automatically add a name to the Address book, display an e-mail message from someone whose name you'd like to add. Choose Tools⇨A_d_d to Address Book⇨Sender from the menu. Outlook instantly adds the name to the Address Book.

Click the Addresses button on the toolbar to display the Address Book window. From there, you can edit or manage the entries in your Address Book.

Using the Address Book when sending a message

The Address Book really comes in handy when you're creating a new message. With the New Message window on the screen, click the To field's button, as shown in the margin. A special Address Book window appears, as shown in Figure 24-5.

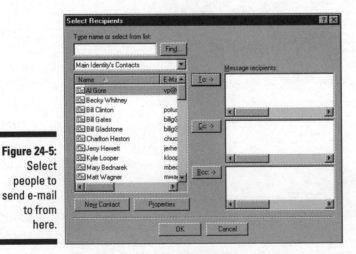

Figure 24-5: Select people to send e-mail to from here.

To add someone to the To field, select that person's name and click the To button. Likewise for the Cc or Bcc fields. To select more than one e-mail address at a time, press the Ctrl key and Ctrl+click to select the names.

When you're done, click OK, and the message's To, Cc, and Bcc fields are already filled in for you.

Creating a group

Oftentimes you'll find yourself sending out e-mail to more than one person. For example, all the folks on your Jokes, Sappy Stories, Family, or whatever lists. By creating a group, you can save yourself some time typing all those addresses over and over.

To create a group, follow these steps:

1. **Choose Tools⇨Address Book to open the Address Book.**
2. **Choose File⇨New Group.**

   A dialog box appears where you can create the group.

3. **Type in a name for the group.**

   Be clever and descriptive. The Jokes group can be called "Jokes." The people you send messages to regarding your Reformed Dirt Eaters group could be called Dirt Eaters.

4. **Add members to the group.**

   Use the Select Members button to pick who you want to be in the group. This displays yet another dialog box from which you can cull your list of e-mail contacts and add them to the group: Select the name/address from the left side of the window and use the Select button to add them to the group on the right side.

5. **Click OK when you're done adding members.**
6. **Click OK to close the group's Properties window.**
7. **Close the Address Book window.**

   Now you're ready to use the group.

To send a message to the group, type the group's name into the To, Cc, or Bcc field. The message is then sent to that group of people automatically.

You can also click the To button, as described in the previous section, to choose a group from the list in your Address Book.

By the way, putting the group in the Bcc field is a wonderful idea; see the sidebar "Putting Bcc to work" for more information.

Blocking Messages

There are some people you really don't want e-mail from. For example, that annoying little person you gave your e-mail address to, the one who keeps asking for money or sending you obscene limericks. Outlook Express has a way to deal with such pests, and it's called blocking messages.

To block e-mail from a specific person, first open or highlight a message from that person. Then choose Message⇨Block Sender from the list. Outlook Express responds by telling you that further messages from said undesirable person will be blocked and, oh by the way, would you also like all messages from that person to be deleted. Click Yes to delete their messages. Lo, you shan't be bothered by that person again.

If you change your mind, or if you accidentally add someone you didn't want to, then you can undo the blocking: choose Tools⇨Message Rules⇨Blocked Senders List. This displays the Message Rules dialog box. Highlight the person you want to unblock, then click the Remove button. Click OK and they're back in.

- ✔ Of course, if the pest changes his or her e-mail address then you'll have to go through the blocking process all over again.

- ✔ Yes, you can use this trick to block some, but not all, junk e-mail or spam. Just add the spammer's name to the blocked list. See the sidebar "Spam, spam, spam, spam" for more spamly information.

- ✔ The Message Rules dialog box can be used to customize how Outlook Express deals with messages. Unfortunately, I don't have the space here to go into its workings in any detail.

Putting Bcc to work

The sneaky Bcc field is used to *blind carbon copy* a message, which involves sending a copy of the message to someone and having that person's name *not* appear in any copy of the e-mail. That way you can clue people into your messages without having the true recipients know the names of everyone who received the message.

To access the Bcc field, choose View⇨All Headers from the New Message window's menu. The people in the Bcc field receive a copy of the e-mail message just like everyone else; however, the people in the To or Cc fields do not see the Bcc field names listed.

A great way to use Bcc is when you send out a message to several people. For example, when sending out That Latest Joke, just put everyone's name in the Bcc field and put your own name into the To field. That way everyone gets the joke (or not as the case may be), but they don't see the huge stack-o-names at the start of the e-mail message.

Spam, spam, spam, spam

Junk e-mail is known as spam. It's a reference to an old Monty Python comedy routine, and regardless of protests from the Hormel company (which makes SPAM, the meat product), it's used as a term for widely distributed, unwanted e-mail solicitations.

Don't let spam bother you. Everyone gets it. Just delete those messages. Read them if you want but delete them. And *never* reply, even if you're requesting to be removed from the spam list; replying to any spam signals the sender that you're a *live one,* and your name will be added to the list of suckers. You'll get more spam in the future. So don't reply! Ever!

Chapter 25

Files to Here, Files from There!

. . . .

. . . .

The Internet was born out of the need to fling files far and wide between the Cro-Magnon computers of the early 1970s. Thank goodness it's much easier to do today. You can send a file to anyone by adding an attachment to your e-mail. You can fetch files either through an e-mail message or by grabbing them from a Web page. This chapter tells you all the details.

Grabbing Stuff from the Internet

The Internet is brimming with files and programs that are just waiting for you to grab a copy. Work some magic, and the file is piped into your PC just as if you copied it from a CD-ROM or floppy disk (but not as fast). You can grab files, programs, fonts, graphics — just about anything and everything you want. And it's as cinchy as clicking your mouse.

    ✔ Copying a file to your computer is known as *downloading*. When the Internet sends you a file, you *download* it. (Think of the other computer as being on top of a hill; it may not be, but it helps to think of it that way.)

    ✔ Sending a file to another computer is known as *uploading*.

    ✔ Complaining to your best friend is known as *unloading*.

Saving a Web page to disk

To save an entire Web page to disk, choose File⇨Save As in Internet Explorer. A Save Web Page dialog box appears, similar to the Save As dialog box in any other application. Use the dialog box to save the Web page to disk.

✔ Saving a Web page actually saves what's called an HTML file to disk. That file contains the formatting instructions for the Web page.

✔ You can view the Web page offline using Internet Explorer, or you can edit it using any Web page editor, such as Microsoft Word or FrontPage.

✔ Because HTML is a text-based file format, you can also view the file using a text editor, like Notepad. Be aware that Web pages look really ugly this way.

Saving part of a Web page to disk

Most Web pages display plain text. You can copy that text and save it to disk just as you'd copy text from one application and paste it into another. Here's how:

1. **Select the text you want to copy.**

   Drag the mouse over the text, which highlights it on the screen. The text is now selected.

2. **Choose Edit⇨Copy.**

   Or you can press the Ctrl+C key combination.

   The text is now copied and ready to be pasted and saved elsewhere.

3. **Start any word processor.**

   You can start Notepad, WordPad, or your word processor, such as Microsoft Word.

4. **Paste the text into your word processor.**

   Choose the Edit⇨Paste command to paste in the text (Ctrl+V is the shortcut key).

5. **Print. Save. Whatever.**

   Use the proper menu commands to save or print or edit the text you copied from the Web page.

I've used this technique a number of times, mostly to copy quotes from famous people and paste them into my books. I then attribute the quote to myself and become very famous for it. For example, "All men are created equal." I made that one up.

Searching for programs

The Internet is a vast storehouse for various programs. It contains applications, programming languages, utilities, games, font files, and lots of programs for using the Internet. It's all out there, free for the taking. The problem usually is finding where the programs are kept.

To find programs, you use a file-searching engine similar to a Web page search engine. Several of these engines are available, though the following example uses CNET's Shareware.com.

As an example, suppose you want to find an Atomic Clock program to set your computer's time to a highly accurate yet alarmingly named atomic clock. Here's how you would search for one:

1. **Visit Shareware.com.**

   Type the following address into your Web browser: `http://shareware.cnet.com`

   In a few moments, the Shareware.com Web page appears on your screen. The Web page changes, so I won't bore you with an antique image of it here. Basically you need to look for the Search text box, a drop-down list of computers or "platforms," and the big Search button. That's the essence of finding a program on the Internet.

2. **Input the type of program you're searching for in the Search box.**

   The more descriptive you are, the better the results, though being vague can help in some circumstances.

   For this example, you're trying to find one of those programs that lets you set your computer's clock based on the Atomic Clock. Type **atomic clock** into the box.

3. **Select your operating system from the drop-down list.**

   Choose `Windows` to search for any Windows programs. If there are options for specific Windows versions, choose whatever matches your Windows version.

4. **Click Search.**

   Doh-dee-doh. . . .

   Eventually you see the Search Results page. On it, you find a list of programs you can download along with a brief description. There may be a link to click to find more information. If so, click it.

   The most important information you need is the file size, which tells you approximately how long it will take to download the file from the Internet into your computer. With a typical 56 kbps modem, a 500K file takes about three minutes to download, more or less.

If more matches are found, you see a link at the bottom of the page titled NEXT 25 (or something). Click it to see even more matches.

5. **Select the file you want to download.**

   Click the link by the file's name. More pages with more information may appear (and remember that this works differently for each search engine on the Web)

6. **Download the file.**

   Follow the instructions on the screen to save the file to disk. A Save As dialog box appears, where you tell the Internet where to save the file on your system.

   I recommend creating a Downloads folder in the My Documents folder for saving downloaded files. You can create that folder using the New Folder button in the Save As dialog box. Then use the dialog box's controls to save the file in that folder on disk.

7. **Wait while the file downloads.**

   The File Download dialog box monitors the download process as the file crawls from the Internet into your computer. Depending on the speed of your modem, this process could take days. (Hey! Get that cable modem, already!)

   Don't disconnect from the Internet until the file has been completely sent! If you do disconnect, you won't have the entire file!

   And don't just sit and watch the screen, either. You can visit other Web pages and do other things on the Internet or work in other applications like Word, while your computer is receiving the file.

After you successfully download the file, you should run it. Most downloaded files are EXE files, which means they're programs. Running the program usually installs it on your computer. Either that, or it blasts the single file out into many little pieces, one of which is a SETUP program you can run to install. Either way, the program is yours!

✔ Downloading the file is free. If the file is shareware, however, you're expected to pay for it if you use it.

✔ Some files you download are called ZIP files. These files are *archives,* or one file that holds several other files as a single, compact unit. After you download a ZIP file, you need to expand or *unzip* it with a ZIP file manager, such as WinZip.

✔ You can find WinZip at: www.winzip.com.

✔ Windows Me and Windows XP treat ZIP files as compressed folders. You can easily open the compressed folder and extract whatever files you need from it after downloading. See Chapter 5 for more information about compressed folders.

✔ Feel free to delete any file you download. If it's a ZIP file (Compressed folder), then you can delete it if it's not been installed or even after installing the program. No problem. (You still, however, need to uninstall the program if you've installed it; see Chapter 19.)

Downloading an MP3 file

MP3, which stands for something, is a file format used to store audio. The quality of the format is such that the music, when played back, sounds nearly perfect. And the file sizes are small, relatively speaking: about 1MB of disk space for every minute of music. That's pretty good; five minutes of audio on a CD occupies only 5MB of disk space in MP3 format, as opposed to 100MB or more for other, similar sound files.

To find MP3 music, visit the MP3 Web page at www.mp3.com.

After you find the music you want, click the download link with the mouse. The file is then sent to your computer.

If clicking the download link causes the Windows Media Player to pop up, stop! You want to save the file to disk and not just hear Media Player play it. (There is no way to save a file in Media Player.) Close the Media Player, and instead, right-click on the download link. A pop-up menu appears, as shown in Figure 25-1.

Figure 25-1:
Choose
Save Target
As to
download
any link.

Choose Save Target As from the menu. Doing so produces a Save As dialog box, which you can use to save the file to a specific spot on disk. (Say! How about an MP3 folder in your Audio folder in your My Documents folder?)

After the file is on disk, you can play it: Double-click its icon to open it and away it goes — provided you have an MP3 player. The latest version of the Windows Media Player will work okay. For other, snazzier players, refer to the same MP3 Web page for some great software to download.

How long does it take to download a file?

Q: As my file is downloading, Windows first says it will take 3 minutes, then 15 minutes. Then after about 5 minutes, things slow to a crawl. Come on! How long does it take to download a file?

A: The answer is the same as for the question, "How long does it take to get to the center of a Tootsie Pop?" The world may never know. The problem is that speed is a variable on the Internet. Despite how fast your modem connects, Internet Explorer can only *guess* as to how long the download will take. It assumes

that your speed won't fluctuate. But it does! Say, for example, a server in Texas goes down in the middle of your download. That means the rest of the Internet gets busier to make up the time and, therefore, the download takes longer.

Bottom line: There's nothing you can do. Consider all time estimates from Internet Explorer (and Windows) to be good guesses only.

✔ Note that some MP3 files are play-only; you can only listen to them on the Web using a program like the Windows Media Player. Such files cannot be saved to disk, unless you obtain specific software that saves the file instead of playing it. Such software can by found on the /www.mp3.com/ Web site.

✔ MP3 files are not zipped; you can play them right away after downloading.

Look, Ma! It's an E-Mail Attachment!

E-mail attachments are fun. They're a convenient way to send files back and forth on the Internet. For example, use your vast scanner knowledge to scan in an image of the kids, save it to disk as a JPEG file, and then attach it to an e-mail message to Grandma! Provided Grandma has read this book, she'll be gazing at her beautiful grandkids in mere Internet moments.

✔ Refer to Chapter 22 for more basic information on e-mail.

✔ At some point, you may receive a file that your PC cannot digest — a file of an unknown format. If so, then the dreaded Open With dialog box appears. Quickly, ignore it! Choose Cancel. Then respond to the e-mail and tell the person that you can't open the file and need to have it re-sent in another format.

✔ Beware of surprise attachments as they could contain viruses or other harmful programs. Most of these may come from people you don't know, though they may also come unexpectedly from your friends or regular e-mail pals. You just need to be careful! Only accept attachments from people you know. Avoid opening attachments ending in VBS or EXE. Otherwise, just delete the e-mail message, and you'll be safe.

✔ I do not accept program files or other large attachments over e-mail.

✔ VBS files are Visual Basic Script programs. Rarely, if ever, will anyone legitimately send you a VBS file.

✔ You can send more than one file at a time — just keep attaching files.

✔ Or instead of sending several small files, consider using the WinZip program to archive your files into one handy ZIP file. Or, if you have Windows Me or Windows XP, put all the files into a compressed folder and e-mail the compressed folder.

✔ Do not send file shortcuts; only send the originals. If you send a shortcut, the people receiving the file won't get the original. Instead they'll get the 296-byte shortcut, which doesn't help.

✔ Try not to move or delete any files you attach to e-mail messages until *after* you send the message. I know this sounds dumb, but too often I'll be waiting for e-mail to send, and (while I'm not busy) I'll start cleaning files. Oops!

✔ This book's word-processor files were written in Idaho, zipped up, and attached to an e-mail message I sent Paul in Indiana. After editing, Paul zipped up the files again and e-mailed them back to me for review. Then they were sent back again to Indiana, attached to an e-mail message.

Grabbing an attachment with Outlook Express

The secret of Outlook Express' attachments is the paper clip icon. When you see the paper clip icon next to the message subject, it indicates that the e-mail message has one or more files attached to it.

When you read the message, you'll find a large paper clip button in the upper-right corner of the message's window, as shown in the margin. Click that button to see a list of files attached to the message, as shown here:

```
📎
┌─────────────────────────────────┐
│ 🔊 Crude noises sound file (30.05 KB) │
├─────────────────────────────────┤
│ Save Attachments...             │
└─────────────────────────────────┘
```

A sound file is attached to the preceding message. Selecting that file from the paper clip button's menu plays the file.

Attached graphics files appear as images below the message body itself. You don't have to do anything; the images just show up. (If not, then the images sent are not JPEG or GIF files.)

All other attached files should probably be saved to disk. To save them, choose the File⇨Save Attachments menu item. A window appears, listing the file(s) attached to the message, as shown in Figure 25-2.

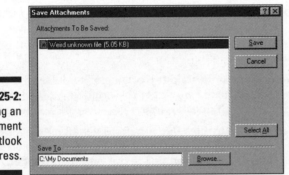

Figure 25-2:
Saving an attachment in Outlook Express.

Note the Save To item at the bottom of the dialog box. Use the Browse button to select another folder; otherwise, the attachment(s) will be saved in whichever folder Outlook Express thinks best (which is a gamble, trust me).

Click the Save button to save the file.

Remember where you saved the file!

With the attachment saved, you can reply to or delete the message as you normally would.

- ✔ I save my attachments in the My Documents folder. After looking at them or examining their contents, I then shuffle them off to the proper folder.

- ✔ Even if Outlook Express displays graphics files right in your message, you may still want to choose File⇨Save Attachments to save them to disk.

Sending an attachment in Outlook Express

You attach a file in Outlook Express by — can you guess? — clicking the big paper clip button in the message composition window. Yup, it's that easy.

Sending colossal files

Q: I'm trying to send my friend a song and it takes *forever* to get to her. Yes, some songs are very huge files. I've tried compressing the file and it went from maybe 3.18MB to 3MB, so that didn't help. Is there a simpler way of sending an attachment of a song? Please help! What am I doing wrong?

A: Well, compression won't help because song files (MP3) are already fairly compressed. But on top of that, your e-mail program converts the raw data into plain text, which makes the resulting file *even larger*, say 5MB, which takes even longer to send. So unless both of you are using high-speed Internet access (DSL, Cable modem, or T1), attaching such a huge file to an e-mail message is utterly inefficient. (In fact, some e-mail programs refuse to send attachments that large.)

As an alternative, you need to save the file to a removable disk and give that disk to your friend. You can use a CD-R to burn a CD and give the file out that way, or if you both have Zip drives, you can save the file to a Zip disk. This may seem like a clunky solution, but it's the best one for now.

Start by creating a new message or replying to a message. (Refer to Chapter 22 for the details.) When you're ready to attach a file, click the paper clip button or choose Insert⇨File Attachment from the menu.

Use the Insert Attachment dialog box to find the file you want to attach. It works exactly like an Open/Browse dialog box. After finding and selecting the file, click the Attach button.

The file you attach appears on a new line in the New Message window, right below the Subject line.

To send the message and the file, click the Send button. And it's off on its way. . . .

✔ Sending a message with a file attached takes longer than sending a regular, text-only message.

✔ It's a good idea to ensure that the recipient of the message can read the type of file you're sending. For example, sending a Word file to a WordPerfect user may not meet with the results you want.

✔ In keeping with my rules mentioned earlier, phone or e-mail someone before you send them a program file so they're certain it's not a random virus being sent.

✔ Send JPEG or GIF pictures. Any other picture format is usually too large and makes the recipient wait a long time to receive the message.

The World of FTP

The traditional way to send files back and forth on the Internet is by using something called FTP, which stands for File Transfer Protocol. How the *Protocol* part got worked in there, I'll never know. It should just be FT for File Transfer, which is what the program does. Maybe FT is trademarked, or they didn't want people saying *fort,* or maybe it's a pun on STP. Who knows?

Receiving files with FTP is easy; your Web browser does that, and it operates in a mode you're very familiar with.

Sending files with FTP is tough. I'll save that gristly morsel for the last section of this chapter.

- ✔ FTP is File Transfer Protocol. Pronounce it *ef-tee-pee.*

- ✔ STP is Scientifically Treated Petroleum. It's the racer's edge.

- ✔ Most of the time, you'll use FTP to get files, usually from some vast file archive somewhere on the Internet.

- ✔ Sending files to the Internet is kind of rare. It's commonly done when you upload information for a Web page. Also some businesses may have an FTP site where you can upload projects, which is still rare.

Browsing an FTP site

When you point your Web browser to an FTP site, it changes modes and operates more like a disk file tool. The difference is that the files you're looking at are on a computer somewhere on the Internet and not on your own PC.

Follow these steps to visit the Simtel FTP site:

1. **Browse to:** `ftp://ftp.simtel.net/`.

   Type the preceding command into the Address bar in Internet Explorer. Type **ftp**, colon, two slashes, **ftp**, period, **simtel**, period, **net**, and a slash.

   The `ftp://` command, like `http://`, tells the Web browser to visit a site on the Internet. Instead of a Web page, however, you see an FTP site. In this case, it's the Simtel archive.

   The archive is shown as a list of files, like the old days of DOS! Sometimes, however, the FTP archive may appear as standard folder and file icons, just the way Windows Explorer shows them. It all depends on the FTP site.

2. **Open the pub folder.**

   Click on the **pub** link. Or if you see a **pub** folder, double-click to open it.

3. **Open the simtelnet folder.**

4. **Open the win95 folder.**

   Finally you're at the Windows 95/98 archive on Simtel. What you see in the browser's window is a list of all the folders, each of which contains a certain category of file.

5. **Open the cursors folder.**

   Inside the cursors folder are various cursor files, which you can use to liven up the desktop.

   Most FTP archives contain at least one index file, which describes all the files in the folder. Locate the index file, which may be called INDEX.TXT or something similar.

   Also notice the other file types. There are mostly ZIP archives, but maybe some EXE, font, or sound files as well.

6. **Download a file.**

   Click the file link you want to download that file. Or if you see an icon, double-click to open the file and download it. The File Download dialog box appears. Select the Save This File to Disk option and click OK. Then use the Save As dialog box to find a spot for the download on disk.

You can continue to peruse the FTP library while the file is downloading, or you can browse the Web, read e-mail — you know the drill. (With Internet Explorer Version 5, use the Back button to return to *Web browsing mode,* or type in a Web page address, or press Alt+Home to get at your home page.)

- Always peruse the Index file in an FTP archive. Note that the Index file may not always be available.

- Not every FTP site lets you browse around. It has to be an *anonymous FTP site,* which means it lets anyone in for browsing purposes.

A few words on FTP programs

Your Web browser lets you cruise FTP sites and download programs, but it does not allow you to upload programs (send files to an Internet computer). That situation is rare to begin with, as described in this section's introduction. But it is possible, provided you use a special FTP program.

Windows comes with a command line (DOS) FTP program called — believe it or not — FTP. It's an ugly and awkward program based on the original UNIX FTP program. I wouldn't wish it on an enemy.

Beyond Windows lousy FTP program, you can get third-party FTP programs that make sending files back and forth between the Internet and your PC as easy as copying a file to a floppy drive.

One third-party FTP program I use and can recommend is CuteFTP. The shareware program costs only $30, and you can download or purchase it from www.cuteftp.com. This is the program I use to update my personal and business Web pages.

Part VI
Something's Wrong!

In this part...

When we finally invent the perfect, faultless computer, it will be our doom. The PC will turn on us. We will have to serve it. And I don't believe that computers will be as forgiving of us as we are of them!

The dilemma with computer problems is that people are too quick to blame themselves for their PC's folly. People assume it's their own fault, that they somehow offended the delicate sensibilities of the PC...

Poppycock! Computers foul up on the slightest whim. Don't mistake their flakiness for anything you've done. Instead, refer to the chapters in this part for remedies. Make this part of the book your place to turn to when the computer up and dies — or just crosses its eyes and says, "Windows exists, so there are problems."

Chapter 26

An Ounce of PC Prevention

The difference between a crisis and an incident is the degree of preparation. If you understand what can go wrong and what you'll need to deal with it, then when anything does go wrong, you'll be far better off than the innocent nudnik who is utterly unaware. For example, I have fire extinguishers all over my house and garage. When the lawn tractor caught fire (sitting beneath a pine tree), we put it out. The lawn tractor was saved, as was the forest around our house, and possibly the house itself.

Being prepared for PC disaster is an important, often sadly neglected, part of using a computer. Yet, armed with a few simple tools and performing some simple tasks can lessen the damage or often prevent many common computer catastrophes. This chapter contains such PC prevention prescriptions. Heed them and live well. (And for the lawn tractor: Always make sure the dealer removes the cleaning rags before you go out and mow.)

The Emergency Boot Disk

The best thing you can create for your PC is the emergency boot disk. That's a disk you can use to start your computer should something dreadful happen to the hard drive. You can direct Windows to create this disk for you, packing it full of diagnostic and startup tools. Every computer you own must have such a disk, and it's a good idea to re-create the disk every few months or so, as well as to try it out and ensure that it works.

Windows 98/Me instructions

Follow these steps to create an Emergency Boot Disk for your PC running Windows 98 or Windows Me:

1. **Stick a fresh floppy disk into drive A.**

   This disk becomes the Emergency Boot disk.

2. **Open the Control Panel's Add/Remove Programs icon.**

   Add/Remove
   Programs

   From the Start menu, choose Settings⇨Control Panel. Double-click on the Add/Remove Programs icon to open it.

3. **Click the Startup Disk tab.**

4. **Click the Create Disk button.**

   Follow the directions on the screen. There is no need to stick a disk into drive A here as you've already done so.

   You may need the original Windows CD for this operation. If so, an annoying dialog box will inform you.

5. **Click OK and close the Control Panel when you're done.**

Skip up to the section, "Now that you have the disk . . ."

Windows 2000/XP instructions

Follow these steps to create an Emergency Recovery Disk for your PC running Windows 2000 or Windows XP:

1. **Stick a fresh floppy disk into drive A.**

   This disk becomes the Emergency Recovery Disk, which is not the same as the Emergency Boot Disk for Windows 98/Me (and I'll explain how in a moment).

2. **Open the Backup program.**

   From the Start menu, choose (More) Programs⇨Accessories⇨System Tools⇨Backup.

3. **Click the Emergency Repair Disk button in the Welcome tab.**

4. **Click OK.**

   Follow the directions on the screen. There is no need to stick a disk into drive A here as you've already done so.

5. **Click OK and close the Backup program when you're done.**

The disk is not a boot disk, as the Windows 98/Me disk is; you cannot start your computer using the disk. Instead, you must start your computer using the CD or startup disks that came with Windows 2000 or Windows XP. Then you use the data on the disk to assist in recovery. This is information a tech support person will assist you with should the need arise.

Carefully label the Emergency Recovery Disk and keep it in a safe place for when you need it. And if you make any additional hardware or software changes to your computer, be sure to re-create the Emergency Recovery Disk.

Now that you have the disk . . .

When the program is done creating the disk, remove it from your floppy drive. Label the disk as the PC's Emergency Boot Disk and keep it in a safe yet handy place.

To test the disk, insert it into your computer's A drive, then restart the computer. (See Chapter 2 for information on how to restart.) Keep the disk in drive A so that the computer starts from that disk.

Eventually you'll see the Emergency Boot Disk's startup menu, something like:

```
   1. Help.
   2. Start computer with CD-ROM support.
   3. Start computer without CD-ROM support.
   4. Minimal Boot

Enter a choice: _
```

Different versions of Windows display different menu items, though your options are basically to start the computer with or without CD-ROM support. If you need the CD-ROM drive to reload Windows or some driver, then you choose that option. Otherwise, choose the no CD-ROM support option. For this exercise, choose the option to start with CD-ROM support.

You'll see some messages displayed as the computer starts itself in DOS or command prompt mode. Eventually you'll see the DOS command prompt:

```
A:\>
```

Run for the hills! Seriously, it's at this point that your PC guru or a tech support person would assist you with further recovery.

To restart your computer back into Windows, remove the Emergency Boot Disk from drive A, then press Ctrl+Alt+Delete (all three keys simultaneously). That's the old DOS reset command, FYI.

✔ If your Emergency Boot Disk doesn't work, create another one. Do it now! Don't be sorry later.

✔ You may never use this disk. In fact, the only people who might use it are the tech-support people or your PC's guru.

✔ Don't forget to label the disk. I believe you'll find that labeling makes the disk easier to find in a panic.

Backing Up Your Files

Backing up is so important to using a computer, it's utterly shocking how many people just don't do it. In fact, I believe that's one of the reasons why Microsoft suddenly stopped including a backup program in Windows. Who bothers with it? But the truth is that you need to keep backup copies of your stuff Just In Case.

I won't rant on and on about backup. And because there is no standard backup program, I'm merely going to rehash the backup mantra for you:

✔ Every day you need to back up the stuff you worked on that day.

✔ Every week you need to back up all your stuff.

✔ Every month you must back up your entire computer, all the files.

Make sense of this! It doesn't matter whether or not you have a backup program or even a fancy tape backup drive. In fact, I use Zip disks and CD-Rs for all my backups. Because all my stuff is kept in the My Documents folder, it's simple for me to drag that folder to a CD-R Direct CD disk or Zip disk. If I'm working on a single project, then I merely make a backup copy of that project's folder at the end of the day on a 250MB Zip disk. Simple.

What about the Norton Utility Emergency Boot Disk?

Q: I dutifully created the Emergency Boot Disk per your book's instructions. However, I also have the Norton Utilities and noticed that it, too, comes with an Emergency Boot Disk. Which should I use?

A: Always use the disk that you created yourself, which is customized for your computer and your version of Windows. The disk that comes with the Norton Utilities is necessary because Norton doesn't know whether or not your PC has an Emergency Boot Disk. If it does, great, then you can use that disk. Otherwise, Norton includes his own diskette for those who, unfortunately, didn't make their own. Also, the Norton disk contains a few handy utilities for diagnosing and data recovery.

The whole notion behind this effort is that you always have a duplicate copy of anything you create. That way, should something awful happen, you can use the duplicate copy for recovery. For example, when my external hard drive died, I wept not; I had a copy of every file on that drive. I lost nothing! It did take me a while to recover (copy) all the files back to the new hard drive replacement, but I didn't lose one byte of data. That was all thanks to the preventative backup practice.

- ✔ I rotate through three sets of 250MB Zip disks for my daily backups. I just keep them in a stack and put today's backup disk on the bottom.

- ✔ As long as you keep all your stuff in the My Documents folder and its subfolders, then backing up your stuff is as easy as making a copy of that folder "tree."

- ✔ Yes, it's possible to backup to a second hard drive, but it's best if that hard drive is a different physical drive than your C drive. For example, if drive D is an external FireWire drive, then backing up to it is okay. But backing up to drive D, which is on the same physical disk as drive C, might not be that safe; if the whole disk drive dies, then both hard drives are lost.

- ✔ Tape backup drives are the easiest things to use for backup. Not only will the tapes hold more information than Zip or CD-R disks, but the backup software that comes with the drive helps make the process wholly automatic.

- ✔ Avoid using floppy disks for backup. Floppy disks are extremely unreliable.

"Does My PC Have a Virus?"

A common question that zips through the mind of a bewildered user facing a silly PC is, "Could this be a virus?" I hate to say it, but yes it could — especially if you can answer *yes* to any of the following:

- ✔ I downloaded files from a Web page on the Internet, specifically a Web page of a questionable nature.

- ✔ I ran a program sent to me as an e-mail attachment, something I wasn't expecting or from someone I didn't know or trust.

- ✔ I ran a program I got from a chat room.

- ✔ I started a game on my PC from a floppy or CD-R boot disk.

- ✔ I used stolen software my friends and co-workers gave me.

- ✔ Other people use my PC.

If you answer *yes* to any of these items, you probably have a virus. Those are all nasty habits, and they're just about the only ways that a virus can infect a PC.

Where you cannot get a virus

You cannot get a virus from any of the following sources:

E-mail. Reading plain e-mail does not give your PC a virus. Various scares and scams have surfaced about reading certain messages and getting a virus, but they're all hoaxes. You cannot get a virus from reading your e-mail, unless your e-mail program (such as Outlook Express) is configured to automatically open attachments. (See the second note at the end of the section.)

A picture file. Picture files cannot infect your PC. JPEGs, GIFs, or even more elaborate graphics file formats cannot infect your PC. Feel free to open these files on the Internet or if they're attached to an e-mail message.

Downloads. Downloading a program that contains a virus won't infect your computer. The virus must be a program you run. If you download the file and don't run it, then you're safe. (Someone sent me such a virus once. I didn't run the program, so my PC was never infected.) To check for a virus, have your anti-virus software scan the file. That way you'll know instantly and can either delete the file or repair it (if that's an option).

Retail software. The stuff they sell at the store is not infected.

Known Web FTP sites. Web sites, such as Shareware.com or any widely used FTP site, will not have infected software on it. And if you doubt that, then download the software and run a virus-checker on it before you run that program. (See the next section.)

Now pay attention: The only way you can get a virus on your PC is to *run* an infected program. That's it! If you don't run the program, you won't get the virus.

There is a potential virus problem with older versions of Outlook Express. In those versions, it's possible to get a virus by reading an e-mail, though it's not really the e-mail that gives you the virus; it's a signature or attachment that's associated with the e-mail that contains the virus. Outlook Express was once configured to automatically open and run any program held in the signature file, which infected your computer despite the fact that you didn't manually open any attachment. This was a bug and Microsoft did fix it.

To be sure your version of Outlook Express is not susceptible to this bug, visit `http://support.microsoft.com`. Search for **Outlook Express** and use the specific article ID number **Q262165**.

Antivirus software

Even if you don't practice any nasty PC program habits, you may sleep better if you get special antivirus software.

Alas, Windows doesn't come with any antivirus software. You need to run down to the Software-o-Rama to buy some or download antivirus software from the Internet.

- ✔ Antivirus software removes the virus from your PC, as well as assists you in spotting such nasty programs before they invade again.

- ✔ Antivirus software also tends to slow down your PC. My advice: Run the software first to scan for viruses. Then configure it so that it scans your system only when you start the PC. Then just use the program to individually scan files you download or get from other people. But turn off the options that monitor your PC's activity 24 hours a day.

- ✔ Believe your antivirus software when it tells you no viruses are in your PC. As long as you've updated your anti-virus software with the latest anti-virus information, you're okay.

- ✔ On the Web, visit McAfee for a sample antivirus program at www.mcafee.com.

- ✔ No, you can't give your PC a virus by sneezing on the monitor. But you should have a box of Kleenex tissues handy for when that does happen.

Using System Restore

I got a flat tire a few months back. Some debris was in the road. I ran over something. I heard the telltale ssp-ssp-ssp as the tire lost air while it was rotating. It was a nice audible clue.

Just like cars, computers should make funny noises before they go south. Computers need thumping thuds or grinding sounds. Or maybe there should be puddles of oil under the mouse. But, no. Computers just stop working. It's maddening.

Sometimes the it-was-working-yesterday syndrome has a cause, only you just forgot it. Ask yourself the following questions:

- ✔ Did I add any new PC hardware recently?
- ✔ Did I add any new software?
- ✔ Did I delete any files recently?

> ✔ Have I changed any software?
>
> ✔ Have I reset any of the Windows options?
>
> ✔ Did I uninstall anything?

Oftentimes you find yourself remembering what happened; that is, "Oh, yeah, I set the printer to print sideways yesterday. No wonder all my correspondence came out looking so funky." Whatever, narrowing down what was changed helps you fix things, or at least leads the tech-support people or your PC guru to the proper cure.

One way you can help is to run the System Restore program before you mess with the computer. By creating a restore point, you perform valuable preventative maintenance for the it-was-working-yesterday syndrome. Basically, you're making a point of telling the computer to remember its settings "yesterday," before you install something new today. That way you can recover, should you need to.

Alas, the System Restore command is only available on Windows Me and Windows XP.

Making a restore point

To set a specific restore point, follow these steps:

1. **Run System Restore.**

   From the Start menu choose (More) Programs⇨Accessories⇨ System Tools⇨System Restore.

2. **Choose "Create a restore point."**

3. **Click the Next button.**

4. **Enter a description.**

   Be creative. Type something, such as, "Before I tried to install that Printer Port CD-R drive." That should do.

5. **Click the Next or Create button.**

   (It's "Next" in Windows Me, "Create" in Windows XP).

   Windows busies itself creating the restore point.

   Soon a message appears on the screen, telling you that the restore point was created.

6. **Click the OK or Close button.**

   (It's "OK" in Windows Me, "Close" in Windows XP).

   System Restore closes.

You're now ready to proceed with your hardware — or software — installation. If anything goes wrong with the system, you can easily restore your system settings to the way they were before. Continue reading in the next section.

Restoring your system

If all goes well with your hardware (or software) installation, very nice. Enjoy the fact that the computer is living up to Microsoft's outrageous promises. Pat yourself on the back. Bow a knee to Redmond, Washington.

If, on the other hand, the gates of Hell crack open and hoards of demons infest your computer like locusts from some Biblical plague, then feel good that you used System Restore. Time to recover:

1. **Run System Restore.**

   From the Start menu choose (More) Programs⇨Accessories⇨ System Tools⇨System Restore.

2. **Choose "Restore my computer to an earlier time."**

3. **Click the Next button.**

   The next screen lets you choose a restore point. Windows creates its own restore points every few days or so, and those are marked on the calendar that appears in the System Restore window (Figure 26-1). Or you can choose a manual restore point, should you have been fortunate enough to create one (see the previous section).

4. **Choose a date from the calendar.**

   The closer to today's date the better.

5. **Choose a restore point from the current day's setting (to the right of the calendar).**

   If you recently created a restore point, then choose it from the list.

6. **Click Next.**

   A warning may appear, begging you to close windows and save your data. Do so! Switch to any open windows or programs and close them. Then click OK in the warning dialog box.

7. **Click Next.**

   The system restores. *Sit still*. Wait.

   Your computer resets. Relax. Wait for it to finish resetting.

   Eventually, after the computer restarts, you'll be dumped back into the System Restore program.

8. **Click OK.**

   You're done.

ASK DAN

How can I protect my system from Internet hackers?

Q: Can anyone access all the files in my computer via my cable modem? Apparently it works just like a network card, and therefore allows free access to my system by my cable company or anyone who knows the address. Is that true?

A: Yes. Cable modems, and most DSL connections, have their own unique "IP address" on the Internet. Anyone who knows the address can PING you or attempt to FTP into your system or do a bunch of nasty things. In fact, they can make that attempt even if they don't know your modem's IP address; various "probe" software exists that constantly hunts for cable or DSL modems. It's a dangerous world.

But don't panic! Inquire your ISP about various forms of "*firewall*" protection, which prevents unauthorized access to your computer. For example, the Norton Internet Security package offers a decent level of firewall protection, which prohibits certain types of nasty people on the Internet from cracking into your computer via the cable or DSL modem.

At this point, your computer should be behaving normally, as it did before you installed or upgraded your hardware or software. Congratulations.

Figure 26-1: System Restore lets you choose a date to restore your previous Windows settings.

System Restore

Choose a Restore Point

Help

The following calendar displays in bold all of the dates that have restore points available. The list displays the restore points that are available for the selected date.

Possible types of restore points are: system checkpoints (scheduled restore points created by your computer), manual restore points (restore points created by you), and installation restore points (automatic restore points created when certain programs are installed).

Select a bold date on the calendar, and then select one of the available restore points from the list.

<	May, 2001					>
Sun	Mon	Tue	Wed	Thu	Fri	Sat
29	30	1	2	3	4	5
6	7	8	9	10	11	12
13	14	15	16	17	18	19
20	21	22	23	24	25	26
27	28	29	30	31	1	2
3	4	5	6	7	8	9

Tuesday, May 29, 2001

2:48 PM a test
4:28 AM System CheckPoint

Back   Next   Cancel

Of course, this still leaves you with the problematic hardware or software that forced you to do a System Restore. At this point you can consider contacting the manufacturer's Web page for support or troubleshooting information, or consider returning the hardware for a refund if it's truly incompatible. The choice is yours, but at least the computer works.

Chapter 27

Troubleshooting Your PC

• •

• •

*W*hy is it that computers run amok? If cars had the same troubles, no one would drive. Heck, no one would walk, sit, or play anywhere near a road. As humans, we count on things to be reliable and consistent. Life is supposed to be that way. Heaven must be that way. Hell? It's probably floor-to-ceiling computers down there.

For millions of reasons, computers go insane and turn on their owners. (Calling Stephen King! Are you dry on ideas?) I can't list them all here, but I can give you general advice plus a few steps to take for regaining control of the beast.

General, Up-Front, Panicky Advice

When your computer screws up, STOP WORKING ON IT!

> ✔ Any time a program crashes or something doesn't work right, save and shut down. Restart your PC. That generally fixes most problems.

> ✔ Don't be a fool and try to continue to work on the system or even play a game. That's nuts.

> ✔ If you're having disk troubles, try saving your file to disk, but also use the Save As command to save the file to another hard drive, floppy disk, or Zip disk.
>
> ✔ Programs that crash don't go away; their corpses stay in memory. Only by resetting your PC do you get that memory back.

Things to Check

Whenever a computer goes haywire, you should do a few things right away.

Check your hardware

Are all the cables connected? Is the monitor (or printer or modem) plugged in?

Printer cables and monitor cables can wiggle loose. Check them!

Modems must be properly plugged into the wall — which is tough because they all have two phone jacks on the back. Ensure you're using the proper one.

The keyboard and mouse cables can loosen. Check them!

Find out how much control you have

Some programs go gently into the dark night. Others are sucked down into the pit of hell with fingernails gouging drag marks into the linoleum.

When a program dies, you may see an error message, notice that things aren't working properly, or receive no response from the computer. If so, you need to determine how much control you still have over the PC.

Move the mouse around. Does it still work? If so, good. If not, try the keyboard.

Does the keyboard work? Try popping up the Start menu in Windows: Press Ctrl+Esc to see whether your keyboard is still functioning. (Press the Esc key to make the Start menu go away.)

You may have to wait for Windows to respond; sometimes a misbehaving program tosses a wrench into the gears, which makes the PC slow to respond.

If you have no mouse or keyboard control, your only resort is to reset. Yes, this is the only time you should manually reset the PC. Refer to Chapter 2.

What's an illegal procedure?

Q: I have been receiving messages that say that this machine is doing something illegal. . . .

A: *Illegal* is a term widely misused by computer programmers. It means *wrong* or *not permitted*

with respect to the way the computer does things. For example, in the filename *this:that*, the colon is an illegal character. That's just the term they use. Sorry it scared you.

Remove that dead program

Windows has the capability to live with dead programs. Even though the program doesn't respond, you can still use the mouse and keyboard, and you can work in other programs. Still, you should rid yourself of the deadware. Here's how:

1. **Press Ctrl+Alt+Delete.**

   In Windows 98/Me, this action brings up the Close Program window. (See Figure 27-1.)

   In Windows 2000, pressing the three-finger-salute (Ctrl+Alt+Delete) summons the Windows Security dialog box, but that's no reason to panic! Simply click the Task Manager button to display the Task Manager window, which has features similar to the Close Program window.

   Pressing Ctrl+Atl+Delete in Windows XP brings up the Windows Task Manager dialog box, which serves the same function as the Close Program window.

2. **Sniff out any recently deceased programs.**

   Look for the words *not responding* after the dead program's name in the list. For example, the program *Government* may be not responding. Click that program's name on the list.

   (If more than one program is not responding, repeat all of these steps to rid yourself of each of them.)

3. **Click the End Task button.**

   The program is killed off.

4. **Close the Close Program or Windows Task Manager window.**

In Windows 98/Me, be careful not to choose the Shut Down button instead of End Task. Sometimes that makes sense — for example, you want to shut down an AWOL program. But the Shut Down button actually shuts down Windows — and without warning. So don't select it casually!

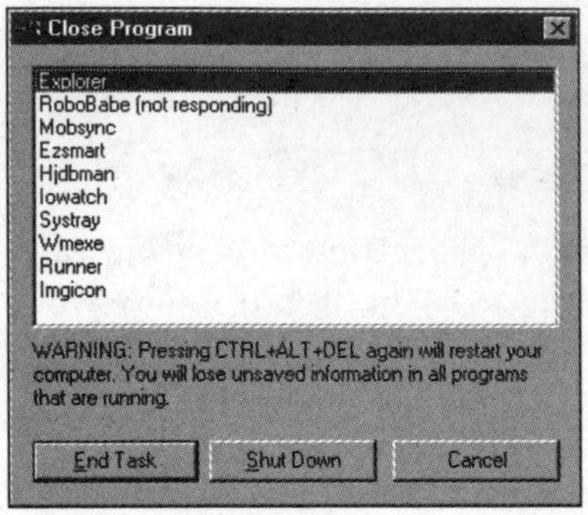

Figure 27-1:
Kill off
stubborn
programs
using the
Task
Manager
window.

At this point, the program is gone. It should be removed from the screen, which makes it easier to get at other programs.

Your next step should be to save and shut down other applications you may be running. Then reset your PC.

Resetting to fix strangeness

Resetting is sometimes the best way to cure just about anything weird. If the mouse pointer is missing, reset. If Explorer dies, reset. If a program hangs, reset — even after you get rid of the dead program.

Follow the instructions in Chapter 2 for resetting your PC. Do it. When the computer comes alive again, the problem may be automagically fixed.

 ✔ Resetting is also known as restarting.

 ✔ Why does resetting work? I have no idea. I think, maybe, the computer just gets tired. It needs to be reset every so often to keep itself awake.

After resetting, check the hard drive

When your computer is up and running after a crash-and-reset, consider running the ScanDisk program. This program checks your hard drives for errors and ensures that the disk system is up to snuff.

To run ScanDisk follow these steps:

1. **Open the My Computer window.**

2. **Right-click on the drive C icon.**

   The pop-up shortcut menu is displayed.

3. **Choose Properties.**

   The disk drive's properties dialog box shows up.

4. **Click the Tools tab.**

5. **Click the Check Now button.**

   In Windows 98/Me, the ScanDisk program is run. Select the hard drive(s) to scan by Ctrl+clicking them in the list. Choose Standard (the Thorough option is good, but takes longer than you need after resetting), and check the "Automatically fix errors" item.

   In Windows 2000/XP, the Check Disk program is run. Check to select both options, "Automatically fix file system errors" and "Scan for and attempt recovery of bad sectors." Click the Start button.

6. **Click the Start button.**

   Your disk is checked for errors, which are automatically fixed if any are found. After that, you're just peachy.

Close the ScanDisk window when you're done.

- ✔ If Check Disk (Windows 2000/XP) is unable to do its job, a warning dialog box appears. Click Yes. That way the disk checking operation continues at a later time.

- ✔ If Scan Disk or Check Disk never seems to run, then you'll need to buy a third party utility to do the job. (Microsoft's utilities just aren't that robust.) I recommend using the Norton Utilities and its version of Scan Disk if you're having trouble. Many of my readers have found that Norton's pulls through where the Microsoft utilities fall way short.

- ✔ ScanDisk is not voodoo. If you have serious disk problems, then it probably won't run at all. In that case, you need to take your PC in for servicing, as covered in Chapter 28.

- ✔ Run ScanDisk every week or so just in case. Windows has a scheduling tool that can run ScanDisk automatically for you. Any good book on Windows will tell you how to do it.

The Perils of Safe Mode

Whenever Windows detects major problems, it starts itself in what's known as Safe mode. Whether or not that implies that normal operation is the unsafe mode, I'll leave for the gurus to debate. The point is that Windows has a special mode you can try should you need to wiggle out of a pickle.

Windows won't let me shut down!

Q: I cannot for the life of me shut down Windows. It gets to the screen that says, "Windows is shutting down" and then . . . nothing! I wait and wait, but eventually I have to reset manually. I'm afraid this is damaging my computer. Can you help?

A: No, it's not damaging your computer when Windows "hangs" on its exit. Like most hams, Windows just refuses to leave the stage!

Honestly, what's happening is that some program is refusing to quit. It gets stuck in memory and Windows cannot remove it, so Windows waits eternally. You're doing the right thing by shutting the power off manually. After all, what else can you do?

It's hard to tell which program gets stuck in memory, but a good guess is that it's your anti-virus software. For some reason, anti-virus software causes more shutdown problems with Windows than I've ever seen. If you disable your anti-virus software (as I recommend in Chapter 26), then the shutdown problem goes away.

Starting safely

Say you screw something up or it screws up by itself. The most common situation I can think of is changing the video display to something you don't want. For example, you have black-on-black text or maybe text so large that you cannot get to the button to change it back. If so, you need to restart in Safe mode.

Shut down the PC as you normally would. If you cannot access the Start button, press Ctrl+Esc. Then press the U key to access the Shut Down command. The Shut Down Windows dialog box appears.

If you cannot see the Shut Down Windows dialog box, press Alt+R to select the Restart option. Then press the Enter key.

As Windows restarts, press and hold the Ctrl key (on some PCs you need to press the F8 key) to display a special Startup menu. Here is the menu that appears with Windows Me:

```
Microsoft Windows Millennium Startup Menu
===================================
 1. Normal
 2. Logged (\BOOTLOG.TXT)
 3. Safe mode
 4. Step-by-step confirmation
Enter a choice:
```

Get a bucket, there's a memory leak!

Seriously, a "memory leak" doesn't involve a bucket or a towel or cleaning up any sort of liquid mess. Instead, a memory leak is a cute name given to a common problem.

When you quit a computer program, the operating system tidies things up. First, it looks for any files opened by that program and closes them. Then it takes all the memory that the computer program used and makes it available for other programs. It's all nice and fair. Well, until some unruly program refuses to shut down properly. In that case, some of the program stubbornly remains in memory. That's a "leak."

A worst-case scenario comes when the program not only refuses to leave memory, but it continues to run and actually consume more and more memory. This type of run amok program eventually crashes the whole computer, resulting in one of those notorious KERNEL32.DLL kind of errors.

The sad part about memory leaks is that you can do nothing to prevent them. (It's really the operating system's job to catch and plug them, but Windows just isn't up to the task.) The thing you can do is to restart Windows (see Chapter 2). If you know which program is causing the leak, then you can report it to the developers and they may have a fix. But otherwise, you're just stuck sitting there, watching memory go bye-bye. (At least there's no annoying drip-drip-drip.)

Search for the Safe mode option (number 3 here). Type that number and press the Enter key.

Safe mode starts, loading only the files necessary to run Windows — it's a no-frills operation. When Windows is finally up, you see it displayed in a low-resolution, low-color mode with the words *Safe mode* splattered on the desktop.

Fix your problem! Safe mode exists to fix problems. Read the dialog box that tells you about Safe mode and how to visit the Control Panel to fix what's bugging you. Generally speaking, all you need to do is undo what it was that you screwed up in the first place.

- Windows 98 has two additional Startup Menu options, both for starting with the command prompt.
- Windows 2000 doesn't have a Startup Menu. If you press the Ctrl key while Windows 2000 boots, you'll eventually see the Windows 2000 Setup screen, where you can adjust or repair the Windows 2000 installation.

Starting safely in Windows XP

Of all Windows editions, XP has the most elaborate Startup menu, full of options to help you recover in times of woe.

When Windows XP is starting, press and hold the F8 key. The following elaborate menu is displayed:

```
Windows Adavnced Options Menu
Please select an option:

     Safe Mode
     Safe Mode with Networking
     Safe Mode with Command Prompt

     Enable Boot Logging
     Enable VGA Mode
     Last Known Good Configuration
     Directory Services Restore Mode (Windows domain
           controllers only)
     Debugging Mode

     Boot Normally
     Reboot
     Return to OS Choices Menu

Use the up or down arrow keys to move the highlight to your
            choice.
Press ENTER to choose.
```

For Safe mode, highlight the top option and press the Enter key.

Another good option to choose is the Last Known Good Configuration, which basically runs the System Restore utility to restore Windows to the last time it was working properly — a wonderful improvement over older versions of Windows.

The final option you're most likely to choose is Boot Normally, which starts up Windows as if nothing is wrong.

When Safe mode starts automatically

If the problem is really bad, Windows may start in Safe mode automatically. Don't let this scare you! Windows has discovered something not quite right in the system and has started in Safe mode to help you fix it.

✔ Safe mode may come up after you install new hardware. That means the software (drivers) required for that hardware is not working properly. Uninstall the software in Safe mode and restart your computer. Contact your dealer to see if new software exists.

✔ Consider running System Restore if Safe Mode rears its ugly head unexpectedly. See Chapter 26.

✔ Refer to the next section, "Checking for Device Conflicts," for more information on why Safe mode may have started automatically.

Starting normally again

If your PC seems to be stuck in *diagnostic* mode, then you may need to manually twist it back into normal mode. Here's how:

1. **Choose the Run command from the Start menu.**

2. **In the Run dialog box, type** MSCONFIG **and press Enter.**

   This action runs the System Configuration Utility, a handy program to help you troubleshoot startup problems.

3. **Click the General tab and ensure that the Normal Startup item is selected.**

This option ensures that Windows starts normally. (You may notice that the Diagnostic Startup is selected, which is the source of your woes.)

4. **Click OK. Your computer should start normally from here on — unless you have another problem.**

Also note that you can use the System Configuration Utility to remove startup programs that may be causing trouble. Refer to the section, "Using MSCONFIG to Troubleshoot Startup Problems" elsewhere in this chapter.

Checking for Device Conflicts

One thing you should check when Windows starts in Safe mode is the Device Manager. It lists all the hardware in your PC and flags any hardware that may be causing trouble.

Viewing the Device Manager

Follow these steps to view the Device Manager:

1. **Right-click on the My Computer icon on the desktop.**

2. **Choose Properties from the shortcut menu.**

3a. **For Windows 98/Me, click on the Device Manager tab.**

3b. **For Windows 2000/XP, click on the Hardware tab, then click the Device Manager button. (Note that you need proper permissions in Windows 2000 to change things in the Device Manager.)**

The Device Manager is shown in Figure 27-2, though it may look subtly different depending on your version of Windows. All the hardware devices attached to or lurking inside of your computer are listed in a tree format. You can open various branches of the tree to see, for example, the various disk drives your computer knows about.

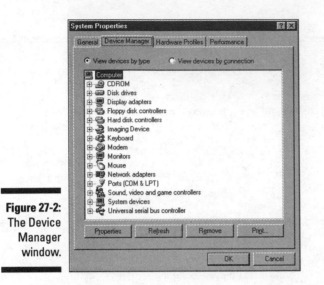

Figure 27-2:
The Device
Manager
window.

If there are any hardware conflicts, they'll be flagged by a tiny exclamation point in a yellow circle:

You don't have to hunt for these items; their branches open automatically to display the errant device.

If you have such a malfunctioning device in your system, double-click it with the mouse. In the center of the device's Properties dialog box is an explanation of the problem (in the Device status area). Sometimes the advice is specific. Sometimes it's just "refer to the device's manual." Sometimes you're asked to run a troubleshooter or conflict manager. Keep reading in the next section.

4. **Close the Device Manager when you're done with it.**

Click the OK button or just close the window.

Another program to check for system conflicts is the System Information utility: From the Start menu choose Programs➪Accessories➪SystemTools➪ System Information. The Hardware Resources/Conflicts/Sharing page lists any trouble spots the Device Manager may miss.

Running a troubleshooter

Troubleshooters are special Q&A programs included in the Help system for Windows. There is no logical or easy way to start them, other than the following:

1. **Choose Help from the Start menu.**

The Windows Help thing appears.

2. **Click to view the Index.**

3. **Type** Trouble **in the text box.**

   The first match might be "troubleshooter," but that's not the one you want.

4. **Scroll down to the word *troubleshooting*.**

   That's not "troubleshooter" but rather "troubleshooting," which you may have to scroll down a bit to find.

5. **Scroll through the list to find the troubleshooter that fits your needs.**

   Modem trouble? Scroll down to the Modem troubleshooter.

   Note that some of the items listed are not troubleshooters but merely display the help information.

6. **Select a topic and click the Display button.**

   And you're off!

   Click the various links and put dots in the proper circles to answer questions and work through the troubleshooter.

7. **Don't forget to close the Help and Troubleshooter windows when you're done.**

I've had about 50-50 luck with the Windows troubleshooters. Sometimes they've pointed me right to the problem. Other times, using the troubleshooter was like trying to herd cats.

Restoring a Device Driver

The most common troubleshooting question I get involves replacing the graphics adapter device driver, which is the software that controls the screen. For some reason, the display's resolution may go bonkers. The resolution is too low and the reader is unable to reset it back. This is a common problem and it has a few easy solutions.

The first solution, providing that you have Windows Me or Windows XP, is to use System Restore to recover the computer's state back when the display was working fine. That works.

The second solution is to reinstall the video device driver, which isn't as horrid as it sounds:

1. **Call up the Device Manager window.**

   Refer to the steps in the section, "Viewing the Device Manager," earlier in this chapter.

2. **Click to open the Display adapters branch on the tree.**

   Your display adapter will be listed, such as NVIDIA GeForce2 GTS or something equally cryptic. That's the name of your graphics adapter.

3. **Double-click your graphics adapter's name.**

   A Properties dialog box for your graphics adapter appears.

4. **Click the Driver tab.**

5. **Click the Update Driver button.**

   The Update Device Driver Wizard runs, which is a simple way to update or reinstall the device drive.

6. **Follow the steps in the Wizard.**

   Work your way through the steps in the Wizard. There is no need to change the pre-selected options unless you know what you're after. Otherwise, the Wizard automatically reinstalls the device driver. For a graphics adapter, chances are that you'll find the proper device driver right there on your hard drive. If so, great; reinstall the driver per the Wizard's instructions.

   Your computer may need to reset; that's okay. Do so.

When you're done, the new driver should be installed, or the old driver reinstated, which gives you back all the glorious graphics you were once used to.

✔ Though these steps are specific to the graphics adapter, they can be followed to update or reinstall the device driver for any device in your computer.

✔ In Windows 2000 you must be logged in as the Administrator to make device driver changes.

✔ Another way to locate device drivers is to visit the device's manufacturer on the Internet. Perform a search in Yahoo for the graphics adapter's name. This eventually leads to the manufacturer's name and Web page. From there you can visit the Technical Support area on the manufacturer's Web page, which contains links to download new device driver files. Remember to bookmark the manufacturer's Web page should you need to visit it again.

Using MSCONFIG to Troubleshoot Startup Problems

Most startup problems have nothing to do with the computer starting properly. They have everything to do with weird messages that appear when the computer starts. For example, you see that some DLL or VBX file is "missing." Huh? Or perhaps an error message tells you that some program tidbit is gone and so the "Frapulator" utility will be unavailable. What?

To troubleshoot any startup problem, you need to use a tool called the System Configuration Utility, or MSCONFIG for short. (Note that Windows 2000 does not have this utility.)

To start MSCONFIG, choose Run from the Start menu. Type **MSCONFIG** into the box and click the OK button. The System Configuration Utility appears, as shown in Figure 27-3.

Figure 27-3 shows the Startup tab, which contains a list of all the secret programs Windows runs when it starts. These are in addition to those listed in the Start menu's Programs/Startup folder. Some of them are System Tray icons, some of them are background tasks, such as anti-virus software, and others are programs that Windows uses to do various things.

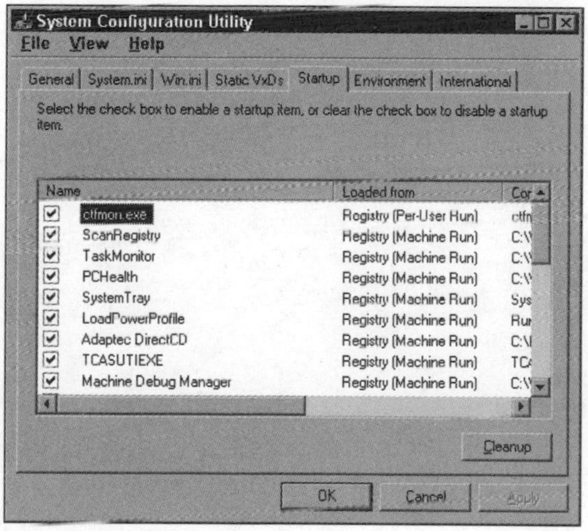

Figure 27-3:
MSCONFIG.

To stop a program from running at start time, remove its checkmark. This does not uninstall the program, but rather disables it from running — which may stop it from displaying an annoying message when the computer starts.

Close the System Configuration Utility window when you're done with it.

✔ Only disable those programs you suspect are causing startup problems. Otherwise, leave the System Configuration Utility alone.

✔ Another place to look for startup programs is in the Win.ini tab: Open the [windows] branch inside the scrolling list and look for items by load= or run=. You can disable those items by removing their checkmarks.

Chapter 28

When to Scream for Help

• •

• •

S hould you scream for help? Of course. The decision to scream should never be questioned. I might add, however, that it helps to know who to scream at.

People scream because they need to be heard. Computers lack ears, so screaming at them doesn't help (even if the computer has a microphone). In fact, because they lack emotions, computers can't tell whether you're really in a bind or just casually pressing the F1 key.

No, it helps to have a person to scream at. Further, it helps to scream in a soft speaking voice. Scream calmly. Describe what's going on. And follow the advice in this chapter to help remove the reason for all that screaming in the first place.

Who Is Your PC Guru?

Your personal computer guru is someone — anyone — who loves computers and knows enough about them to offer help when you need it. Your guru is an important person to know and respect. Everyone has one — even the gurus themselves! If you don't have one, you need one.

At work. At the office, the guru is probably the computer manager, but ask around to see whether anyone else can do the job. Quite a few computer zanies may be lurking around the office. If you find one, he or she may be able to offer help and advice more quickly than the computer manager (who goes by a schedule). Especially for help on particular types of software, turn to people who use the programs regularly; they may know tricks they can pass along.

At home. For the home, finding a guru can be more difficult. Usually a neighbor, friend, or relative will know enough about computers to help you install hardware or software, or at least give you advice about some program.

Whatever your situation, identify your guru and keep that person in mind for troubled times or for extracting advice and tips. It's like having a good mechanic handy or knowing a friendly doctor. You may not use your guru all the time, but knowing that he or she is available makes computing easier.

A certain amount of finesse is involved when using your computer guru's talents; a line must be drawn between getting occasional help and taxing your guru's patience.

Other Places You Can Look for Help

Computer gurus aren't everywhere. Suppose you live on Pitcairn Island, and your PC just came mail order from PCs Limited (along with your absentee ballot for the 2000 presidential elections). Who's going to be your guru? Definitely not the lady who makes festive pot holders out of palm fronds.

When you don't have a real guru handy, look for alternatives. Here's a bunch I can think of right off the top of my head:

✔ Some computer stores may offer classes or have coffee groups where you can ask questions. But keep in mind that they're a limited source of information.

✔ Local computer clubs dot the nation. Don't be afraid to show up at one and ask a few questions. You may even adopt a guru there or learn about special sessions for beginners. Many computer clubs or special interest groups (SIGs) are designed specifically for questions and answers. Check the local paper or computer flyer at the store.

✔ Community colleges offer introductory courses on computers and some software programs. Come armed with your questions.

✔ Don't forget the gurus you already paid for: the technical-support people at your computer store or the telephone support you get with every piece of software you buy. Everything comes with support; it's part of the purchase price (or so they claim). Especially for software, call the support department if you're having trouble. (But don't abuse phone support; it's not an excuse for not reading the manual.) Also, watch out for phone support you must pay for, either from the long distance call or on a per-minute charge.

✔ If these traditional avenues fail, consider the unconventional. Search for help on the Internet or access a newsgroup particular to the thing that's bothering you.

Figure Out Whether It's a Hardware or Software Problem

Your guru, or even you, may be able to fix hardware problems: Check the cables, listen for noises, watch for sparks, and so on.

Software problems, on the other hand, can generally be cured by your guru or by a phone call to the developer's technical-support hot line (or wait-on-hold line). But which is which? It's important to know which problem you're experiencing because computer doctors get irked when you hand them a PC with a software problem. Here are the clues:

1. **Does the problem happen consistently, no matter which program you're running?**

   For example, do Word, Excel, and your accounting package all refuse to send stuff to the printer? If so, it's a hardware problem; more specifically the printer is being stupid. Check the power. Check the cables. Check the printer.

2. **Did the problem just crop up?**

   For example, did the Print Preview mode work last week but not today? If so, it could be a hardware problem, it could be a network problem, or it could be a software driver problem — provided that you haven't changed anything on your computer or added any new software since the last time the program worked properly.

3. **Does the problem happen with only one application?**

   For example, does the computer always reset when you try to print using your photo editor? If so, it's a software problem. Call the developer.

Generally speaking, if the problem happens in only one program, it's the software. If it's consistent across all your applications or it happens at random times, it's the hardware.

Calling Tech Support

Tech support can be good or bad — or both! It used to be good and free. There were 800 numbers and lots of eager, young people willing to help you to do anything from writing a printer driver to removing the cellophane off the computer box.

Today, tech support is either pay-as-you-go or nonexistent. Before you call tech support, try to find out how much it's going to cost you and how busy the staff usually is. Asking around is the best way to discover this info.

Also, try visiting the company's Web page. Look for support information or a FAQ (Frequently Asked Questions) page. You may find your answer there. I discovered, for example, how best to configure my PC for two monitors by visiting a Web page instead of dialing up the pricey tech support.

If you finally give in and call tech support, you should be armed with the following knowledge:

- Be near the computer when you call. The tech person will doubtless want you to work through some problems or try solutions.

- For hardware problems, gather a description of the hardware that's ailing you: how much memory is installed, the microprocessor name and number, the computer type or brand name, and the serial number of the device.

- For software trouble, they'll want a serial number, version number, and maybe a registration number.

- Be able to reproduce the problem.

- Act calm and civil.

- Be prepared to take advice.

The tech-support person will work you through the problem and provide a solution. Hopefully that will fix the problem.

- You may want to write down the solution so that you don't have to phone tech support again.

- Tech support is available for just about every hardware or software product sold. Please don't abuse it! Always try every possible resource (the Web, the manual) before calling up technical support.

- Right-click the My Computer icon and choose Properties from the short-cut menu. Most major computer manufacturers put a button in the System Properties/General dialog box called Support Information. Click that button to find out how to get help with your computer.

- Never use tech support as a substitute for reading the manual. Too many people did that in the early 1990s, which is probably why all the free tech support disappeared and today you generally have to pay for it.

- Don't forget your computer dealer! You paid them for service and support. If you're in a bind, the folks there should be who you call first.

Part VII
The Part of Tens

In this part . . .

Our love affair with the number ten probably has to do with our ten fingers. Throughout history we've listed things by tens: Ten Commandments, ten-gallon hats, ten-speed bikes. Almost every civilization has its ten-somethings. Well, except for the Sumerians. For some reason they got stuck on the number 12. Who knows? Ten fingers and two ears? The mind boggles!

This is The Part of Tens, which would have been The Part of Twelves had I lived in ancient Sumer and had there been a need for a book like *The Abacus For Dummies*. In any case, the chapters in this part of the book each list ten items that help you deal with your computer. All useful information.

Chapter 29

Ten Common Beginner Mistakes

*S*ure, you can make a gazillion mistakes with a computer, whether it's deleting the wrong file or dropping the printer on your foot. But I've narrowed the list down to ten. These are the day-to-day operating mistakes that people tend to repeat until they're told not to.

Not Properly Quitting Windows

When you're done with Windows, shut it down. Choose the Shut Down command from the Start menu, click OK, and wait until the screen says that it's safe to turn off your PC.

- Don't just flip the power switch when you're done.

- In the same vein, if your PC has a hardware reset button, don't use it unless you absolutely have to.

- Refer to Chapter 2 for proper PC shutdown instructions.

Buying Too Much Software

Your PC probably came out of the box with dozens of programs preinstalled. (No, you're not required to use them; see Chapter 19 on uninstalling software.) Even with all that software preinstalled, don't overwhelm yourself by getting *more* software right away.

Buying too much software isn't really the sin here. The sin is buying too much software and trying to learn it all at once. The buy-it-all-at-once habit probably comes from buying music, where it's okay to lug home a whole stack of CDs from the store. You can listen to several CDs over the course of a few days. They're enjoyable the first time, and they age well. Software, on the other hand, is gruesome on the first day and can take months to come to grips with.

Have mercy on yourself at the checkout counter and buy software at a moderate rate. Buy one package and learn it. Then move on and buy something else. You learn faster that way.

Buying Incompatible Hardware

Whoops! Did you forget to notice that that new keyboard you bought was for a Macintosh? Or maybe you thought you were getting a deal on that USB modem, and lo, your PC doesn't have a USB port. And the biggest disappointment: You buy a new AGP expansion card, but all you have available are PCI slots.

Always check your hardware before you buy it! Especially if you're shopping online; if you're not sure that the hardware is compatible, phone up the dealer and ask those folks specifically.

Not Buying Enough Supplies

Buy printer paper in those big boxes. You *will* run out. Buy extra floppy disks, Zip disks, CD-Rs, and whatever type of disks your PC's disk drives eat.

Not Saving Your Work

Whenever you're creating something blazingly original, choose the Save command and save your document to the hard disk. When you write something dumb that you're going to patch up later, choose the Save command, too. The idea here is to choose Save whenever you think about it — hopefully, every few minutes or sooner.

You never know when your computer will meander off to watch Barney while you're hoping to finish the last few paragraphs of that report. Save your work as often as possible. And always save it whenever you get up from your computer — even if it's just to grab a Fig Newton from the other room.

Not Backing Up Files

Saving work on a computer is a many-tiered process. First, save the work to your hard drive as you create it. Then, at the end of the day, back up your work to floppy or Zip disks. Always keep a safety copy somewhere, because you never know.

At the end of the week (or monthly), run the backup program that came with your PC's tape backup drive. I know this is a pain, but it's much more automated and easier to do than in years past. If your PC lacks a tape backup unit, *buy one!* You can back up to Zip disks, but that's expensive; backing up to floppy disks is crazy; and backing up to a CD-R or a Jaz drive is okay, especially if you have software that can perform the backup for you.

Opening or Deleting Unknown Things

There are both hardware and software rules about opening or deleting unknown things. On the software side, I have a rule:

If you didn't create the file, don't delete it.

Windows is brimming with unusual and unknown files. Don't mess with 'em. Don't delete them. Don't move them. Don't rename them. And especially don't open them to see what they are. Sometimes opening an unknown icon can lead to trouble.

On the hardware side, don't open anything attached to your PC unless you absolutely know what you're doing. Some hardware is meant to open. New console cases actually have pop-off and flip-top lids for easy access. They make upgrading things a snap. And if you do open a console, remember to unplug it! It's okay to open your printer to undo a jam or install new ink or a toner cartridge. Even so, do not open the ink or toner cartridges.

Other hardware items have *do not open* written all over them: the monitor, keyboard, and modem.

Booting from an Alien Disk

The number-one way to get a computer virus is to start your computer from a strange floppy disk. I'm not talking about starting the PC using a boot disk that you create or one that comes in a hermetically sealed software box. I'm talking about that — wink, wink — *game* Bob slipped you last week. You know the one. (Heh, heh.) Boot from that disk, and you're inviting who-knows-what into your PC. Don't.

Replying to spam E-Mail

Do not reply to any spam e-mail unless you want more spam. A popular trick is for the spammers to put some text that says, "reply to this message if you do not want to receive any further messages. . . ." Don't! Replying to spam signals the spammers that they have a "live one," and you will get even more spam. Never, ever reply to spam!

Opening a Program Attached to an E-Mail Message

You can receive photos via e-mail. You can receive sound files. You can receive any type of document. You can even receive ZIP file archives or compressed folders. These are all okay to receive. But if you receive a program (EXE or COM) file or a Visual Basic Script (VBS), do not open it!

The only way to get a virus on a PC is to *run* an infected program file. You can receive the file okay. But if you open it, you're dead. My rule is: Don't open any EXE file you're sent through e-mail.

- ✔ ZIP files (compressed folders) are okay to receive. You can open them and see what's in them. If they contain programs you're unsure of, then just delete the whole deal. You're safe.

- ✔ If you have to send a program file through e-mail, write or phone the recipient in advance to let him or her know it's coming.

- ✔ When in doubt, run antivirus software on the file before you run it.

- ✔ Some types of viruses can come in Microsoft Word documents. Antivirus software may catch these viruses, but in any case, confirm that the sender meant to send you the file before you open it.

Chapter 30

Ten Things Worth Buying for Your PC

I'm not trying to sell you anything, and I'm pretty sure that you're not ready to burst out and spend, spend, spend on something like a new computer (unless it's someone else's money). But you may want to consider buying some nifty little things for Mr. Computer. Like ten things worth buying for a dog (leash, cat-shaped squeeze toys, pooper-scooper, and so on), these ten things will make working with the beast more enjoyable.

Software

Never neglect software. Jillions of different types of software programs are available, each of them designed to perform a specific task for a certain type of user. If you ever find yourself frustrated by the way the computer does something, consider looking for a piece of software that does it better.

Wrist Pad

A wrist pad fits right below your keyboard. It enables you to comfortably rest your wrists while you type. This may help alleviate some repetitive motion injuries that are common to keyboard users. What more can I say?

Antiglare Screen

Tawdry as it may sound, an antiglare screen is nothing more than a nylon stocking stretched over the front of your monitor. Okay, these are *professional* nylons in fancy holders that adhere themselves to your screen. The net result is no garish glare from the lights in the room or outside. It's such a good idea that some monitors come with built-in antiglare screens.

Glare is the number one cause of eyestrain while you're using a computer. Lights usually reflect in the glass, either from above or from a window. The antiglare screen cuts down on the reflections and makes the stuff on the monitor easier to see.

Some antiglare screens also incorporate anti-radiation shielding. I'm serious: They provide protection from the harmful electromagnetic rays that are spewing out of your monitor even as you read this! Is this necessary? No.

Keyboard Cover

If you're klutzy with a coffee cup or have small children or others with peanut-butter-smudged fingers using the keyboard, keyboard covers are a great idea. You may have even seen them used in department stores: They cover the keyboard snugly but still enable you to type. A great idea, because without a keyboard cover, all this disgusting gunk falls between the keys. Yech!

In the same vein, you can also buy a generic dust cover for your computer. This item preserves the computer's appearance but has no other true value. Use a computer cover only when the computer is turned off (and I don't recommend turning it off). If you put the cover on the PC while the PC is turned on, you create a mini-greenhouse, and the computer will — sometimes — melt. Nasty. This result doesn't happen to the keyboard, which is a cool character anyway.

More Memory

Any PC works better with more memory installed. An upper limit on some computers is over 1GB of RAM, which seems ridiculous now but who knows about five years from now? Still, upgrading your system to 128MB or 256MB of RAM is a good idea. Almost immediately you notice the improvement in Windows and various graphics applications and games. Make someone else do the upgrading for you; you just buy the memory.

Larger, Faster Hard Drive

Hard drives fill up quickly. The first time it's because you've kept a lot of junk on your hard drive: games, things people give you, old files, and old programs you don't use anymore. So you can delete those or copy them to Zip disks for long-term storage. Then, after a time, your hard drive fills up again. The second time, it has stuff you really use. Argh! What can you delete?

The answer is to buy a larger hard drive. If you can, install a second hard drive and start filling it up. Otherwise, replace your first hard drive with a larger, faster model. Actually, buying a faster model is a great way to improve the performance of any older PC without throwing it out entirely.

Ergonomic Keyboard

The traditional computer keyboard is based on the old typewriter keyboard (the IBM Selectric, by the way). Why? It doesn't have to be. No mechanics inside the keyboard require the keys to be laid out staggered or in a cascading style. Repetitive typing on such a keyboard can lead to various ugly motion disorders (VUMDs).

To help you type more comfortably, you can get an ergonomic keyboard, such as the Microsoft Natural Keyboard. These keyboards arrange the keys in a manner that's comfortable for your hands, keeping everything lined up and not tweaked out like on a regular computer keyboard.

My wife loves her Microsoft Natural keyboard. She raves about it. On the other hand, I'm a purist and refuse to use it. In fact, I use an old IBM 101-key keyboard on my typing computer because I love all the noise it makes.

Larger or Secondary Monitor

Ever see a 19-inch computer monitor? How about the 21-inch model? They're *wonderful*. The 17-inch monitor you have was probably a good choice for when you bought your computer. But check out the screen real estate on that larger monitor.

The nifty thing about Windows and buying a new monitor is that you don't have to toss out the old one. You can use *both* monitors at once. You need a second video adapter to drive the second monitor, but it's absolutely wonderful.

See Chapter 11 for more information on dueling monitors.

USB Expansion Card

USB is the *thing* to have for expanding your PC. If your computer lacks a USB port, then you can buy a USB expansion card.

My advice: Get a two-port USB PCI card. (Sorry about all the acronyms and jargon.) Two ports is enough to start. If you get more than two USB devices, you can either swap them out or just buy a USB hub to continue expanding your system. See Chapter 8 for more USB information.

Scanner or Digital Camera

If you want the latest PC toy, then buy a scanner or digital camera.

Scanners are wonderful if you enjoy graphics and want to send pictures over the Internet. Digital cameras are great toys, but they're expensive. And they take some getting used to.

My advice: If you already have a nice camera and take lots of pictures, get a scanner. Wait for digital cameras to drop a bit in price before you make the investment. (See Chapter 17 for more information on scanners and digital cameras.)

Chapter 31

Ten Tips from a PC Guru

1 don't consider myself a computer expert or genius or guru, though many have called me all those terms. I'm just a guy who understands how computers work. Or, better than that, I understand how computer people think. They may not be able to express an idea, but I can see what they mean and translate it into English for you. Given that, here are some final tips and suggestions before you and your PC go off on your merry way.

You Control the Computer

You bought the computer. You clean up after its messes. You feed it floppy disks when it asks for them. You control the computer, simple as that. Don't let that computer try to boss you around with its bizarre conversations and funny idiosyncrasies. It's really pretty dopey; the computer is an idiot.

If somebody shoved a flattened can of motor oil in your mouth, would you try to taste it? Of course not. But stick a flattened can of motor oil into a disk drive, and the computer will try to read information from it, thinking it's a floppy disk. See? It's dumb.

You control that mindless computer just like you control an infant. You must treat it the same way, with respect and caring attention. Don't feel like the computer's bossing you around any more than you feel like a baby's bossing you around during 3 a.m. feedings. They're both helpless creatures, subject to your every whim. Be gentle. But be in charge.

Most Computer Nerds Love to Help Beginners

It's sad, but almost all computer nerds spend most of their waking hours in front of a computer. They know that's kind of an oddball thing to do, but they can't help it.

Their guilty consciences are what usually make them happy to help beginners. By passing on knowledge, they can legitimize the hours they whiled away on their computer stools. Plus, it gives them a chance to brush up on a social skill that's slowly slipping away: the art of actually talking to a person.

✔ Always be grateful when given help.

✔ Beware of False Nerds. These are people who don't love computers but who went to some sort of school to learn a few by-rote tricks. They may not be helpful nor know anything about computers other than what they're told. You can tell False Nerds because they lack the enthusiasm of the True Nerd, the one who will help you.

Get a UPS

The Uninterruptable Power Supply (UPS) is a boon to computing anywhere in the world where the power is less than reliable. Plug your console in the UPS. Plug your monitor in the UPS. If it has extra battery-backed-up sockets, plug your modem into the UPS as well.

✔ See Chapter 2 for information on using a UPS as well as using a power strip.

✔ Using a UPS does not affect the performance of your PC. The computer could care less whether it is plugged into the wall or a UPS.

Upgrading Software Isn't an Absolute Necessity

Just as the models on the cover of *Vogue* change their clothes each season (or maybe that should be change their *fashions* each season), software companies issue perpetual upgrades. Should you automatically buy the upgrade?

Of course not! If you're comfortable with your old software, there's no reason to buy the new version. None!

The software upgrade probably has a few new features in it (although you still haven't had a chance to check out all the features in the current version). And the upgrade probably has some new bugs in it, too, making it crash in new and different ways. Feel free to look at the box, just as you stare at the ladies on the cover of *Vogue*. But don't feel obliged to buy something you don't need. (And I apologize for all the parentheticals.)

Don't Ever Reinstall Windows

There's a myth floating around the tech support sites that the solution to all your ills is to reinstall Windows. Some suspect tech support people even claim that it's common for most Windows users to reinstall at least once a year. This is rubbish.

You *never* need to reinstall Windows. All problems are fixable. It's just that the so-called tech support people are lazy and resort to a drastic solution as opposed to really discovering what the problem is. If you press them, then they *will* tell you what's wrong and how to fix it.

In all my years of using a computer, I've never reinstalled Windows or had to reformat the hard drive. Everything is fixable. Anyone who tells you otherwise is full of horse poop.

Perfectly Adjusting Your Monitor

I don't have much explaining to do here. Keeping the monitor turned up too bright is bad for the eyes, and it wears out the monitor more quickly.

To adjust the monitor to pink perfection, turn the brightness (the button with the little sun) all the way up and adjust the contrast (the button with the half moon) until the display looks pleasing. Then turn the brightness down until you like what you see. That's it!

Unplug Your PC When You Upgrade Hardware

The new PCs don't have a flippable on/off switch like the older models. When you open the case to upgrade or add an expansion card, your belly (if it's like my belly) may punch the power-on button, and lo, you're working in a hazardous electrical environment. To prevent that, unplug the console before you open it for upgrading.

You don't need to unplug the console or even turn off the PC when you add a USB or FireWire device. (You do need to unplug it if you add a USB expansion card, however.)

Subscribe to a Computer Magazine

Oh, why not? Browse the stacks at your local coffeehouse-slash-music-store-slash-bookstore. Try to find a computer magazine that matches your tastes.

- I haven't found a good beginner's magazine in a while. (One may be out there since I last looked.)
- What sells me on a magazine are the columns and the *newsy* stuff they put up front.
- Some magazines are all ads. That can be great if you like ads, or it can be boring.
- Avoid the nerdier magazines, but I probably didn't need to tell you that.

Shun the Hype

The computer industry is rife with hype. Even if you subscribe to a family-oriented computer magazine, you'll still read about the latest this or the next biggest trend that. Ignore it!

My gauge for hype is whether or not the thing hyped is shipping as a standard part of a PC. I check the ads. If they're shipping it, then I write about it. Otherwise, it's a myth and may not happen. Avoid being lured by the hype.

- When hype becomes reality, you'll read about it here in this book.
- Former hype I've successfully ignored: Pen Windows; Push technology; Shockwave; Microsoft Bob; Windows CE, Home wireless networking.

▶ Hype that eventually became reality: USB; CD-R; Zip drives; shopping on the Web or *e-commerce;* DVD drives; digital cameras.

Don't Take It So Seriously

Hey, simmer down. Computers aren't part of life. They're nothing more than mineral deposits and petroleum products. Close your eyes and take a few deep breaths. Listen to the ocean spray against the deck on the patio; listen to the gurgle of the marble Jacuzzi tub in the master bedroom.

Pretend you're driving the convertible through a grove of sequoias on a sunny day with the wind whipping through your hair and curling over your ears. Pretend you're lying on the deck under the sun as the Pacific Princess chugs south toward the islands with friendly, wide-eyed monkeys that eat coconut chunks from the palm of your hand.

You're up in a hot-air balloon, swirling the first sip of champagne and feeling the bubbles explode atop your tongue. Ahead, to the far left, the castle's spire rises through the clouds, and you can smell Chef Meisterbrau's awaiting banquet.

Then slowly open your eyes. It's just a dumb computer. Really. Don't take it too seriously.

Index

• C •

Notes

Notes